Developing Resourceful Humans

Equating human capital to machine capital is a thing of the past. *Developing Resourceful Humans* reaches beyond the historic approach of human resource development to developing resourceful humans – a new philosophy of learner empowerment.

The contributors draw on their experience as adult educators from Canada, the United States, and Europe to present perspectives on the dimensions of this change. The first part of the book establishes the historical position of adult education within the economic context. The contributors discuss human capital propositions and project into the broader context for change. This context sets the tone for the second part of the book, where the contributors examine the learning dimensions of the change environment.

A unique dialectic format is used to draw on the range of positions taken by the contributors. Each chapter is followed by a commentary, which takes the ideas in the previous chapter as its starting point.

With an understanding of the emerging world economic order and the changes in education and employment this brings, this book will be of interest to students of adult education and to administrators of human resource development.

The editor, **Lynn Elen Burton**, is the Executive Coordinator of the Canadian Task Force on Incomes and Adjustment in the Atlantic Fishery. She has taught at all levels of education and has written widely on human resource development. Much of her work has been directly involved with the adult education policy of the Canadian government.

Developing Resourceful Humans

Adult Education Within the Economic Context

Edited by Lynn Elen Burton

ROUTLEDGE

London and New York

First published 1992
by Routledge
11 New Fetter Lane, London EC4P 4EE

Simultaneously published in the USA and Canada
by Routledge
a division of Routledge, Chapman and Hall, Inc.
29 West 35th Street, New York, NY 10001

Typeset in Times by J&L Composition Ltd, Filey, North Yorkshire
Printed and bound in Great Britain by
Mackays of Chatham plc, Chatham, Kent

British Library Cataloguing in Publication Data

A catalogue record for this book is available from the British Library.

ISBN 0-415-00121-8

Library of Congress Cataloging-in-Publication Data

Developing resourceful humans: adult education within the economic context / edited by Lynn Elen Burton.
p. cm.—(International perspectives on adult and continuing education)
Includes bibliographical references and index.
ISBN 0-415-00121-8
1. Adult education—Economic aspects—Canada. 2. Economic development, Effect of education on. 3. Human Capital.
I. Burton, Lynn Elen, 1946– . II. Series.
LC5254.D47 1992
374—dc20

91-45393
CIP

This book is dedicated to the multitude of professional adult educators working towards a better world and the empowerment of people through learning. Royalties will be contributed towards this end.

Appreciation goes to all of the authors for their contributions and for their patience with the time required to use this unique dialogic approach. A special thank you goes to Ian Morrison, Executive Director of the Canadian Association for Adult Education and to Dr Jack Mezirow, Past Chairman of the Adult and Higher Education Department at Columbia University, for their ongoing confidence and advice. Marlene Gandhi provided invaluable support throughout the publication production.

A special thanks goes to Daisy Izene Austin and Donald Burton, my mentors, models, and mom and dad.

Lynn Elen Burton
1992

Contents

Figures and Tables

FIGURES

TABLES

Contributors

Stephen Brookfield is Visiting Scholar at St Mary's University in St Paul, Minnesota. He was recently Associate Professor within the Department of Higher and Adult Education, and Associate Director of the Center for Adult Education at Columbia University in New York City. With his Ph.D. from the University of Leicester in the United Kingdom, he also holds postgraduate diplomas from the Universities of London and Nottingham. Dr Brookfield's main research activities are in the fields of adult learning, community education, comparative adult education, and qualitative research. A prolific writer, his books include: *The Skillful Teacher* (1991), *Developing Critical Thinkers* (1987), *Understanding and Facilitating Adult Learning* (1986), *Learning Democracy* (1987), *Self-Directed Learning: From Theory to Practice* (1985), *Adult Learners, Adult Education and the Community* (1984), and *Independent Adult Learning* (1982).

Lynn Elen Burton is the Executive Coordinator of the Task Force on Incomes and Adjustment in the Atlantic Fishery. She was recently Director of Environmental Education, Environment Canada. She was Senior Advisor to the Prime Minister's National Advisory Board on Science and Technology. She directed the major sector Task Force and Panel work that produced the reports, *Learning a Living in Canada* and *Learning for Life*. She is on the Board of Directors for the Canadian Association for Adult Education and the Education Sub-Committee for the Canadian Commission for UNESCO.

Anthony Patrick Carnevale is the Chief Economist and Vice President of the American Society for Training and Development in Alexandria, Virginia. He writes extensively on human resource development, including the watershed publication, *Human Capital: A High Yield Corporate Investment.*

Ivan Charner is Director of Research and Development at the National Institute for Work and Learning in Washington, DC. He has written extensively on human resource development, adult learning, and business–education partnerships. He is author of *Responding to the Educational Needs of Today's Workplace* (1987), *Variations by Theme: The Life Transitions of Clerical Workers* (1986), and *Different Strokes for Different Folks: Access and Barriers to Adult Education and Training* (1984). He has a special interest in older workers and the labor movement.

Arthur Cordell is a Special Advisor on Information Technology Policy for the Canadian Department of Communications. Known for his vision of the future, he has also played key roles in the development of Science Policy in Canada.

Beverly Witter Du Gas was the Director of the School of Nursing at the University of Ottawa in Canada. Dr Du Gas has been operationally involved in distance education to link practicing nurses through continuing education. She served on the Board of Directors for the Canadian Association for the Study of Adult Education.

Frank Feather is a business consultant with an international roster of clients including *Fortune* 500 companies, the United Nations, and numerous governments. He was a strategic planner with international banks for over 20 years and served as the Chairman of the First Global Conference on the Future held in Toronto in 1980. His recent book, *G-Forces: Re-Inventing the World,* has an entire chapter on education in the twenty-first century.

Elisabeth Gerver is the past Director of the Scottish Institute of Adult and Continuing Education. She has taught many years in higher education in Scotland, England, and Canada. She is Vice President of the European Bureau of Adult Education and Chair of the Board of the *International Journal of Computers in Adult Education and Training*. The author of *Computers and Adult Learning and Humanising Technology,* she is currently writing *Strategic Women.*

Gerard G. Gold is Senior Program Officer at the National Institute for Work and Learning in Washington, DC. He is the author of publications such as: *Employment Based Tuition Assistance* (1985), and *Business and Higher Education: Toward New Alliances* (1981). As a fellow of the Indo–US Subcommission on Education and Culture, he has also looked at industry–education collaboration in India.

Linda MacDonald is the Assistant Director of Continuing Education at St Mary's University in Halifax, Nova Scotia. She has spent much of her working life involved in women's issues and access for women to learning opportunities. While at Mount St Vincent's University in Halifax, she became a special doctoral candidate through distance education in the Adult Education Guided Independent Study program (AEGIS) at Columbia University in New York City. A key player in the Canadian Congress for Learning Opportunities for Women (CCLOW), Linda combines both concerns for women and learning in her work.

Teresa MacNeil is Chairman of Adult Education at St Francis Xavier University in Nova Scotia. She has held executive positions with the Advisory Committee on the Cape Breton Economy, Frontier College, the Board of Governors of Atlantic Provinces Economic Council, the Cape Breton Development Corporation, and the Canadian Commission for UNESCO. She is the recent past President of the Canadian Association for Adult Education.

Nicole Morgan is an independent author and consultant specializing in long-term planning. She has to her credit several widely acclaimed books: *Nowhere to Go*, one of the first forecasts of plateauing in large organizations; *Implosion*, an analysis of the growth and downsizing in the Canadian public service; and *The Equality Game*, an analysis of major labor market trends in the federal bureaucracy in Canada as they relate to women. She has taught philosophy in France and worked for the prestigious organization "Futuribles."

Derek Portwood is an academic consultant in higher education and is currently working with the South East England Consortium for Credit Accumulation and Transfer. He was Director of the Centre for Unemployment Studies at the Polytechnic of Wolverhampton. Dr Portwood has taught in a variety of further and higher education institutions in the United Kingdom. Much of his work emphasizes action research.

Kjell Rubenson is Professor of Adult Education at the University of British Columbia. Dr Rubenson was the King's Advisor on Adult Education in Sweden and a Professor at the University of Linkoping. He has been instrumental in the development of public policy in Canada and has provided policy advice on human resource development to the Prime Minister's National Advisory Board on Science and Technology.

Hans Schutze was Senior Counsellor for the Centre for Education Research and Innovation for the OECD. Dr Schutze also served as Senior Advisor to the Head of the Social Democratic Party of the Federal Republic of Germany. He has published extensively on the subject of recurrent education and is currently teaching at the University of British Columbia in Canada.

Dale E. Shuttleworth is involved in community education, including the linking of communities around the world through telecommunications hook-ups. Dr Shuttleworth was the Assistant Superintendent of Community Service for the Board of Education for the City of York in Ontario, Canada. He was the recipient of awards such as: the Dag Hammarskjöld Gold Medal for Excellence in Education and the Norman High Award from the Ontario Association for Continuing Education.

Stuart Smith is the Chairman of the Commission on Post-Secondary Education in Canada. Dr Smith was the Chairperson of the Science Council of Canada and the leader of the Liberal Party in Ontario. He is the President of Rockcliffe Research, a scientific management company. Dr Smith has a number of honorary degrees and has been recognized for his substantial contributions to Canada and other countries.

Erik Solem was the Chairman of the Canadian Association for the Club of Rome. A futurist, Dr Solem was the Chairman of the Inter-Departmental Committee on Futures Forecasting in Canada. He provides strategic advice to Canadian leadership in defense and the environment.

Linda Sweet is Principal of Glenburnie School, a private elementary school in Mississauga, Ontario. She has forged new territory for women in sports and was the first Vice President of Racing for the Canadian Yachting Association. She played an important role in entrenching women's rights in the Canadian Constitution.

Maurice Taylor is a Professor of Adult Education at the University of Ottawa. Dr Taylor was a Teaching Master at Algonquin Community College in the Adult Basic Education Department and has served as a consultant to community and institutional literacy programs in Canada and the United Kingdom. In addition to his Ph.D. degree from the Ontario Institute for Studies in Education, he also holds a *diplôme de langue et lettres françaises* from the Université d'Aix-en-Provence in France.

Preface

The only constant in the emerging world is change – and the accelerating rate of that change. Hierarchical corporate structures under the old economic order are being replaced by a spider web of activity whose strands reach all over the world. A technology induced redefinition and reorganization of work, coupled with the need to manage change will inevitably break up the present boxes of school, work, and retirement. The coming interweaving of work, learning, and life calls for new flexibility and a re-thinking of our industrial-aged institutions – political, economic, and social.

Learning to learn becomes the cornerstone of learning for life. The traditional 3R's of reading, 'riting, and 'rithmetic must merge with the 3R's of the future – reasoning, relating, and redefining.

The control implied in the traditional philosophy of *human resource development* will be overtaken by the decentralized power inherent in the new concept of *developing resourceful humans*. Past investment favoring machines and natural resources over people, could prove to be a very serious mistake for nations in the emerging post-industrial world. The political, economic, and social return on investing in people and their skills is expected to be high.

> "The coming of the post-industrial world will not eclipse industrial production, nor the importance of the more highly skilled workers who will remain in industrial production. Agriculture did not disappear with the advance of industry. It became mechanized and more productive. In 1850, for instance, one farmer provided for four other people. In 1982, one farmer provided for seventy-eight others."
> (Anthony Patrick Carnevale, *Human Capital: A High Yield Corporate Investment*, ASTD, 1982).

The purpose of this book, *Developing Resourceful Humans: Adult Education within the Economic Context*, is to explore the shifting paradigm from human resource development to developing resourceful humans. Part One, Human Resource Development, will establish the historical position of adult education within the economic context, discuss human capital propositions, and project into the broader context for change. Part Two, Developing Resourceful Humans, will examine the learning dimensions of that change.

While an editorial effort has been made to secure the most complete referencing possible, the writing style and citations in this book are as varied as the authors themselves. A unique dialectic format has been utilized to draw on the diverse perspectives of adult educators from Canada, the United States, and Europe. An optimistic commentary, which uses the author's ideas as a "jumping off point," follows each chapter. The complex nature of this process means that some of the research has greater currency than others. This approach will hopefully provide the food for ongoing discussions of the controversies, contrasts and consensus in perspectives on human resource development and developing resourceful humans.

Part I

Human Resource Development

Chapter 1

Human Resource Development: A Historical Perspective

Kjell Rubenson

"Adult-education: the economic context" is a wide topic containing several of the most crucial questions in the social sciences. Despite that, it is seldom discussed within the "adult education family."

The economics of education developed into a subfield of its own in the early 1960s, concerning itself primarily with the relationship between investment in education, on the one hand, and economic development and income distribution on the other. Theories on education and economic development apply also to adult education. However, adult education raises issues above and beyond those dealt with in the mainstream economics of education, e.g. the impact of adult education on working life and the role of adult education in cooperatives.

Economic theories have a more profound effect on public policy than is often realized. Economic concepts have come to regulate the way administrators and policymakers structure their thinking. Also, economic theories are permeated with social and individual values and are an expression of a certain ideology. The discussion of the merit of the various economic paradigms can ultimately be seen as "ideological warfare."

Today, when many developed societies are faced with their worst economic crises since the Great Depression, the focus once again is on education. Education is the solution to the unemployment problem and it is through education that Canada – like the rest of the world – is going to be able to compete in the world markets in a time of rapid technological restructuring. This raises the question: "To what extent and under what conditions can education and especially adult education be part of an answer to today's economic crises?"

The purpose of this chapter is to use recent findings to problematize the issue. It will not give firm directions, but with the help of recent research it will imply alternative policy directions. It is important not to neglect earlier discussions in the social sciences on the merit of the human capital theory in educational planning. Reviewing what was said at that time can give a perspective on today's policy alternatives. Further, it is important to be observant of that shift in the economic thinking that, in my opinion, has occurred on issues like social equality.

This chapter starts with a discussion of the human capital theory, its history and present status. The analyses will then shift to adult education and the new technology and will be followed by some thoughts on adult education for alternative economic development. The chapter concludes with some comments concerning adult education and public policy.

HUMAN CAPITAL THEORY

When Schultz (1961) presented his paper "Investment in Human Capital," he began what has become known as the human investment revolution in economic thought (Sobel 1982). Two years later, Dennison's "The Sources of Economic Growth in the United States" established a strong link between investment in education and economic growth. Together with Schultz's work, this book had a profound impact on educational policymakers around the world.

In Canada, the Economic Council of Canada, under the chairmanship of J. Deutsch, repeatedly pointed out the role of education in the growth of the national economy. In its first annual review in 1964, the Council stressed the vital need for creating and maintaining an adequate supply of professional, technical, and other highly skilled manpower as a basis for future growth of the Canadian economy. Increased investment in human resources to improve knowledge and skills was proclaimed as the most essential ingredient for attaining the goal of faster and better sustained productivity and growth. Almost 30 years later, the Council, under the leadership of Judith Maxwell, is currently in the final stages of completing a major study, which examines this area further. In Deutsch's analysis, it is most probable that the existing educational structure gave rise to grave concerns in view of two of the dominant themes of the time:

1 that education is a central production factor, and
2 that continued rapid structural change with considerable demands for the improvement of the qualifications of the Canadian labor force can be expected.

It is not surprising then that the Minister of Education, W.G. Davis, in a 1966 speech, indicated that the human capital approach was one of the major factors that influenced the organization of the Community College system.

> Dr Deutsch, as I told him not so many weeks ago, successfully placed most of the problems facing the developing economy of this province and this country at the doorstep of education. I said this imposed quite a large load on educators and that we would do our best to respond. But I think it is very encouraging for those of you who are devoting your time and effort to education to realize that there is a very direct relationship between what we are attempting to do within the field of education and the economic, and just as importantly, the social development of this province and of course this nation.
>
> (Davis 1978: 162)

The enthusiastic recognition of the human capital theory arose, as Sobel (1982: 56) points out, because it provided a framework for incorporating the economics of education, the economics of discrimination, and the economics of poverty into an applied branch of microeconomics termed "the economics of human resources". The concept also provided an umbrella to cover both the conservative elements interested primarily in economic growth and the reformists who saw in educational expansion equalization of opportunity, income and, ultimately, power. In short, the human capital theory was seen to explain economic development as well as inequality in earnings.

Schultz proposed that a more equal distribution of investments in education would equalize individual earnings and stated:

> The hypothesis here proposed is that these changes in the investment in human capital are the basic factors reducing the inequality in the distribution of personal income.
>
> (Schultz 1961: 2)

The belief in equalization through education led Schultz to question the appropriateness of using modification in income transfers, in progressive taxation, and in the distribution of privately owned wealth as factors in altering the distribution of personal income. Instead, Schultz contended that the best way of achieving even greater future income equality was by increasing the availability of free or low-tuition education. The hypothesis is that the structure of wages and salaries is primarily determined by investment in schooling, health, on-the-job training, searching for information about job opportunities, and by investment in migration.

The crucial question with regard to earning inequalities is how to explain the individual demand for investment in human capital. According to Mincer (1970, reported in Osberg 1981: 120) human-capital theory brings, among other things, the following perspectives to the issue of demand and inequality:

1 Individuals invest in their own future income, primarily by acquiring schooling and on-the-job training. The amount they invest and the return they receive is, however, dependent both on their abilities and on their opportunities.
2 The aggregate degree of inequality in earnings distribution can be seen as the summation of individual decisions on human-capital investments and labor supply.
3 Since individuals have differing tastes, opportunities, and abilities, they will make different investments in human capital. In the absence of government intervention, an inequality of economic results is therefore inevitable in a capitalistic market system.
4 Families acquire different resources and make different decisions regarding investments in their children. In the absence of government intervention, which equalizes investments in the human capital of children, inequality of opportunity is inevitable in a capitalistic market system.

To sum up, at the time of the large increases in public expenditure on adult and higher education in Canada in the 1960s one did not perceive any conflicts between economic efficiency and social and economic equality or, expressed in different terms, between the private and social demand for education. In fact, both forces went in the same direction – increased investments in adult and higher education. As a background to today's policy environment, it is worthwhile to remember that the 1960s were dominated by the neo-Keynesian perspective which stressed increased government intervention in the market place in order to stimulate economic growth, increase general welfare and create a somewhat more equal society. Today, as will be discussed below, the situation is the reverse. Government intervention is seen as the dragon and the free-market forces as the savior. With this change, the notion of equity which was a crucial part of the human capital thinking in the 1960s, has vanished.

The balmy days of education came to an end at the beginning of the 1970s (somewhat later for adult education) and the enthusiasm with which the human capital theory and its related policies were met turned into criticism. The romantic 1950s and 1960s were replaced by the cynical 1970s. Investment in education had not generated the expected economic growth and worse, there was a realization that more and more schooling did not necessarily equalize access to the available goods and services of society.

Table 1.1 describes what has happened in Canada with regard to the inequality of income from 1951 to 1978 (Osberg 1981: 11). The population is divided into five equal groups or "quintiles," each representing 20 per cent of the family units. An equal distribution of income would imply that each quantity received 20 per cent of total Canadian family incomes – i.e. the poorest 20 per cent would receive 20 per cent of the total income, as would the richest 20 per cent of family units.

Table 1.1 Income shares of Canadians – families and unattached individuals – in various years

Year	*Lowest 20 %*	*Second Quintile*	*Third Quintile*	*Fourth Quintile*	*Top 20 %*
1951	4.4	11.2	18.3	23.3	42.8
1957	4.2	11.9	18.0	24.5	41.4
1961	4.2	11.9	18.3	24.5	41.1
1965	4.4	11.8	18.0	24.5	41.4
1967	4.2	11.4	17.8	24.6	42.0
1971	3.6	10.6	17.6	24.9	43.3
1975	4.0	10.6	17.6	25.1	42.6
1976	4.3	10.7	17.4	24.7	42.9
1977	3.8	10.7	17.9	25.6	42.0
1978	4.1	10.4	17.6	25.2	42.7

Sources: Podoluk (1968: 294)
Statistics Canada 13–207– (1980: 85)

The share of the poorest has remained more or less stable at around 4 per cent while the share of the richest has remained constant at around 42 per cent. If anything, there has been a tendency to a reduced share for the poorest. Even taking into account the fact that the increase in single-person households may have led to an overestimation of income inequality, the results clearly indicate that the increased investment in human capital has not been accompanied by any major developments towards greater equalization in individual incomes.

The crises in education in the 1970s led to a shift in theoretical orientation and a renewed interest in approaching the relationship between education–work–society from a conflict perspective. In the economics of education, the screening hypothesis was presented as an alternative to the human capital theory. I will give a short review of this theory since it provides an alternative starting point from which to suggest solutions to today's crises.

THE SCREENING HYPOTHESIS – AN ALTERNATIVE THEORY

The screening theory seeks to explain what the human capital theory cannot – that is, why there is such a persistent preference of employers for workers with ever higher levels of education (Blaugh 1976: 46). The reason may be that such workers possess scarce cognitive skills, and desirable personality traits such as self-reliance and achievement drive. It could be because they display compliance with organizational rules. The point is, however, as Blaugh states, that all of these desirable attributes are not known at the time of hiring. Faced with a selection problem, the theory postulates that employers treat educational qualifications as a screening device to distinguish new workers in terms of personality traits rather than cognitive skills. The cognitive skills are supposed to be acquired on the jobs. Thurow (1975: 79) claims that 60 per cent of US workers acquire all their job skills on the job. Thus the employers are basically selecting job applicants in terms of their trainability.

Therefore, Blaugh (1976: 46) argues, the observed correlation between earnings and length of schooling, which is so prominent in the human capital literature, disguises a more fundamental correlation between schooling and the attributes that characterize trainability. The contribution of education to economic growth, he goes on, is simply that of providing a selection mechanism for employers. The issue then becomes whether or not education is the most efficient selection device.

The reason why the screening or credentialism hypothesis explains not only initial salaries but also lifelong earnings is that most workers are part of an internal labor market with clearly defined and regulated job ladders (see Doeringer and Piore 1971).

The screening theory is promoted by two different schools of thought – the neo-Marxists and the neo-institutionalists. While the two schools agree that a primary role of education is the role of a selection mechanism, they differ in their explanation of the phenomenon. The starting point for the neo-Marxists is the class structure and they focus therefore on how the ruling class can maintain control of the means of production. The role of the education system according to this view, is to legitimate the existing division of labor. This, according to Bowles and Gintis (1976: 103), is done by ostensibly providing an open and objective mechanism for assigning individuals to unequal economic positions. The educational system is viewed as an integral element in the reproduction of the prevailing class structure of society. The educational system integrates the students into the economic system through a structured correspondence between its social relationships and those of production (Bowles and Gintis 1976: 131). The division of labor is not seen as primarily guaranteeing efficiency; rather it allows the capitalists to control the market production process. Division of labor is thus more a result of class conflicts than of technology. Neo-institutionalists, while agreeing that the market forces will produce neither equality of opportunity nor equality of results, do not look to radical political change but see politics and governmental actions to reduce inequalities as possible within the capitalist market.

The screening theory has far-reaching policy consequences. The importance of credentialism implies that a person's actual level of education is of less importance than his or her relative level of education. The theory suggests that educational expansion is unlikely to have a significant impact on differentials in earnings. What will happen is that the hiring standards will increase. Further, the theory implies that increases in the average level of education will not result in any substantial economic growth (Blaugh 1976: 47). As Osberg (1981: 129f) rightly points out, the controversy is really about the degree to which education creates credentials versus skills, since few would deny that it does both.

The two theories discussed here, human capital and screening, provide two fundamentally different perspectives from which to approach today's main social and economic problems – the technological revolution.

THE TECHNOLOGICAL REVOLUTION AND ADULT EDUCATION

The revolution within microelectronics, together with recent major developments within telecommunications, push toward an information economy and form the basis for the information revolution.

It is widely anticipated that information technology will affect all aspects of life and raise serious economic, social, and political issues. As a response to the move of less-developed countries into capital-intensive production, the "old" industrialized countries have tried to meet this challenge by shifting their industrial base toward products and processes that require highly skilled workers. Recent governmental reports have pointed out that Canada's competitiveness on the world market will to a large degree depend on its national resources in terms of knowledge, learning, information, and skilled intelligence (National Advisory Board on Science and Technology, 1988, 1989, 1991; Department of Finance, 1984; Royal Commission on the Economic Union 1984; Minister Employment and Immigration 1984).

The choice of the title *Learning a Living in Canada* by the Skill Development Leave Task Force (1983) reflects the renewed interest in linking education to economic development. It is from this perspective that one should understand the growing fear among business and labor leaders, government officials and educators that the present education system is ill-suited to respond to the new demands created by the information technology. The US National Commission on Excellence in Education stated in its final report that:

> In a world of ever-accelerating competition and change in the conditions of the workplace, of ever-greater danger, and of ever-larger opportunities for those prepared to meet them, educational reform should focus on the goal of creating a learning society.

> In our view, formal schooling in youth is the essential foundation for learning throughout one's life. But without lifelong learning, one's skills will become rapidly dated.
>
> (National Commission 1983)

Once again education – now in the shape of lifelong learning – has been proclaimed the panacea for all the problems that society faces. Statements such as those appearing in government documents are seldom based on any serious quantitative or qualitative analyses of the deficiencies in the present pool of human resources, however there are some voices in the scholarly community that warn that the available evidence contradicts popular beliefs (Levin and Rumberger 1983). These scholars argue against the policymakers' common perceptions that structural changes and the changes in the present jobs will result in a major demand for sophisticated job skills.

There are several issues involved here: how educationally demanding are the new jobs that will be created in comparison with the ones that will disappear; what is the overall employment effect of the new technology; and what will happen with existing jobs?

Employment effect

There have been many alarming reports, especially from Western Europe, that the micro-revolution will bring about dramatic changes for large portions of the presently employed work force. An often quoted French study (Nora and Minc 1980) forecasts that 30 per cent of the employees in banks and insurance companies could be unemployed within 10 years. Similar estimates in Britain are in the range of 16–25 per cent by 1990 (Science Council of Canada 1982). There has been much less concern for the displacement power of microprocessors in North America than in Europe. There is no consensus as to what extent microelectronics will displace labor. This is partly because the shorter and longer impacts tend to be confused and, further, that most predictions are based on aggregate data which hide many structural issues, such as freer trade. However, it is evident that new technologies increase productivity and therefore have a labor-saving effect.

The overwhelming problem rests in the prediction of the ratio of new jobs created by the technology to jobs lost as a result of the new technology. There are basically three sources of information on which to base a study of the employment effects of the new technology:

1 labor market forecasts of the growth and composition of future employment of the kind the Labour Market Outlook and Structural Analysis (LMOSA) group in Canada provides;
2 studies of the employment effects, within a factory or office, of the introduction of the new technology, e.g. industrial robots; and
3 attempts to estimate the effects not only within an industry or office but also to take into account the external employment effects linked to the production, distribution, and if applicable, the installation of the technology itself.

Available information is almost exclusively based on type 1 studies and there hardly exists any research of type 3. Thus the evidence used against the prevailing "educational sentiment" is to a large extent based on official occupational projections. The research group at Stanford University has, based on analyses of US Bureau of Labor Statistics (BLS), shattered the belief that the development is resulting in a great increase in the high-technology sector (Levin and Rumberger 1983). Their argument is that while it is true that the high-technology jobs will be the fastest growing occupations, their relative number in the labor market is very small. Instead of looking at relative numbers, one ought to focus on the absolute number of jobs. In that case the BLS data reveal that there are 800,000 new jobs expected for fast food workers and kitchen helpers, 600,000 new jobs for janitors and sextons but only 150,000 new jobs for computer programmers.

Figures presented in a Consultation Paper on Training from the Minister of Employment and Immigration show that the same pattern is true in Canada. The prediction by the LMOSA reveals that a relatively small number of jobs will account for much of job growth. One outlook suggests 30 large occupations could provide 40 per cent of all new jobs. These occupations are not, as a whole, very educationally demanding and thus the report states:

> Many of the growth occupations have, however, little impact on training volumes. For many of them, there are numbers of

unemployed people who can take the jobs without major training. Others involve low skill levels.

(Minister Employment and Immigration 1984).

Instead, the report concludes, the pressure on training will come from some rapidly growing occupations, which are unlikely to create large numbers of jobs but which will be critical to the successful introduction of technological change and to Canada's overall competitiveness.

Labor market projections provide a rough estimate of the direction the labor market is going but do not directly address the employment effects of the new technology. Further occupational classifications as used in labor market forecasts can, to a certain extent, mask the impact of the new technology. A study by the Swedish Bureau of Statistics found that as many as four out of five jobs directed somewhat to the use of computers would not be identified as such if the estimation were based on occupational group (SOU 1984: 20). This study indicates the problem of assessing the implications of the new technology using only data categorized according to occupational group.

The type 2 studies have primarily dealt with robotization within manufacturing. An OECD report cited the number of workplaces suppressed per robot as between 0.8 and 6.2, depending on the type of application (Schutze 1984). The limitations with these kind of estimates are that they do not take into account how many jobs would have been lost had the firm not increased its productivity by introducing robots.

It is almost impossible to find any such comprehensive studies of the total effects, i.e. not only the effects within a firm but also the creation of new jobs involved in producing and distributing the technology. Schutze (1984) refers to a German case study that attempted to take a broader look and found that for each robot introduced, the loss of working places was an average of four workers over two shifts, while the number of working places created within the firm was 0.09 and the working places created in production of industrial robots were just over 0.5.

The experts are divided on the net employment effects of the new technology and many maintain that it is more or less impossible to estimate these. However, there is evidence that the new technology may have greater impact on some sectors than others and that women will be more affected than men. Women are largely concentrated in a very narrow range of occupations and industries such as office work and the information industry which may be hard hit by the technological revolution. Those who continue to choose traditional women's occupations during the coming 5–15 years will carry a disproportionately large burden of the adjustment to the technological revolution.

It is important to stress that the vulnerable situation for women is not only a problem of the new technology but ultimately a reflection of sex-bound career selection. Unless women can acquire skills for other areas, they will not be able to capitalize on any employment compensation effects that the technology will have since the employment created will not match their skills.

To sum up the employment effects:

1 the labor market forecasts predict that the majority of the jobs in the next 10 years will be in low-skill areas;
2 there will be a fast expansion of high-technology jobs but the absolute number of these jobs is not as high as is commonly believed;
3 the classification system used in labor forecasts masks the full effect of the new technology;
4 the net employment effects of the new technology are very difficult to estimate; and
5 studies show that women, over the next 5–15 years may be extremely hard hit by office automation.

Changes in Job Content and Skill Requirement

It is evident that information technology is already influencing most sectors of the economy: offices, factories, stores, schools, etc.

The following data from Sweden tell something of the speed with which information technology is hitting the industrialized world. Every third Swede in the ages 16–65 had used some kind of computer and one in four had over one year of experience and regular use. More than half of these had acquired their knowledge since 1980 (SOU 1984: 20). Looking at the workplace, one out of four were using computers in their work.

While there is a widespread agreement that most people, as indicated in the Swedish study, will come into contact with the new technology, experts disagree whether this will require a more skilled work force or not. Those who do not believe in a general upskilling of the work force refer to the way that technology historically has been applied at the workplace (Levin and Rumberger 1983). According to this view the application of technology is part of the process of dividing work tasks into simplified operations that require few skills to perform – the so-called "Taylorism." Advances in microelectronics are seen as further threats to fragmentation which would not only reduce production costs but also increase the employers' control over the production process.

The foundation for this kind of reasoning originates from research on effects of the automation that took place during the 1960s as well as scattered case studies of the application of the new information technology.

An often cited example is the application of the computer itself. Initially the handling of the computer required knowledge in programming. Today most users can rely on ready-made program packages that can be handled with little knowledge of computer language. While the technology has become more advanced the actual handling of it has become simplified, requiring fewer skills. This view has been called the deskilling hypothesis, and it can be contrasted with the broadly proclaimed need for general upskilling, which seems to assume that increased complexity and sophistication in the development of the technology results in a corresponding increase in skill requirement among the users (see figure 1.1).

> These data imply that we may be able to absorb more highly educated people by redefining the requirements for employment, if not the job itself, and thus, in fashion of Humpty Dumpty, make the content of work what we say it is.
>
> (Berg 1970: 80)

Paradoxically, as the investment value of education slumps, the importance of its credentialing function soars (O'Toole 1977: 64).

Berg's and O'Toole's conclusions imply that the educational demands from the labor market are quite different from the demands for actually doing the work (Broady and Gintis 1983: 123). Berg's study deals with the latter while O'Toole addresses the former. On the market, where a person sells his or her labor, the educational demand could be very high regardless of what is really required at the workplace. Treated as a zero-sum

Figure 1.1 Relationship between technological advancement and skills required for the application of the new information technology.

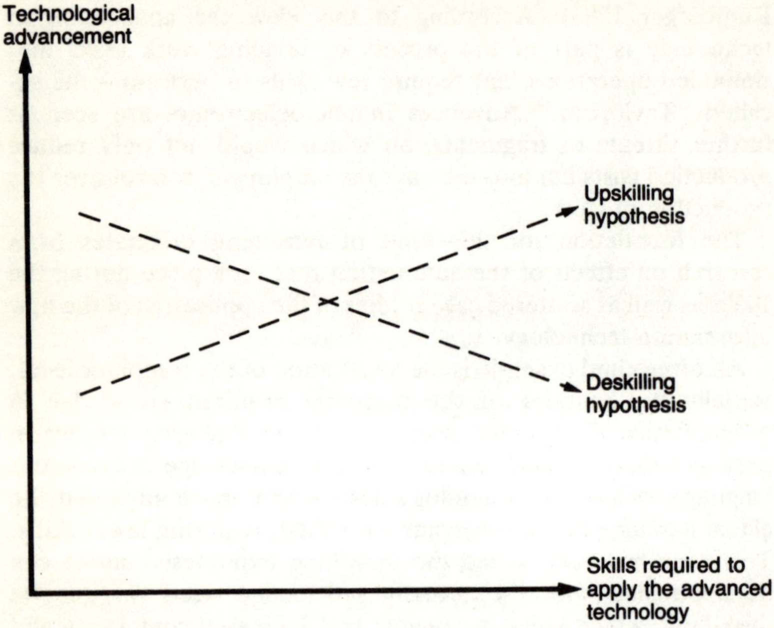

game it follows that education is a necessary but not sufficient condition to secure work.

Advocates for the screening theory stress that education in itself does not create jobs and that it is the position in the educational hierarchy rather than educational level that is important. Thus there is some truth in both of the following commonly made statements: "Educate the unemployed in order to give them a job" and "Education can't solve the unemployment problem."

Whether the problem is defined as overeducation or underemployment, the essence of the concern is that there is an unused capacity in the work force. Accepting this, one has to remember that the phenomenon only concerns recent graduates. The interesting thing is how educational attainment is distributed across age cohorts.

Table 1.2 shows that there are large groups among the 35-and-over cohort that have not gone beyond elementary education. Looking at the 45–54 cohort almost one out of three have only

Table 1.2 Educational attainment by age

	None-Elementary	*High School*	*Some Post-Sec*	*Post-Sec Diploma*	*Univ*
20–24	4	55	19	16	6*
25–34	7	49	11	17	16
35–44	17	46	7	14	16
45–54	30	46	5	10	9
55–64	39	43	4	8	6
Percentage of total Canadian population 17 and older	21	48	9	12	10

Source: Statistics Canada's 1983 Adult Education survey.
Note: * The low figure can be explained by the fact that many of the 20–24 had not yet finished their university studies.

elementary education. This ought to give rise to some concern remembering that on the average they have 15 years left before retirement. One rather surprising result is that the relative number of highly educated is as high among the 35–45 cohort as in the 25–34 age group.

There are at least two unresolved issues in the present discussion on the implications of the new technology for adult education. The first has to do with how much unused capacity there is in the present labor force and the second is the relationship between the organization of work and the utilization of skills. In the arguments around the deskilling – upskilling polarization, the organization of work is often treated as a fixed entity and the consequences of alternative organizational paradigms are left out. Further, the impact of the new technology is seen as deterministic, following more or less the same pattern with little or no possibility for the employees to intervene. However, it is important here to link this discussion to the movement towards industrial democratization with its struggle for greater participation of the employees in altering the production and work organization. In the ultimate analysis, the crucial question will be whether work is organized in such a way as to facilitate a more even distribution of knowledge within the work force. It is telling that the Swedish labor unions regard the matter of education and training of their members as one of the most crucial issues in their struggle for industrial democracy and successful and equitable adjustment to the information technology.

There are several reasons why the question of skills ought to be approached from this broad perspective. It is evident from the Minister of Finance's consultation paper "Challenges and Choices" that labor relations in Canada represent one of the threats not only to economic prosperity but also, as the Science Council earlier pointed out, to the ability to introduce the new technology. Thus the problem for Canada is as much how to organize work so that existing skills can be fully utilized as how to develop new skills.

It is interesting to observe that the approach to the new technology is very different between the United States and Sweden. Thus Levin and Rumberger's negative conclusions – presented above – are based on the assumption that the organization is constant and no changes are likely, whereas the Swedish research departs from considering the interaction between technology and organization. The differences are a reflection of dissimilarities in the two societies at large and in working life specifically. The important point from a Canadian perspective is that the two traditions provide different policy implications.

I have attempted in figures 1.2 and 1.3 to conceptualize the discussion graphically. A distinction is made between the existing skills a person possesses (figure 1.2) and the capacity to learn the "necessary" skills (figure 1.3). Further, a separation is made between skills for the actual handling of the new technology (hands-on skills) and skills for the understanding of the broader implications of the technology and the control of it. Naturally this is a simplified picture of a complex phenomenon. To talk about skills for the understanding is not to imply that the question of control and power can be reduced to knowledge and attitudes among employees.

Starting with figure 1.2, those arguing that there is no great need for new skills are mainly focusing on point A, whereas those demanding efforts to increase the skills are concerned with how to go from point C to point A. The interesting aspect, however, is how one chooses to deal with point B. Does a person have a broad understanding of how the technological innovations exert an influence on his work, which alternatives exist, possibilities or lack thereof to control the technology? It could be maintained that this broader knowledge ought to be treated as twenty-first century "civic education," something necessary for a society to maintain

Figure 1.2 Assumptions regarding existing skills

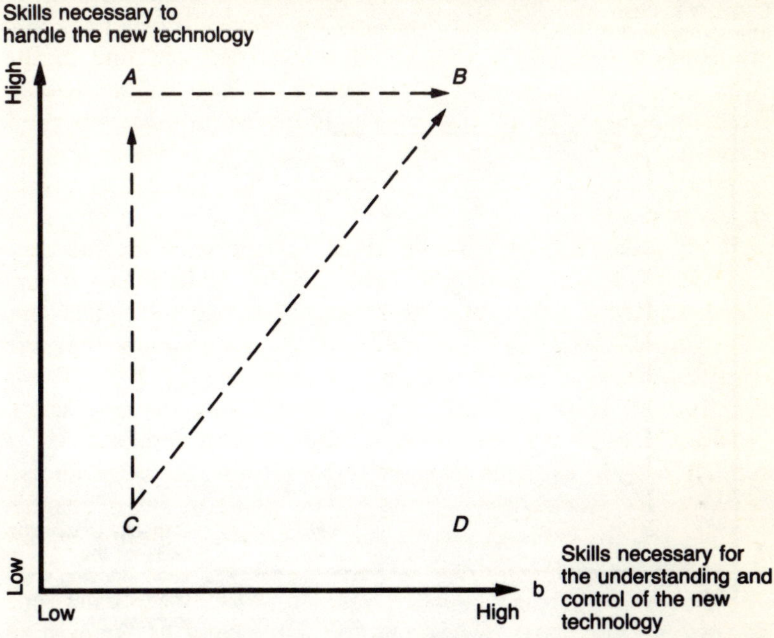

its democratic structure. One could also, strictly from an economic efficiency perspective, claim that to fully use the flexibility of the new technology and quickly adapt the production and the organization to constant changes a broad knowledge is essential.

Looking at the kind of courses offered by the various providers of adult education the most important thing seems to be how to go from C to A without approaching B. Most of the courses contain technical information and/or instructions on how to use the new technology but nothing on the broader implications of the new technology.

Assuming that a person lacks skills and needs to move from C to A, C to B, or A to B, the capacity to acquire the missing skills (figure 1.3) becomes relevant. The intention here, however, is not to get into the vast literature on adults' learning but rather to restrict the presentation to a few comments related to the context of this chapter.

Adult educators have fought hard to destroy the myth that the capacity to learn starts to deteriorate at an early age and have

Figure 1.3 Assumptions regarding the capacity to learn required skills

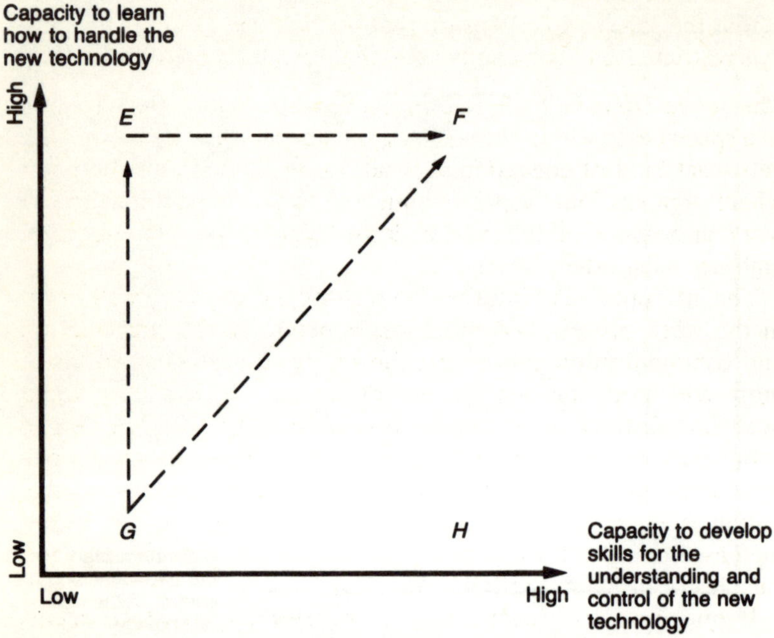

rightly pointed to methodological flaws in earlier research designs. However, in the eagerness to do this they have neglected to consider existing individual differences. A person's ability to learn after having left school is partly related to the kind of environment one lives in. Thus the initial differences in ability widen with age and a deterioration has been observed among those who enter jobs that do not require the acquisition of new knowledge (Härnqvist 1977). Thus there has been a deterioration in the human capital or, using the terminology of the screening perspective, the trainability has decreased. This is not to say that there has occurred any biological or physiological changes that have resulted in loss of capacity. Further, when the scope for personal initiative on the job has been limited by factors in the work process, then the individual's ability to participate during leisure time in activities which call for personal initiative seems to decrease (Meissner 1971). In conclusion, various studies indicate two things:

1 that there can be some problems, at least initially, to move from G to E or from G to F, and
2 that the safest way to ensure that the wastage in human capital is restricted is to constantly keep the learning process operating.

The move from G to F is especially problematic. Best treated as a special case within the sociology of education, it concerns who gets what kind of education in what forms. This is also the point where organizational aspects connected to the democratization of work and issues of the role of knowledge and adult education embrace each other.

The introduction of information technology may very well result in the work process becoming less concrete as the presentation and communication concerning the production process are done more and more through the use of symbols. Thus there would occur an abstraction of the knowledge through which a person commands his or her work situation. This would require a work force that has general theoretical knowledge as well as knowledge around the actual work process. As well, there would be an increased demand for abstract thinking, information-seeking, and calculus of probability (SOU 1984: 20).

If one were to accept this line of reasoning – which seems reasonable with regard to point B in figure 1.2 – then it could be argued that the world of education and the world of work are coming close to each other. This happens, not because education is becoming more practical but because work is becoming more abstract. It is in this perspective that the existence of large groups of adults with very short education and jobs that reduce rather than increase their capacity to study, is troublesome.

ALTERNATIVE ECONOMIC DEVELOPMENT

As a result of the recent economic crisis, with its devastating effect on the employment situation, there is a growing interest in trying alternative ways to create jobs. There are two main streams in this development "entrepreneurship" and cooperatives. In the general debate this distinction is often blurred and entrepreneurship has come to stand for both directions. However, I think it is important to treat them separately as they are embedded in conflicting ideologies and value systems. Thus the role of adult education is, or rather ought to be, quite different depending on which concept the provider subscribes to.

Entrepreneurship is part of what has become known as the "new economics," but which really is a return to nineteenth-century classical economics (Seldon 1983). An emphasis of this "new economics," which presently guides policy making in Great Britain and the United States, is the skeptical view of the ability of government to know how, or even wish, to do public good. Instead, according to this view, it is only the free play of the market forces that can create general wealth. Seldon (1983) maintains that the welfare state has suppressed the emergence of voluntary welfare organizations that could have catered more effectively for the requirements of the poorest and points to the need for commercial entrepreneurship. The new economics favors private ownership as a better safeguard against the state than public ownership.

The new economics treats entrepreneurship as one of the pillars of the capitalistic philosophy. The aim of adult education in this situation is, stated somewhat simply, to equip the individual with the skills with which to become as successful as possible in terms of (1) creating and maintaining the job, and (2) making as high a profit as possible. This perspective can be contrasted with the cooperative model, which shares some of the same goals but partly has other aims.

The link between adult education and the cooperative movement goes back to the days of Robert Owen. At that time cooperative education was defined as "primarily the formation of cooperative character and opinion; and secondarily, though not necessarily of less importance, the training of men and women to take part in industrial and social reforms and municipal life generally" (WEA 1918: 374). Further, as the 1918 WEA yearbook stated, a special feature of cooperative education is that of the training of cooperative employees in technical and general subjects. This latter kind of education can be seen as providing "instrumental knowledge" necessary for running a cooperative. This double purpose of cooperative adult education, the instrumental and the philosophical, is what distinguishes it from the entrepreneurial approach, which only contains the instrumental aspect.

As an aside, it could be mentioned that education has played a very important role in the history of the Mondragon group – perhaps the most fascinating of modern cooperatives. It is interesting that the educational programs provided by Mondragon have much in common with the educational model proposed by Robert Owen and the consumers' cooperatives of the Rochdale pioneers. Thus the two functions of cooperative education are clearly visible in Mondragon (see Thomas and Logan 1982).

The interest in worker cooperatives is presently growing rapidly in most western industrialized countries. It is therefore of interest to take a look at Conforth's (1983) review of research on the success and failure of worker cooperatives. Four types of worker cooperatives were distinguished:

1 *Endowed cooperatives*: firms that have been "given away" by their original owners to the employees.
2 *Defensive cooperatives*: cooperatives formed by employees in order to preserve jobs on the closure of a business.
3 *"Alternative" cooperatives*: cooperatives that grew out of the alternative movements of the 1960s and 1970s. The members are usually middle-class, well-educated, and have a strong commitment to democratic ideals and are producing for social needs rather than profit.
4 *Job-creation cooperatives*: cooperatives formed in order to create new jobs.

It is an open question how the success of these cooperatives should be measured because of the mixture of commercial and social objectives.

Conforth's review showed that most of the problems faced by the early cooperatives (see Webb and Webb 1920) are as acute today. The defensive and job-creation cooperatives were often undercapitalized and lacked or failed to appreciate the management skills needed to run the business. The job-creation cooperatives were often "paternalistic", lacked worker participation, and demonstrated the problem of initiating democracy from above. The job-creation cooperatives that failed often had an undertrained work force. Conforth concluded that in some defensive and job-creation cooperatives the pursuit of social objectives, such as maintaining jobs or youth training, hurt their financial performance and reduced their chances of survival. If one were to argue that a main function of these cooperatives is to be educative, and thereby help the young and unemployed to learn new skills, then a strong point could be made that they should receive some public funding, at least during the initial phase. When new cooperatives have got some assistance by local cooperative development agencies, a number of the defensive and job-creation cooperatives have become successful.

The endowed cooperatives had the fewest financial problems, which is quite understandable as they were well established businesses before they became cooperatives. Their problem rested on how to achieve a system of democratic control and increased worker participation.

The alternative cooperatives showed poor financial performance but survived thanks to the members' high commitment to the goals of their cooperative. They often lacked productive skills, produced for need rather than profit, and chose methods more on grounds of democracy than efficiency.

What, if any, are the implications for adult education from the above review? It seems quite obvious that primarily, the adult education component must take into account that cooperatives do not form a homogeneous, organizational group but differ according to their objectives, organizational characteristics, and economic circumstances. In some cases the emphasis ought to be on how to create a democratic and participative work organization while in others the main objective is to develop skills necessary to manage and run the cooperative. No factory, regardless of spirit, is able to utilize even unsophisticated equipment and tools without an appropriate study of skills. Vanek argues that:

> At all times, but especially in its early stages, the effort of introducing self-management, must be accompanied by an educational effort.
>
> (Vanek 1975: 36)

A crucial and very sensitive question is whether the Canadian adult education establishment has much to offer in terms of cooperative education. The recent survey of adult education in Canada revealed the enormous domination by the formal educational institutions (Secretary of State 1984: 38). Together the colleges/CEGEPs, school boards, and universities attracted 40 per cent of the participants; the voluntary sector, 16 per cent; employers 18 per cent; private schools, 12 per cent; and union and professional associations 9 per cent (5 per cent did not state provider).

The formal institutions select, classify, distribute, transmit, and evaluate all that is considered to be "public knowledge." This system reproduces the cultural and social structure in society (Rubenson 1980: 37). Cooperatives such as Mondragon can be seen as a revitalization movement that through education transmits a culture which is in conflict with the dominant culture. In fact what Mondragon has done from the beginning is to select, classify, distribute, transmit, and evaluate all that is considered to be the "movement's knowledge" and in this way reproduced the cultural and social standing of the movement. The educational system is in the hands of the cooperative and provides an alternative to what the formal system offers. Not only the content but also the teaching methods are a reflection of the Mondragon philosophy (see Thomas and Logan 1982: chapter 3).

The voluntary organizations in Canada cater to personal development/general interests and hobby/craft/recreation. Some 84 per cent of their participants take part in this type of adult education courses. The voluntary sector is not involved in job-related activities and is oriented toward the individual, not the collective (Secretary of State 1984).

It could be argued that the present provision for adult education is better set up to serve an entrepreneurial than a cooperative approach to alternative economic development. If a stronger emphasis is to be put on cooperative adult education a great deal of consideration must be devoted to an analysis of the possibilities to use and/or alter the present provision of adult education. In this process the role of the labor unions cannot be neglected. Throughout the history of the cooperatives, the relationship of labor unions has raised broad theoretical questions such as: what is the role of the cooperatives within a predominantly capitalistic context, do they increase or decrease the workers' solidarity with other workers? Hochner's (1983) analyses showed that although unions in the United States usually perform a traditional collective bargaining role there is mounting evidence that unions can and do act to facilitate conversion to worker ownership, and that when the unions are initiators, they often act to push for changes in management style and structure. I will not go further into the role of the labor unions here as a more in-depth analysis cannot be provided within this overview. However, the link between adult education and the labor movement, as well as other popular movements, is important when trying to find new ways toward cooperative adult education.

CONCLUSION

The Massachusetts Institute of Technology Commission on Industrial Productivity concluded in its recent report, *Made in America: Regaining the Productive Edge:*

> Without major changes in the ways schools and firms train workers over the course of a lifetime, no amount of macro-economic fine-tuning or technological innovation will be able to produce significantly improved economic performance and a rising standard of living.
>
> (Devtouzos, *et al.* 1989: 81)

In conclusion, instead of minor tinkering and often contradictory policy solutions, it is high time to consider seriously what the OECD's concept of recurrent education really implies. In its broadest definition, recurrent education can be defined as follows:

> A comprehensive educational strategy for all post-compulsory or post-basic education, the essential characteristic of which is the distribution of education over the total life span of the individual in a recurring way, i.e. the alteration with other activities such as work, but also with leisure and retirement.
>
> (OECD 1973: 24)

This definition contains three essential elements: first, it offers an alternative educational strategy to the conventional concentration of all information and full-time education in youth. It proposes to spread post-compulsory education over the full life span of the individual, and thus accepts the principle of lifelong learning. Second, it proposes a framework with which lifelong learning will be organized, this being the alteration and effective interaction between education (as a structural learning situation) and other social activities during which learning occurs. Third, it proposes a coherent strategy for what at present are three unrelated sectors: the conventional post-compulsory educational system, adult education, and labor market training, including on-the-job training of all kinds and at all levels.

If the major societal change at present is the accelerated speed with which change occurs then it ought to be obvious that the accompanying educational revolution requires an acceptance of the view of education as a recurring phenomenon. Although it is common to admire concepts such as recurrent and lifelong education, in truth these principles have had very little concrete input into educational policies.

One of the concerns expressed in the preceding analysis was that there may occur a further polarization in the labor market as a consequence of new technology. Referring back to the presentation of the screening hypothesis the implication is that the internal labor market will play an increased role as training costs increase. Thus those who enter dead-end positions or those trying to enter the labor market late in life are facing increased problems. Employers can be expected to give even more consideration to education as a screening device since the role of training will be – or at least will be perceived to be – more crucial in the economy.

There is today, as was said earlier, an enormous belief in the market forces. However, the technological development is creating a situation where policymakers ought to take a more comprehensive view of the education traditionally provided by the employers and the publicly governed education. This calls for more, rather than less, governmental involvement.

A company's educational decisions are governed by considerations regarding productivity and profit. Goals like equity seldom enter the discussions. Education for broader skills and general knowledge, as distinct from company- or product-oriented training, is rare and generally directed toward managers and other skilled white-collar groups. However, in a strict economic sense a more comprehensive employers' program could be beneficial from a societal point of view. The increased pressure on the economy stemming from the rapid technological progress has in some countries spurred an interest to build a more elaborate and at the same time more flexible system of work-related education and training (SOU 1983: 22). In these cases the development toward financing and institutional arrangements lies somewhere in the zone between the state and that which is purely private (Clement 1983).

The danger with trusting the market force is, as was discussed in connection with the human capital theory, that in the absence of governmental intervention, which equalizes investment in the human capital, inequality of opportunity is inevitable. With a system of lifelong education these inequalities will constantly increase. Finally there is no indication that the "market forces" will address the question of skills for understanding the broader implications of the technology – what was called the "civic education" component of computer education. Anything more drastic that will occur in this area will depend on the democratization of working life. This implies that adult education can have an important indirect economic role. The earlier discussion in this section has dealt with adult education as a means to improve the individual's skills and in this way increase his/her productivity and/or possibility to compete in the labor market. The indirect effect of adult education on economic resources has to do with the redistribution of political resources and the use of these resources. Economic equality can thus come about by changing the way of setting salaries, creating jobs, etc., e.g. through a strengthened labor union.

The role adult education can play in creating alternative means to achieve economic development will depend on its choice of the entrepreneurial or cooperative model. The possibility of choosing between these approaches may be more limited and more socially determined than adult educators realize. Have the proud Canadian traditions of cooperative education as a force for social and economic change vanished for good or . . .?

REFERENCES

Berg, I. (1970) *Education and jobs: The Great Training Robbery*. Boston, MA: Beacon Press.

Blaugh, M. (1976) "Human Capital Theory – A Slightly Jaundiced Survey," *Journal of Economic Literature*. September, 827–55.

Bowles, S. and Gintis, H. (1976) *Schooling in Capitalist America*. New York: Basic Books.

Broady, D. and Gintis, H. (1983) "Samband mellan arbetsliv och utbildning. Några Aktuella Vägar för Forskningen," in TCO (ed.) *Kan Utbildning Förändra Arbestslivet*. Stockholm: TCO.

Clement, W. (1983) "Intermediate ('Parafiscal') Financing Schemes", in H. Levin and H. Schutze (eds) *Financing Recurrent Education*. Beverly Hills, CA: Sage Publications.

Conforth, C. (1983) "Some Factors Affecting the Success or Failure of Worker Co-operation," *Economic and Industrial Democracy*. 4:2, 163–90.

Davis, W.G. (1978) "Colleges of Applied Arts and Technology in Ontario," in R. Kidd and G. Selman (eds) *Coming of Age*. Toronto: CAAE.

Denison, Edward F. (1962) *The Sources of Economic Growth in the US and the Alternatives Before Us*. Supplementary Paper No. 13, New York: Committee for Economic Development.

Department of Communications (1983) *The Information Revolution and Its Implications for Canada*. Ottawa: Supply and Services Canada.

Department of Finance (1984) *A New Direction for Canada: An Agenda for Economic Renewal.* Ottawa: Supply and Services Canada.

Devtouzos, M., Lester, R., and Solow, L. (1989) *Made in America: Regaining the Competitive Edge*. Cambridge, MA: MIT Press.

Doeringer, P.B. and Piore, M.J. (1971) *Internal Labor Markets and Manpower Analysis.* Lexington, MA: D.C. Heath & Co.

Drambo, L. and Bark, A. (1983) *Kontorsautomation och Kvinnors Framtida Arbetsmarknad.* Stockholm: Data-effektutredningen Ds A.

Härnqvist, K. (1977) "Enduring Effects of Schooling – A Neglected Area in Educational Research," *Educational Researcher*, 6:10, 5–11.

Hochner A. (1983) "Worker Ownership, Community Ownership and Labor Unions: Two Examples," *Economic and Industrial Democracy*, 4:3, 345–70.

Levin, H. and Rumberger, R. (1983) *The Educational Implications of High Technology.* Palo Alto: IFG Stanford University.

Meissner, M. (1971) "The Long Arm of the Job: A Study of Work and Leisure," *Industrial Relations*, 10, 239–60.

Mincer, J. (1970) "The Distribution of Labor Incomes – A Survey with Special References to Human Capital," *Journal of Economic Literature*, March 1–26.

Minister Employment and Immigration (1984) *Consultation Paper: Training.* Ottawa: Supply and Services Canada.

National Advisory Board on Science and Technology (1988) Report of the Industry Committee to the Prime Minister, Ottawa.

—— (1989) Report of the Private Sector Challenge Committee to the Prime Minister, *Keeping Canada Competitive: The Innovation Imperative.* Ottawa.

—— (1991) Report of the Human Resource Development Committee, *Learning to Win: Education, Training and National Prosperity.* Ottawa.

National Commission on Excellence in Education (1983) *A Nation at Risk: The Imperative of Educational Reform.* Washington DC: US Department of Education.

Nora, S. and Minc, A. (1989), *The Computerization of Society: A Report to the President of France*, Cambridge, Mass: MIT Press.

OECD (1973) *Recurrent Education.* Paris: OECD.

—— (1983) *Industrial Robots.* Paris: OECD.

Osberg, L. (1981) *Economic Inequality in Canada.* Toronto: Butterworth.

O'Toole, J. (1977) *Work, Learning and the American Future.* London: Jossey-Bass.

Royal Commission on the Economic Union and Development Prospects for Canada (1984) *Challenges and Choices, Interim Report.* Commissioner-Donald MacDonald. Ottawa: Supply and Services Canada.

Rubenson, K. (1980) "Theoretical Framework," in R. Hoghielm and K. Rubenson (eds) *Adult Education and Social Change.* Lund: Gleerup.

Schultz, T. (1960) "Capital Formation by Education," *Journal of Political Economy*, 68:4, 1026–39.

—— (1961) "Investment in Human Capital," *The American Economic Review*, 1:2, 1–17.

Schutze, H. (1984) "Adult Education and the Changing Workplace," in

ICAE (ed.) *International Symposium on Adult Education.* Shanghai, Toronto: ICAE.

Science Council of Canada (1982) *Planning Now for an Information Society: Tomorrow is Too Late.* Report No.33, Ottawa.

Secretary of State (1984) *One in Every Five.* Ottawa: Education Support Sector, Secretary of State.

Seldon, A. (1983) "The New Economics," *Journal of Social, Political and Economic Studies*, 8:1, 3–40.

Skill Development Leave Task Force (1983) *Learning a Living in Canada*, report to the Minister of Employment and Immigration, Ottawa.

Sobel, I. (1982) "The Human Capital Revolution in Economic Development," in P. Altbach, R. Arnove and G. Kelly (eds), *Comparative Education.* New York: Macmillan.

SOU (1983) *Utbildning för Arbetslivet.*

—— (1984) *Datorer och Arbestslivets Förändring.* 1984: 20.

Thomas, H. and Logan, C. (1982) *Mondragon – an Economic Analysis.* London: George Allen & Unwin.

Thurow, L.C. (1975) *Generating Inequality – Mechanisms of Distribution in the U.S. Economy.* New York: Basic Books.

Vanek, J. (ed.) (1975) *Self-management, Economic Liberation of Man.* London: Penguin Books.

WEA (1918) *The WEA Education Yearbook, 1918.* Nottingham: Nottingham Studies in the Theory and Practice of the Education of Adults.

Webb, S. and Webb, B. (1920) *A Constitution for the Socialist Commonwealth of Great Britain.*

Commentary

Human Resource Development: Education and the World of Work

Hans Schutze

Using Kjell Rubenson's historical framework for Human Resource Development, this commentary will focus on education and the world of work.

There is a growing general awareness that the industrialized world is in the midst of a massive transformation. For the industrialized countries, the last decade has been characterized by major upheavals and great changes. The energy and environment crises, the modifications in the worldwide division of economic and industrial power, the emergence of new social aspirations and values and the slowdown in economic and productivity growth have created conditions in many respects very different from the situation ten years ago. Moreover, due to the demographic developments, the increased rate of participation of women in the labor force, new labor-saving production methods, and slackening overall economic growth, OECD countries have experienced a level of unemployment that was unprecedented since the early 1930s. Structural and technological change are profoundly transforming industries and occupations: a great number of jobs have disappeared and others have been created, the workplaces of many people have undergone important changes. In many cases, these changes in the workplace imply a major educational and training challenge as skill requirements are also changing.

Relating these new economic and social trends to education and training is more than ever pertinent. The need for a highly trained work force which can rapidly adjust to the changing demands of production seems now pressing. Labor laws and collective agreements have resulted in heavy reliance on existing manpower and on increasingly firm-specific training. Now that the labor force needs to be both skilled and flexible, greater education and training opportunities are needed to enhance the mobility and flexibility of the work force.

Before looking into what is happening to the workplace, let us first cast a glance at the labor market in general. In recent years, the labor market in OECD countries has been characterized by a number of important developments, some of which have a direct impact both on the workplace and the job skill requirements. A few figures will suffice to illustrate these changes.

The OECD has prepared figure 1.4 to illustrate changes over time in the composition of the working age population in selected countries by educational level (OECD 1989c: 56).

Although unemployment had risen in OECD countries to a level unprecedented since the Second World War (around 32 million people, or 8.8 per cent) in 1983, the number of jobs had also dramatically increased over the previous decade. The absolute growth of jobs between 1970 and 1983 totaled 34 million (or 10 million more than the entire population of Canada). This seeming contradiction – more jobs, but more unemployment – is explained by three factors: a demographic one (the total number of the working age population, i.e. people between 15 and 64 years rose by 75 million, or 14 per cent, between 1970 and 1983); the fact that women have entered the work force in increasing numbers (the general participation rate rose from 40 per cent in 1950 to 55 per cent in 1983); and third, the fact that the number

Figure 1.4 Changes over time in the composition of the working age populations in selected countries (by educational level)

Notes:
a. Educational attainment is classified on the basis of data submitted by national authorities. The classifications presented here may not reflect the full diversity of education and training systems in cases where data provided are not sufficiently detailed. For further information on the classification of educational attainment for each country. see Annex 2.C.
b. A number of countries in their data included persons whose level of attainment cannot be determined. For the purpose of the analysis, those persons have been omitted. They comprise the following percentage of working age population: Australia (1983) 3.7% (1988) 4.6% (students): Japan (1974) 9%, (1987) 10% (students): the Netherlands (1987) 13.5% (students): Portugal (1987) 0.3% (other qualification): Sweden (1971) 1.1%, (1987) 1.9% (other qualification or no answer): United Kingdom (1987) 5.6% (other qualification or no answer).
c. Data refer to persons 20 and over, with the following exceptions: 15 and over in Australia: 15–74 in Finland: 20–64 in Italy, the Netherlands, Sweden (1987) and the United Kingdom (males): 20–60 in the United Kingdom (females): 20–74 in Norway (1971) and Sweden (1971).
Source: OECD Annex 2.D 1989.

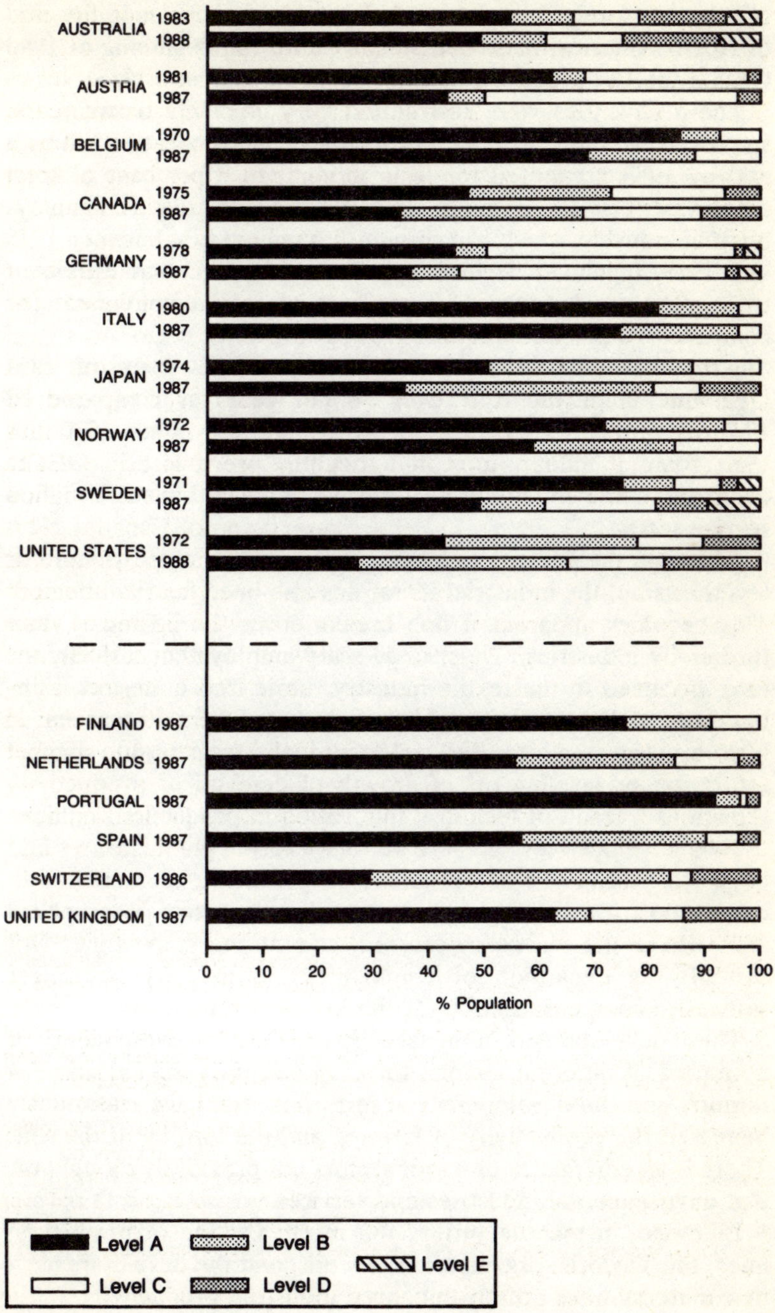

AUSTRALIA 1983
1988
AUSTRIA 1981
1987
BELGIUM 1970
1987
CANADA 1975
1987
GERMANY 1978
1987
ITALY 1980
1987
JAPAN 1974
1987
NORWAY 1972
1987
SWEDEN 1971
1987
UNITED STATES 1972
1988
FINLAND 1987
NETHERLANDS 1987
PORTUGAL 1987
SPAIN 1987
SWITZERLAND 1986
UNITED KINGDOM 1987
0 10 20 30 40 50 60 70 80 90 100
% Population
Level A
Level B
Level C
Level D
Level E

of migrant (foreign) workers, or of immigrant workers in the case of North America, had risen steadily until the beginning of 1980 (with a total of around 15 million between 1970 and 1983).

These new jobs were distributed very unevenly between the sectors of economic activity. Agricultural employment had shrunk and by 1983 accounted for little more than 8 per cent of total employment (as compared to almost 14 per cent in 1970). Employment in industry, which had risen by 3.6 million jobs between 1975 and 1979, began to decline in 1980 and in 1983 was estimated to account for less than 31 per cent of total employment (as compared to 37 per cent in 1970). The service sector was thus the major source of net job creation, and its share of total area-wide employment is over 58 per cent (as compared to 49.2 per cent in 1970). In other words, while between 1970 and 1983 some 9 million jobs in agriculture were lost in OECD countries, some 45 million new jobs were created in the so-called service sector.

Although the number of jobs in industry has remained more or less the same, the industrial sector has also been heavily affected. This becomes apparent if one breaks down the aggregate data further by industries. Thus, large-scale employment dislocations have occurred in the textile industry, basic iron and steel, shipbuilding, and the motor vehicle industry. Due to a variety of factors, such as increased international competition, market saturation or leveling off of growth of demand or productivity growth as a result of technical innovation in production, millions of jobs have been lost in these sectors, causing plant closures and large-scale dismissals of workers. New jobs have been created in other industries, although not necessarily in the same geographical area where the closures occurred, nor at the same time. But overall, the expansion of employment in industry no longer suffices to compensate fully for the losses of jobs.

These developments in the labor market are the consequence of a number of different factors, for example, the mechanization of farming and the development of fertilizers that have enormously increased the productivity of farming and the fertility of the soil. There is an emergence of major sectors not previously thought of, e.g. environmental industries and services.

Likewise, in manufacturing, the mechanization of production lines, the Taylorist organization of work, and the development of new material have greatly enhanced industrial productivity.

But now, a new generation of technologies has been developed and is increasingly penetrating all sectors of economic activity.

Microcomputers, numerically controlled machines (in particular, machine tools), industrial robots, CAD/CAM (Computer-Aided Design/Computer-Aided Manufacturing systems) and other high-technology equipment and processes are having a profound impact not only on the number of jobs in the industries affected, but also on the content of jobs, work organization, and professional job and skill requirements.

"New technologies" consist, then, of a number of different systems and processes and, in order to discuss their impact on the workplace and the employment structure, it is useful to give a few concrete examples. Most spectacular is probably the industrial robot, i.e. "a reprogrammable, multifunctional manipulator designed to move material, parts, tools or specialized devices through variable programmed motions for the performance of a variety of tasks." Robots have penetrated particularly the manufacture of machinery in the automobile industry where they are used for machine tooling, spray painting, spot and arc welding, die-casting, press work, forging, pallet loading, plastic molding, etc. While robots have primarily been allocated to do dirty, dangerous, unhealthy, or boring jobs, thus generally improving working conditions, their implantation has resulted in a considerable restructuring of work skills, and where certain skill profiles, both high and low skilled, have disappeared (e.g. casters, painters, welders), new ones have been created, such as system operators or technical personnel for repair and maintenance.

Another example are the CAD/CAM systems which consist of computerized design, including graphic design, process planning, and parts programming systems, numerical controls, and groups of machine tools interconnected and supervised by computers. Computer-aided design systems are not only used for product design, but also for modeling and simulation, and direct linkage can be installed from the design system to the manufacturing system, i.e., the design can be automatically converted into instruction for a machine tool system. Computer-aided manufacturing systems are used for numerical control of machine tools, welding, spraying, etc., automated inspection and grading of raw material, inspection of machine parts, inventory control, and automated warehousing.

A third example concerns office communication systems, which are increasingly affecting and transforming office jobs. Word processors, micro-, mini-, and mainframe computers, video display terminals, photocopying, microfiche, digital telephone, private branch exchanges and closed circuit television find applications in the preparation, storage, and transmission of documents. Data-banks, information networks, telephone-line-based data retrieval and computer analysis serve to store, retrieve, analyze, and use data and information. Long-distance communication and mailings are done by use of electronic mail/tele-conferencing.

The emergence of microcomputing and telecommunications as principal factors of production and management have contradictory effects upon the organization of firms. In the area of production, the tendency is toward the reduction of the extent of economies of scale. Rapid retooling and the economical tracking of different products within a single production system permit small-scale plants to compete on relatively favorable terms with the mass production units which have dominated most of manufacturing. The trend toward heightened consumer interest in product variety and quality has complemented such technical developments: therefore, the economic advantages of standardized products and large plants are declining rapidly in many markets.

At the same time, the speed and low cost of long-distance data transmission made possible by the combination of the microcomputer and telecommunications have greatly eased the task of coordinating the activities of large multinational enterprises. The center can check up on, and make corrective adjustments to, the activities of the divisions, plants, and even individual employees in a way which was previously impossible. Thus, there is a seemingly paradoxical combination of shrinking minimum plant size and growing maximum corporate size.

Within the enterprise, the relative weight of tasks has been changing steadily as a result of technical and market developments. The actual physical handling of materials now accounts for less than one-half of the total activity within large advanced firms in production industries – and is set to fall still further in the future. The functions that have grown in relative importance include product development, marketing, and finance, all of which are intensive of both information handling and highly qualified manpower. The ability of the organization to apply information systems effectively to the operation and integration of these diverse functions is central to corporate performance – as is the availability of suitably qualified personnel.

Organizational change is also visible lower down the scale, within the plant and the department. The flexible variant of automation made possible by the microcomputer has already eliminated the jobs of an army of less skilled workers in both factory and office. The more repetitive the job, the technically easier it is to automate it. Semi-skilled and clerical work is already being replaced on a grand scale. At the same time, the installation, operation, and improvement of computerized equipment requires considerable inputs of highly educated and well-trained personnel such as programmers, technicians, and systems engineers. This compositional upskilling of the labor force is not new. What the microprocessor adds to the process is a considerable widening of the range of automation possibilities, and, given the intensity of international competition, a potential increase in the speed of change.

At the level of the job itself, the range of possibilities is considerable. In particular, there can be no presumption of an automatic increase in skill requirements in particular jobs as the result of the advent of flexible computerization, it depends upon two sets of factors: the economic context of the innovation and the strategy pursued by corporate management and unions. The enhancement of skill requirements is particularly likely in cases where the new equipment is costly relative both to the old machinery it replaces and to the labor which works with it. In such cases, the cost of the incremental downtime and scrappage associated with less skilled labor toward the use of skilled labor on the new equipment. However, many firms still espouse the view of employee motivation and control associated with the names of Taylor and Ford: namely, that the best way to get workers to work is to give them as narrow a set of job tasks as possible and to supervise closely their performance on those tasks.

Under such strategies, the use of information technology tends to become slanted toward the intensification of existing systems of monitoring and control. There is, however, already evidence that such managerial strategy is itself subject to revision in the light of the experience of new technology. In several instances firms that have used new technologies to maintain or intensify deskilled forms of work organization have been prodded into changing course by unforeseen consequences – notably poor quality of output and high employee dissatisfaction. Based on a broad range of experience, it is therefore likely that new technologies do simultaneously broaden the range of possibilities in job design and slant outcomes toward decentralized, skill-using forms of work organization.

At the same time, the variety of applications, along with the entrenched nature of Taylorist assumptions and methods, cautions against expecting too rapid changes in this respect. Not only will there remain a large domain beyond the reach of computerization (particularly in low-wage manufacturing and personal services), but, even within the area of application of new technology, many managers will by preference or habit apply it with a view to minimizing rather than increasing skill requirements.

The relationship between technical change and human resource development is a complicated one. Changes in products, processes, and organizations will require different skills, and also more skills. Systems of education and vocational training will be influenced accordingly. In practice, however, the ability of education and training systems to meet even current requirements for skilled manpower varies considerably across OECD countries. In the case of the more radical demands posed by information technology, the limited adaptability the national systems may prove one of the most severe constraints upon an economy's ability to adopt new products and processes.

Concerning the volume of education and training undertaken in the economy, the expectation of continued compositional upskilling of the labor force, as low-skilled occupations decline and high-skilled ones rise, implies a steadily increasing load upon educational and training systems. A higher proportion of the labor force will require education beyond minimal levels, as well as more systematic and formal training on the job. According to some recent estimates, about 80 per cent of the work force needs to be literate in order to meet tomorrow's skill requirements, compared to around 30 per cent at present. Thus, the accelerating rate of industrial retraining and technological change is bound to increase investments in education and training significantly, both within the formal education system and at the workplace.

Another important indicator, as reported in "Human Resources Development and a Competitive Economy" (CAAE, 1990) is how adult education and training – including employer and government-sponsored training – is distributed among the labor force. While adult education and training can provide opportunities for under-educated and under-employed adults to improve themselves, some evidence suggests that formal learning reinforces the gap between educational "haves" and "have nots." Citing the Canadian example, recent surveys (reported below) confirm the conventional wisdom that certain segments of the Canadian labor force are significantly under-represented in adult education and training.

Canadian Adult Education Survey

The 1983 Survey of Adult Education found that persons with a university degree were eight times more likely than those with only an elementary education to participate in adult education courses (Secretary of State 1984). Prime age (25–34) adults were three times (at 29 per cent) more likely than older workers (55–64) to participate in such learning. Blue-collar workers were less than half as likely as white-collar workers to participate in an adult education course (16 per cent vs 33 per cent). While 19 per cent of all adults in Canada and 24 per cent of adults in Alberta were engaged in adult education, the adult participation rate was only 9 per cent in Newfoundland and Labrador.

Canadian Adult Training Survey

The results of the 1985 Adult Training Survey (StatsCan 1986) indicate that adults with a university degree were 15 times more likely to participate in part-time job-related training than those with only an elementary education. In Alberta, 14 per cent of adults participated in part-time/short-term job-related training in 1985, compared to only 3 per cent in Newfoundland.

Workers in public administration jobs and finance had an employer-sponsored training rate of 15 per cent while workers in utilities, and community services had participation rates of 14 per cent and 13 per cent respectively. Only 4 per cent of construction and agriculture workers participated in such training. Blue-collar workers and older workers were significantly underrepresented in job-related training in 1985.

While the participation rate for women in part-time/short-term training (8 per cent) was marginally lower than that of men (9 per cent), the survey yielded significant gender differences. In all types of adult training, employers were more likely to reimburse tuition fees of male rather than female employees, particularly in the governmental sector. Men were twice as likely as women to participate in full-time employer-sponsored training.

Other Canadian Employer Surveys

Statistics from employer surveys on worker participation in training are consistent with adult education research. The lower-skilled, the lower-paid, visible minorities, women, youth, and the educationally disadvantaged are under-represented in employer-sponsored training. Employees in the upper end of the organizational hierarchy (executive, managerial, professional, and other white-collar workers) are over-represented. The 25–44 year old group has the highest industrial training participation rates (EIC 1987; Ontario 1989).

A 1985 survey of industry training indicated that 17 per cent of professional/technical workers and 16 per cent of managerial employees participated in formal training, whereas only 6 per cent of construction workers and 4 per cent of transportation workers did so (EIC 1987).

The Canadian Labour Market and Productivity Centre (CLMPC) survey, *Speaking Out on Training*, indicates that 53 per cent of unskilled workers, as opposed to 41 per cent of all workers and 37 per cent of professional and administrative workers, received no job training in the last two years (CLMPC 1989). Fifty-two per cent of unskilled workers, as opposed to 30 per cent of all workers and 20 per cent of professional and administrative workers, considered that they were not adequately prepared to adapt to workplace change due to lack of training, education and experience.

Another indicator of the under-representation of certain groups in industry training is participation rates in apprenticeship training. Although these are increasing, women currently account for only 4 per cent of all apprentices in Canada, while they represent 46 per cent of the labor force (CLMPC 1989).

Further Considerations from OECD

As the developed world faces a general situation of declining youth-cohorts entering its labor market, a warning from OECD's 1989 *Employment Outlook* appears pertinent:

> There may be a great challenge in achieving higher levels of educational attainment for low achievers in those countries in which declining sizes of youth cohorts promise to contribute to labour shortages. This development may bid up wages for entry level jobs, tempting young persons to leave school early, even if their educational attainment is sufficient for immediate employment but inadequate for long-term career preparation. Interventions may therefore be necessary to make education sufficiently interesting to compete with labour market opportunities, or, where labour market shortages may be unavoidable, flexible enough (with provisions for income replacement if need be) to be able to be combined with employment throughout working life.
>
> (OECD 1989: 82)

In this context, dropping out is potentially most serious if it has the effect of inhibiting the capacity of a young person to function as a lifelong learner. The economic and social costs of high failure and drop out rates in the front end model deserve serious attention. Any enterprise with a 33 per cent "failure scrapping" rate would be out of business very soon.

The focus of attention in the past has been almost exclusively on seeking ways to retain young people in the education system. Altogether too little attention has been devoted to policy changes to enable dropouts to obtain second chances at a later date when they may be once again motivated to learn.

And finally, figure 1.5 compares levels of unemployment by gender for 1975 and 1987. Note that:

1 unemployment rates tend to decline with age;
2 that women's unemployment is higher than men's; and
3 that the relative disadvantage of low educational attainment has increased from 1975 to 1987 (OECD 1989c, 61).

Given the changing map of the labor force and the emerging work force literacy needs, what then are the qualifications needed for the jobs which are affected by technological innovation? One feature on which most experts seem to agree is that, given the rapidity of changes affecting the workplace, it is impossible precisely to anticipate future job contents and hence qualification requirements. It is therefore pointed out that, generally, emphasis will have to be put on generic skills, in particular the ability

Figure 1.5 Levels of unemployment by gender for 1975 (above) and 1987.

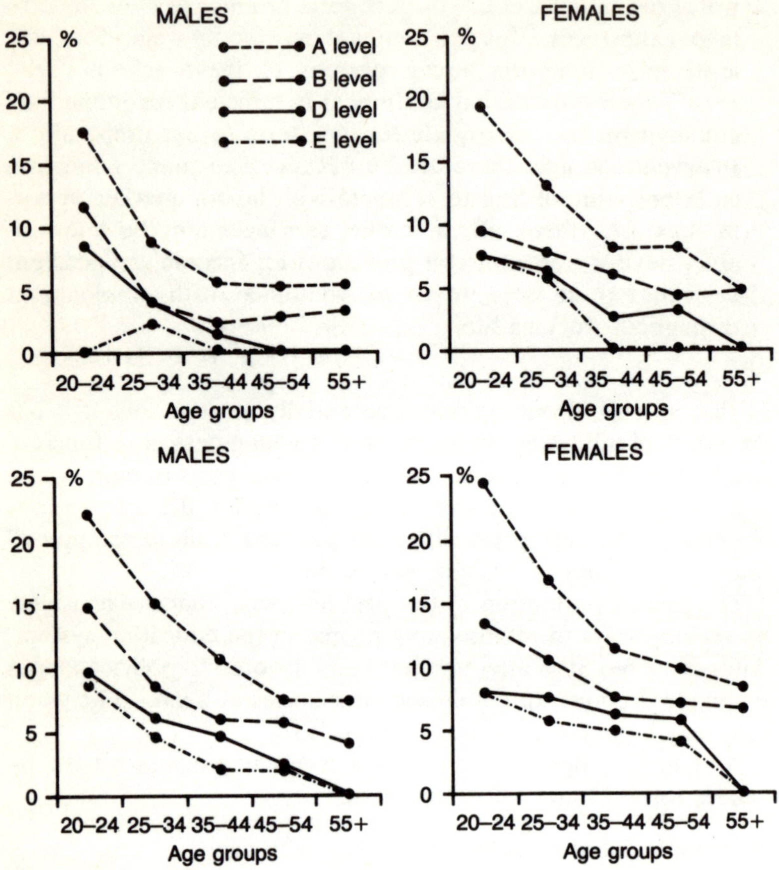

Source: OECD 1989.

to adapt and learn, rather than on narrow occupation-specific training.

A recent survey, commissioned by the European Community and based on a questionnaire to industry, lists a number of general qualities which industry believes will be required from the work force involved with computer-based systems or equipment:

1 the capability for analytic thinking applied to different processes of work;

2 a sense of quantitative appreciation of different processes;
3 a sense of responsibility and a capacity for autonomous work;
4 the ability to link technical, economic, and social considerations in the appreciation of equipment and working methods; and
5 a planned and methodical approach to work.

Many experts agree that "computer literacy," i.e. knowledge of the computer as a tool for managing massive amounts of information, is becoming increasingly important and, in fact, equivalent in importance to basic literacy. Others think that even computer literacy is not sufficient to cope with the new technological developments and hence use the term "technological literacy" to describe a level of understanding of technology in its various forms that goes beyond a familiarity with computers.

Thus, a recent study of the US Congress Office of Technology Assessment suggests that technological literacy will indeed soon be required of all members of the work force as broader and more extensive applications of information technology are made in offices and plants. According to these experts, basic electronics and informatics expertise will be crucial for the great majority of jobs, alongside general capabilities, i.e. broad basic knowledge and skills, high ability to learn, flexibility, and thinking in terms of abstract, complex systems and processes.

Other researchers are less convinced that these, in fact, will constitute general skill requirements applicable to the whole work force. They point out, for instance, that in the US, manpower projections by the Department of Labor suggest that the growth of jobs for computer system analysts, data processing machine mechanics, and computer programmers will be relatively small in comparison with such unskilled or semi-skilled job categories as janitors, nurses' aides, fast-food workers, and waiters. However, these researchers, too, stress the increasing importance of a basic foundation in logic, analytical reasoning, expressive and communicative skills, and in general the ability to learn and to adapt to changing workplaces and production processes.

The problem of human resource development concerns the content of skills as well as the quantity of skill. The implementation of information technology in the workplace tends to alter the demands placed upon both managers and workers. For lower level employees, there is a tendency for experiential skills (such as the feel for materials and machines) to be replaced by cognitive (such as the knowledge of the principles of a particular process) and affective (such as the willingness to be vigilant and responsive).

It was already mentioned that, to the extent that work becomes increasingly organized around a team basis, social skills such as communication and cooperativeness become increasingly important. To the extent that the pace of restructuring continues to develop, the ability to learn new ways of doing old things, and even new things altogether, becomes more important. With such changes being a reality, the content of schooling and training will be affected.

The shift from experiential to cognitive and affective requirements implies an increase in the importance of formal schooling relative to job experience. The need for individual openness to change requires a more creative and flexible content in the school or training curriculum.

Although technological innovation has massively increased the productive capacity of machines, human knowledge and skills are no less important than in the past; on the contrary, the development and application of automated and flexible systems, as well as the full realization of their productive potential, depend on the way human resources are developed and utilized. Particularly at the level of enterprise strategies, human resources policies, not least through education and training, are being considered as a new competitive parameter in a situation of increasing international competition.

The introduction of new technologies at the workplace clearly eliminates a broad range of repetitive and routine jobs both in the area of blue- and white-collar jobs. This in turn creates a trend of general upskilling of the remaining jobs as well as problems and tensions in relation to traditional modes of work organization where, in particular, the roles of supervisors and middle management have to be redefined to take into account, on the one hand the trend of upskilling and, on the other hand, the more direct and flexible flow of information due to the utilization of new technologies.

There is strong evidence that there is no technological determinism when it comes to the impact of new technologies on work organization and skill developments. On the contrary, the introduction of new technologies creates a wide range of options concerning work organization and the development of skills and qualifications of the people affected. Even if numerous cases exist where the introduction of new technologies in an initial phase leads to increased hierarchical control and preservation of the existing work organization, such a phase is usually abandoned after a period of costly underutilization of the existing potential of the new technologies. The implications of this are simply that when the introduction of new technologies is being considered, equal attention has to be given to the consequences for work organization and skills as to the new technology per se.

There is a clear trend toward more teamwork in relation to new technologies both in blue- and white-collar work areas. The concept of one man/one machine/desk is increasingly being replaced by the concept and practice of one team/one technical system.

The trend toward teamwork puts a premium upon broadening the competence profile of the individual worker. Increased emphasis on education and training is being directed toward communication and social skills and the need to complement necessary technical skills with a more holistic view.

Related to the trend to more teamwork is also a trend toward increased emphasis on polyvalent skills, meaning the ability of an individual worker to perform all the tasks in the framework of a team.

There seems, in general, to be an important relationship between investment in education and training and changes in work organization. Investment in education and training without consequent changes in work organization and responsibilities seems on the whole to be an unwise investment. In other words, education and training at the enterprise level cannot be separated from changes in work organization.

Since enterprises are increasingly obliged by either law or collective agreement to keep their work force (i.e. they have less freedom to hire and fire), the internal labor market is increasing in importance and poses particular problems of the responsibility of individual enterprises concerning education and training, not only of their own work force, but also of those workers who will be made redundant. Traditionally it has been considered that it is the role of governments to provide the training for such workers (i.e. labor market training). However, new and interesting initiatives are being taken by some of the enterprises in providing education and training also for those who will be laid off. This opens up new perspectives on the respective role of public and private training initiatives directed to those who will have to change their jobs.

Among those enterprises where a deliberate policy exists to consider their human resources as one of the most important resources of the enterprise, there exists also a policy of considering investment in education and training of crucial importance. This has led to the recognition, within the enterprise, of the high costs being associated with a policy of underinvestment in education and training in relation to the introduction of new technologies. In other words, "human capital" is increasingly seen as being of the same importance as physical capital as they are essential to the full realization of the expected benefits of the technology.

Enterprise-sponsored training opportunities are not available for the great bulk of those out of employment, or workers in small and medium-sized firms. Training for these groups must be provided by education and training institutions. Adult education must also cater to the specific needs of those adults who do not possess the basic literacy and numerical skills that are increasingly becoming minimum prerequisites for obtaining or holding a job.

In response to this demand, institutions for adult education and training must develop appropriate programs and courses that provide participants with broadly based polyvalent and flexible qualifications. Government and the private sector must initiate policies and strategies with a view to creating mechanisms and incentives that enable and induce adults to effectively participate in such programs. The use of new educational technologies will help to overcome some of the existing barriers to adult participation in recurrent training programs.

Technological change at the workplace and the need for the recurrent adaptation of workers' skills are thus rigorously reinforcing the concept of lifelong learning and recurrent education. In saying this, it must be stressed, however, that lifelong learning embraces a far broader range of educational and social objectives than training for change in the workplace and, therefore, the concepts of recurrent education and lifelong learning must not be understood as mere instruments to adapt workers to the changing skill demands of the labor market, but rather remain basic strategies for the enhancement of personal fulfillment, development, and equal opportunity and life chances.

REFERENCES

Canadian Association for Adult Education (1990) *Human Resources Development and a Competitive Economy*. Toronto.

Canadian Labour Market and Productivity Centre (CLMPC) (1989) *Report of the Task Force on Apprenticeship*. Ottawa: CLMPC.

Employment and Immigration Canada (EIC) (1987) *Electrical and Electronics Manufacturing Industry: Human Resources Study*. Ottawa: Supply and Services Canada.

OECD (1989) *Employment Outlook*. Paris: OECD.

Ontario Ministry of Skills Development (1989) *The Training Lecision: Training in the Private Sector*. Toronto: Queen's Printer.

Statistics Canada (1985) *Resources for Research and Development with Estimates*. Ottawa: Supply and Services Canada.

—— (1986) *Adult Training Survey*. Ottawa: Education Culture and Tourism Division.

—— (1989) *Advance Statistics of Education 1989–90*. Ottawa: Supply and Services Canada.

—— (1989) *Education in Canada: A Statistical Review for 1987–88*. Ottawa: Supply and Services Canada.

—— (1989) *Financial Statistics of Education 1985–86*. Ottawa: Supply and Services Canada.

—— (1989) *Community Colleges and Related Institutions: Post-Secondary Graduates and Enrolment: 1987*. Ottawa: Supply and Services Canada.

—— (1990) *Human Resource Training and Development Survey*. Ottawa: Supply and Services Canada.

Chapter 2

Human Capital: A High-yield Investment

Anthony Patrick Carnevale

It is human nature to waste anything that seems abundantly supplied. At the moment, there seems to be an overabundance of North American workers. Our economies apparently are overflowing with underemployed, unemployed, and expendable people. As unseemly rates of unemployment hover in double digits, we are told that labor-saving machinery will soon make us all redundant. The bogeyman of technology is loose again.

Developed nations are predisposed to the view that there are too many people. Our recent history encourages us to accept the notion that people are superfluous while machinery, financial capital, and the tangible fruits of the earth are scarce. Since 1946, we in North America have been forced persistently to reshape our economic and social structures in order to bear, feed, clothe, educate, employ, and house the 76 million members of the American baby boom. As a result, while we have learned to value people for their purchasing power, we have not seen them as critical resources for production.

Things are rarely as they first appear. Upon closer examination, the apparent oversupply of Americans proves illusory. Unfortunately, our misconceptions and the biases of our recent history are threatening the economic future of the United States. There is some risk that we will be misled by the notion that people are oversupplied and beguiled by our recent past into a national investment strategy that favors machines and resources extracted from the earth over people. This would surely prove a serious economic error.

In fact, the economic and social yield from investing in human resources is high and increasing. Our economic growth and productivity are becoming ever more dependent on our human resources.

Educated, healthy, trained, and spirited people are the ultimate source of economic growth. They are not simply the passive consumers of an autonomous and inhuman economic yield. The nation's economic history tells us with deadening statistical regularity of the increasing yield from human capital investment. The evidence (shown in figure 2.1) demonstrates clearly the overwhelming historical and projected contribution of human resource factors to the increase in national income. By way of comparison, human resource inputs are shown to be consistently more important than capital.

People – not machines – are the wellspring of productivity. Productivity is the human art of getting more with the same or fewer resources. This can be accomplished by increasing the intensity with which we utilize resources (working harder) or by increasing the efficiency with which we mix and use available resources (working smarter). Both depend on the skill and work effort of labor and management. In short, productivity at its roots, turns on human decisions and work attitudes.

Growth in on-the-job know-how, the reallocation of labor, and the increase in the quality of labor through education, training, and health care have consistently accounted for more than three quarters of productivity increases since 1929, and for most of our growth in national income. By comparison, the amount of machine capital per worker has contributed a consistent, and disappointing 20 per cent or less.

Human motivation is a key economic resource. The evidence of the economic impact of human motivation is compelling. Convincing data show that the key difference in productivity among firms and nations can be attributed not to the quantity of resource inputs but to some unmeasurable qualitative human "factor x." Research shows that productivity differences between workers in the same plants with the same pay and equipment can vary by a factor of four, and differences between plants with identical equipment, labor, and pay can vary by 50 per cent. According to available research, the variation in "x" efficiency is rooted in motivational and cultural differences. Recent advances in the measurement of motivational factors in the workplace suggest that a 10 per cent improvement in motivational factors allows for a 1 per cent reduction in product prices.

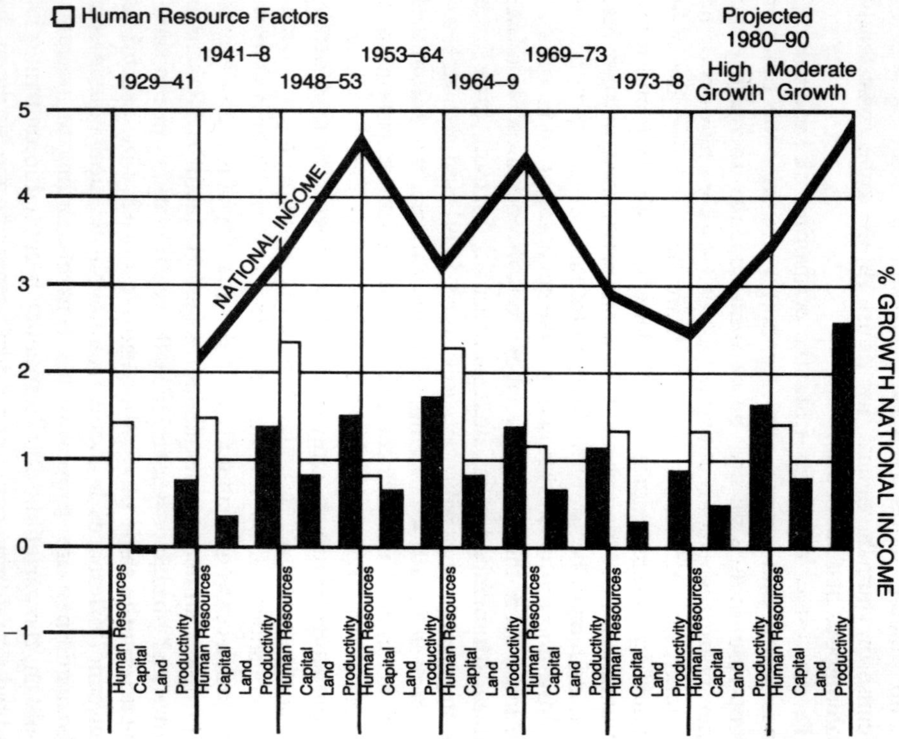

Figure 2.1 Components of growth in national income (1929–90)

Historically, human resources have been gradually replacing all others. The economic history of the modern world is a tale of the inexorable shift from natural and machine resources to acquired human skills as the basic building blocks of production. In 1890, resources from the earth, including minerals, energy, and food, accounted for 50 per cent of the gross national product. Today, these same resources account for less than 10 per cent. Over the same period, human resources grew to account for more than four-fifths of US total economic output. The acquired skills and abilities of the human population have become the master resource, because they are the agents that transform the environment into usable goods and services.

In the last century, for instance, economists routinely listed land, labor, and capital as the factors essential for economic production. In the shift from an economy based on agriculture and other resources extracted from the earth to the post-industrial economy, land has virtually been eliminated as a prime factor of production. Available data suggest that land played no part in the productivity increases between 1948 and 1966, and because the economic contributions of land declined, thereafter, it had a negative impact on productivity between 1966 and 1978.

As the economic value of all other resources has declined, the value of human time has increased. In the United States, real earnings per hour of work have increased fivefold since 1900. Fully 75 per cent of national income, now derives from earnings. Nobel laureate Simon Kuznets's classic studies of economic growth show a rapid growth in the value added by the human factor relative to other factors of production. Kuznets finds that over this century, the share of national income attributed to property declined from 45 per cent to 25 per cent, while the human contribution to national income increased from 55 per cent to 75 per cent.

In 1817, an American laborer earned the equivalent of two bushels of wheat per week. By 1890, weekly wages were equivalent to nine bushels of wheat. Wheat dropped in price by half between 1900 and 1970, which means that if human labor had remained in rough proportion to agricultural output, workers could have expected the equivalent of 18 bushels per week in 1970. Instead, the weekly compensation of manufacturing workers was equivalent to 96 bushels.

Not only has the economic system demanded an increased quantity of human capital, it has rewarded an ever-increasing quality. Manufacturing workers received only two cents per hour more than unskilled workers in 1900. By 1970, the absolute difference was 79 cents. Teachers, the Nation's lowest-salaried professional, received only 24 cents per hour more than unskilled labor in 1900. Their margin had increased to $1.90 per hour in 1970.

The historical dominance of the human factor in economic growth and productivity will persist and grow. In the latter portion of the twentieth century, the dominance of human resources in the American economy will continue and accelerate. We are presently in the midst of a shift to a post-industrial service and information economy where productivity will increasingly be embodied in persons not raw resources or machines.

We already have come full circle since the early nineteenth century. In 1820, more than 70 per cent of the labor force worked on the farm. In 1980, only 3 per cent worked on the farm, and 70 per cent of the work force had moved through manufacturing and into services and information industries. What is more, the current shift from manufacturing to the service and knowledge industries will likely accelerate with new labor saving technologies.

The coming of post-industrial society will not eclipse industrial production, nor the importance of the more highly skilled workers who will remain in manufacturing. Agriculture did not disappear with the advance of industry. It became mechanized and more productive. In 1850, for instance, one farmer provided for four other people. In 1982, one farmer provided for 78 others. In much the same fashion, manufacturing and basic industries will rely more heavily on machinery and a smaller, more highly skilled work force for increased productivity.

An inevitable and accelerating economic trend underlies these data. That trend is what economists refer to as the "rationalization" of the world economy. Rationalization is the process by which high-skilled, high-technology-intensive production concentrates in developed countries and, correspondingly, lesser skilled, technology-poor production concentrates in lesser-developed nations. It is the sorting out of national competitive advantage in the world economy.

The competitive advantage of the lesser-developed nations begins with their low-wage, low-skill labor pool. Our own competitive advantage relies on the application of technological advances and our ability to maintain and accelerate the skill level of our labor force. In the long term, the United States cannot protect its share of unskilled production. Ultimately, we cannot match "sweat equity" with 950 million Chinese. We cannot compete for low wage, low-skill production markets.

Our real competitors are the other, "more developed" countries. As the pace of technological change accelerates, competitive advantage depends on our ability to adapt, to apply new technologies to production, and to integrate human skills with new machine technology. Adaption will be all the more difficult as product life and skill life become shorter and shorter. Ultimately it is the rate at which we apply new technologies and integrate them with ready labor that will determine our success. As the international rationalization process accelerates, the constant and optimal shifting of human and machine resources will be required, as will the constant retraining of the workforce.

In the future, workers – not natural resources – will be scarce. The world of "standing room only" will never come. Births are influenced heavily by economic and social conditions. Births rose with income during the early agricultural development of economic systems and declined with the coming of industry and urbanization. In fact, declining birth-rates have characterized the United States and other industrial nations for more than 200 years. The single exception to that trend occurred in the United States between 1946, and 1964, when 76,441,000 babies were born. This was 20,000,000 more births than in the previous 20 years (1926–45). By all reports, however, the "baby boom" is an exception. It passes into history while the dominant trend toward low birth rates reasserts itself.

The economic effects of population decline are already upon us. Overall shortages of workers are hidden, however, under the cloak of the current high rates of unemployment. Recovery from our "double dip" recession of the early 1990s will reveal this overall shortage quickly and dramatically. In the 1970s, for instance, slower rates of growth produced 19 million jobs for new workers. One can only speculate on the impact on available jobs of major structural change, demographic realities, and new global competitiveness into the 1990s.

The human resource is inexhaustible. It guarantees that there are no permanent limits to economic growth. The anxious notion that we draw our resources from increasingly inaccessible reservoirs is scientifically unfounded and statistically unproven. Human economic and social institutions always will adjust to the available supply of economic resources. Increased prices for scarce resources create incentives to expand supply. When rising prices fail to generate new supplies, substitutes become cost-effective and available resources can be remixed in the production process. In the rare cases where the costs of extracting more resources becomes prohibitive, human tastes will adjust to accept substitutes or other goods and services.

ECONOMIC BENEFIT FROM FORMAL EDUCATION

Perhaps the most remarkable finding is the sizable, positive influence of increased formal education on growth in US national income. The nation's commitment to educational attainment has increased at an accelerating rate. Between 1940 and 1978, the median number of school years completed among American workers increased from 9.1 to 12.7. Over the same period, the proportion of all workers with a grade school education increased from 50 per cent to 91 per cent, those with a high school diploma from 19.7 per cent to 41.4 per cent and those with four or more years of college from 5.7 per cent to 17.7 per cent.

Let's take a closer look at the numbers. Of what economic value is this nation's $250 billion education enterprise? Well, first the obvious; the American education system is one of the nation's largest employers. Only health care, at roughly $400 billion a year, exceeds education as a proportion of the gross national product. For the sake of clarity, I'll divide education's other economic benefits into some arbitrary categories. First, we'll look at education's economic benefits to society, then to employers, then to communities, then to families, and then to individuals.

The Society

From the point of view of the society, the question is whether the resources used in education add to the total size of the economic pie. The answer, at least in economic literature, is consistent and flattering. Formal education has consistently out-performed machine capital in its contribution to overall growth in national income since 1929. For instance, between 1948 and 1973 almost a fifth of the growth in national product was due to formal education, mostly due to an increased proportion of Americans with a high school diploma or some higher education. In the period between 1973 and 1981, when productivity growth mysteriously declined, education still contributed substantially to the gross national product and out-performed machine capital. In fact, economists agree that increases in educational attainment accounted for a third of the total growth in gross national product during that period.

Before we leave our brief discussion of the economic impact of education on the whole society, let me leave you with two important perspectives on the future of the economic relationship between education and the society. First, over the long term, the educator's economic role is crucial. Indeed, the numbers I just quoted probably understate the contribution of education to the nation's long-term economic growth prospects. For instance, the distinction between the economic contribution from education and machine capital is an artificial distinction. Machines, after all, are human creations. In the long term, it is the education system that shoulders the principal responsibility for maintaining, disseminating, and advancing the state of human knowledge that ultimately creates the next machine and dreams up the next economy.

The short-term relationship, however, is less certain. In the short term, the economy leverages education more than education leverages the economy. In the short term, the quantity and quality of jobs are usually given. It is the educator's task to fit young people with the skills necessary to fill specific job slots and to retrain adults as skill requirements change. In the short term, education doesn't create jobs but jobs create the need for specific kinds of education. In the short term, if there are no jobs for magicians and engineers, there will be little educational demand for magic or engineering.

In addition, in the short term, demographic and economic factors beyond the educator's control can create a buyer's or seller's market. In the 1970s, with the baby boom entering the work force and inflation and unemployment high, there were many more job seekers than jobs. The oldest of economic laws was in operation: that which was amply supplied – in this case young people – was not valued. Employers could substitute a greater quantity of less educated labor for more educated labor.

If all goes well, the buyer's market of the 1970s will have become the seller's market of the 1990s. As the baby boom is finally absorbed into the workplace, the number of young people available for entry-level jobs is declining rapidly. In addition, the disappearance of the oil inflation of the 1970s suggests that we can generate lower unemployment levels without encouraging runaway inflation. We could arrive at a point where there are many more entry-level jobs than entry-level job seekers. From the educator's point of view, these are "happy problems." Entry-level labor scarcity will mean the products of the schools will be valued, that the school's clientele – its students – will have good reason to stay in school and achieve in school with a job at the end of the tunnel. What is more, your consumers, the employers, the military, and others will be anxious to coalesce with you to build workable partnerships and garner resources.

The second perspective I would offer on the changing nature of the economic relationship between education and society is that if we are to continue the economic contributions from education, in general, we will have to pursue different strategies in elementary-secondary and post-secondary education. The elementary-secondary strategy will have to emphasize quality, and the post-secondary strategy will have to emphasize higher volume. We'll need better elementary-secondary education and more post-secondary education. Let me explain. Until recently, the main source of growth in elementary-secondary education's contribution to the economy has been the extension in the numbers of school years completed by all Americans. Opportunities for economic growth from increasing high school graduation rates are going to become smaller over the next decades, because there aren't that many more people to get through high school. As we achieve our goals of universal free public education, the opportunities for growth in the economy, for increasing the proportion of the work force with a high school diploma, diminishes.

We can continue the economic contributions from educational attainment by rapidly increasing the proportion of the Nation's population that goes on to post-secondary education. But under current conditions, that's unlikely. The public subsidy for college, unlike elementary-secondary schooling, is relatively small and the non-public costs are incurred by individuals. In addition, if we greatly expanded the proportion of the work force going to college, the economic benefits to the economy would increase but the competitive value of a college education for individuals would go down creating an offsetting disincentive for college going. This suggests that potential economic growth from the education sector will have to come from greater post-secondary subsidies or from improvements in the quality of elementary-secondary education. One hopeful sign is that "quality" seems to be the essential thrust of this latest round of educational reform. The bad news is that we must find the resources to pay for "quality" in elementary-secondary education or a general expansion in post-secondary education.

The Employer

Now let's shift our focus from the aggregate economic contribution of education to education's economic contributions to groups within society. The economic benefits to employers occur in the principle areas of employee work effort, sorting, and skill acquisition. First, education has always correlated strongly with the work ethic. Sixty-three per cent of college graduates show a strong work ethic as compared to 47 per cent of those with high school or less. And only 18 per cent of college graduates find no inherent value to working as compared to 31 per cent of those with high school or less. Second, employers have always utilized educational attainment and educational achievement as sorting devices to help them pick and choose among those who offer themselves as prospective employees. Third, and perhaps most important, education is a major provider of job-specific and occupation-specific skills. The skill training partnership between education and employers is longstanding and successful.

We spend roughly $250 billion a year on formal education in the United States – roughly $150 billion for elementary-secondary and $95 billion for post-secondary. Employers spend roughly $180 billion a year on informal training on the job and an additional $30 billion on formalized courses of instruction. Thirty-eight per cent, or $11.4 billion, of that formalized training provided by employers, is bought from outside providers. Employers buy 63.5 per cent, or $7.24 billion worth of their outside training from schools.

Employers and educators share the role of preparing the nation's entry-level workers and retraining experienced workers. When asked where they learned what they needed to know to qualify for their initial job, Americans said they learned what they need to know in school and on the job. The more professional and white-collar employees tend to get more of their preparation for their initial job in school and less through formal and informal employer-based training.

Service workers – farming, forestry, and fishing – craft workers and machine operators and laborers tended to rely on a mix of schooling and workplace learning that emphasized the workplace as a learning experience more than schooling. But in all cases, there was a mix of schooling and workplace learning in preparation for entry-level jobs. When asked where they got retrained to meet skill requirements beyond entry level, Americans tend to respond with a mix of schooling and workplace learning with the decided shift towards learning on the job – as one would expect among experienced employees.

Let's look at the data. When managers, professionals, and technical and sales workers were asked how they qualified for their initial jobs, 66 per cent said they learned some or all they needed to know in schools, 15 per cent said they learned some or all they needed in order to do the job in formalized company programs, and 44 per cent said they learned some or all they needed to know informally on the job. As you can see, service, farming, craft, machine operators, and laborers tended to rely less on schooling and more on formal company programs and informal on-the-job learning.

When asked where they were retrained, managerial, professional, technical, and sales employees said they learned 40 per cent of what they needed to know to be retrained in school, 32 per cent in company-based formal training, and 35 per cent of what they needed to know, they learned informally on the job. In general, when we look at retraining, there is a decline in the participation of schools and an increase in formal and informal on-the-job learning as a source of new skill acquisition. What I find most remarkable about these data is the extent of the employer's activity in providing initial training for entry-level jobs, and the extent of the school system's involvement in retraining. In general, these data suggest to me that the training partnership between employers and the school system is more robust than any of us has ever supposed.

Communities

Now let's look at education and its economic contribution to communities. There are three kinds of economic benefits that come to mind. First, education provides a certain amount of socialization that allows us to live together in dense urban communities efficiently and effectively. Second, education teaches people to defer gratification in favor of benefits that accrue later in life. The ability to defer gratification in the interest of encouraging economic gain somewhere down the road is at the root of the community's ability to save human, machine, and financial capital. Deferred gratification is the emotional principle that underlies entrepreneurial behavior and our economic notion of investment. The third economic benefit that education delivers to the community is a reduction in dependency. Better-educated people make better economic decisions, do better career planning for themselves, and as citizens make better economic decisions for the community as a whole. In addition, as we already discussed, education provides people with occupational and job skills that encourage employment and reduce public dependency. Obviously, education correlates strongly with employment. Sometimes we forget just how strongly. For instance, a single year for early childhood education, targeted on a disadvantaged child, will return as much as $23,852 a year in reduced costs to taxpayers after the child reaches twenty years of age.

Education also benefits the community to the extent that it raises property values and attracts business. Studies show that people are willing to pay for a good education system and that, next to low taxes, new or relocating business firms are interested most in good schools for the children of their employees and retraining facilities for personnel. Indeed, one study suggests that for every dollar invested in education there is $1.60 returned to communities that make that investment.

Families

Education also benefits families and ultimately the American economy, because the family is the incubator for the nation's human capital and our primary and cheapest provider of human services. Exactly how does education encourage the development of human capital through the family? Available literature tells us that educational attainment and achievement correlate with less domestic violence, better child-rearing practices, better nutrition, and smaller families in which, some would argue, economic resources are more effectively concentrated on fewer children.

Individuals

Happily, education also benefits its primary client – the individual. Every year of schooling completed correlates with a 2.73 increase in life expectancy for females and 2.48 increase in life expectancy for males. A single year of pre-school education will eventually result in annual earnings of $19,200 for disadvantaged clientele – $5,200 per annum over the $14,000 they would have made on welfare. Over a lifetime, a high school degree is worth an additional $189,000 in earnings. High school plus a few years of post-secondary education is worth an additional $109,000. A four-year college degree adds yet another $226,000 to lifetime earnings, and college plus some adult education beyond college can add another $107,000. The difference in lifetime earnings between the average American who doesn't complete high school and the average American who completes college and continues to participate in some form of adult education is roughly $631,000 over a lifetime.

What is even more hopeful is that the relationship between education and earnings is strongest for females and minorities. For instance, high school completion is worth 7 per cent in terms of increased lifetime earnings for white males, 9.4 per cent in increased lifetime earnings for white females, 9 per cent in increased lifetime earnings for black males, and 9.1 per cent in increased lifetime earnings for black females.

Studies of disadvantaged youth have shown remarkable effects from schooling on youth employment and wages. One study of the labor market experiences of 16 through 21 year-olds showed that students who are disadvantaged but received "B" and "C" grades earned 39 per cent more in youth jobs than students who received "D's" and "F's". The same study showed that students who are disadvantaged but received "A" and "B" grades received 54 per cent more than students who are similar in terms of their socioeconomic profile but who earned "D's" and "F's". Still another study points out that students with low grades tend to have the worst work habits and highest rates of absenteeism. Education is still the best means of leveraging the nation's minority and underpaid female majority up the income ladder.

THE FUTURE

Can we expect the relationships between education and its various economic beneficiaries to change in the future? We have already touched on two of those changes. First, we have already realized most of the economic benefit from the remarkable expansion in the number of years of schooling completed by Americans. In the future, we'll have to rely more on quality increases to leverage economic gains from education. The second change in the economic context for education is the scarcity in the number of young people that will encourage lower unemployment rates. This happy problem is both the educator's greatest opportunity and greatest challenge, because while there will be high demand for scarce young people, more and more of those people will come to school and to work with human capital deficits.

Let's look at the numbers. The proportion of the population under 5 years will decline from its peak in 1960, at 11.2 per cent, to a low of 6.8 per cent by 2020. Similarly, the number of 5 through 17 year-olds will decline from a peak of 25.7 in 1970, to a low of 17.8 per cent by 2020. Scarcity of young people, however, is likely to result in both a reduction in the quantity of entry-level job seekers and a reduction in the quality of young job seekers. In the likely low-unemployment economy that will result, more and more of the available entry-level employees will be found among populations in whom we have made the least human capital investments. In 1984, 38 per cent of the babies born in the United States were minority – black, hispanic, or native American. By the year 2000, 38 per cent of those under the age of 18 years will be minority.

In the future, there will be many fewer whites and many more blacks and hispanics in entry-level jobs. Evidence of our deficient investment in these two groups is not hard to find. For instance, when one looks at the overall American adult population, one discovers happily that in 1985, 83.5 per cent had graduated from high school. Yet only 63.8 per cent graduated by the age of 19. The rest received GED (adult high school equivalency) or other forms of certification. When one looks at blacks and hispanics the story becomes even more pessimistic. While 83.5 per cent of all Americans had graduated from high school and 63.8 per cent graduated by the age of 19, only 51.8 per cent of blacks and 40.3 per cent of hispanics graduated from high school by age 19. Should we be concerned about the quality of learning among GEDs and those others who do not graduate by 19? I think so.

Reading scores are another indication. In a 1985 national assessment of 9 year-olds, we discover that virtually all Americans have rudimentary basic reading skills. Seventy-one per cent of whites have basic reading skills compared to 39 per cent for blacks and 44 per cent for hispanics. Twenty-two per cent of whites have intermediate reading skills compared to 4 per cent for blacks and 4 per cent for hispanics, and 1.2 per cent of whites have adept reading skills compared to one-tenth of one per cent for blacks and none for hispanics. When we look at reading scores for 17 year-olds, there is improvement for all races and ethnic groups and the gap between whites, blacks, and hispanics seems to decline. A second look suggests, however, that the relatively minor closing of the gap between blacks, hispanics, and whites results, in fact, from the substantial number of low achieving blacks and hispanics who dropped out of the school system by that time. Pre-school programs provide another pessimistic piece of evidence.

Early childhood education works. One study showed that a single year of pre-school could reduce unemployment in later life by half; increase high school completion by 30 per cent, reduce arrests by almost 50 per cent; make disadvantaged pupils 50 per cent more likely to score above national averages on achievement tests; and, as stated previously, result in social benefits as high as $28,000 per annum per child. Our problem is that we are underinvesting in early childhood education. Thirty-seven per cent of the nation's children under the age of 5 are enrolled in pre-school programs, and yet only 19 per cent of children under the age of 5 from families who earn less than $10,000 are enrolled in those programs.

MORE EVIDENCE

We know as a result of recent work that short durations of poverty have little effect on long-term social and economic performance. We also know that long bouts of poverty can have disastrous consequences, both in terms of economic and social performance over a lifetime. The disturbing news is that only 5 per cent of white children ever live in poverty for more than five years, while 46 per cent of the nation's black children live in poverty for more than five years at some point during their childhood. We also know that the culture of poverty requires a critical mass of people in the same deracinated condition in order to result in its most disastrous economic and social effects. This notion, after all, is the basic rationale behind the integration strategies of the 1950s and the 1960s. The culture of poverty is beginning to assert itself again as we develop even larger urban ghettos cut off from the mainstream society. We know, for instance, that children raised in poor families where someone worked, have a much reduced chance of remaining poor themselves as adults as compared with children raised in poor families where no one works. We know, for instance, that when there are less than 7 per cent poor in a local school, 28 per cent of the poor students will achieve in the bottom quartile and 12 per cent of the non-poor students will achieve in the bottom quartile. At the same time, when the proportion of poor children increases in a school system, both the poor children and the non-poor children tend to perform less well. For instance, of the 24 per cent poor children in the school, 56 per cent of the poor students achieve in the lowest quartile and 48 per cent of the non-poor students achieve in the lowest quartile.

WORKPLACE LEARNING

As stated earlier, American employers manage a learning system that includes as much as $180 billion in informal on-the-job training and an additional $30 billion in formalized learning paid for by employers. By way of comparison, this $210 billion learning system is roughly the same size as the nation's public elementary, secondary, and higher education institutions.

This learning system is the first line of defense against economic and technological change. The ability of American employees to adapt to new technologies and other forms of economic change is largely dependent on their ability to learn on the job. Economic and technological change occurs incrementally; its first impact is on employers and employees on the job. As a result, our ability to respond to competitive challenges is largely dependent on the quantity and quality of formal and informal learning in the workplace. More effective and timely workplace learning systems would not only allow us to keep pace better with changing technologies and economic circumstances, but would also encourage more self-conscious career development from employees, as well as minimize dislocation.

As you can see in figures 2.2 and 2.3, Americans learn what they need to know to do their jobs in schools and on the job, formally and informally. School tends to be most important for managers,

Figure 2.2 Sources of training by occupational group

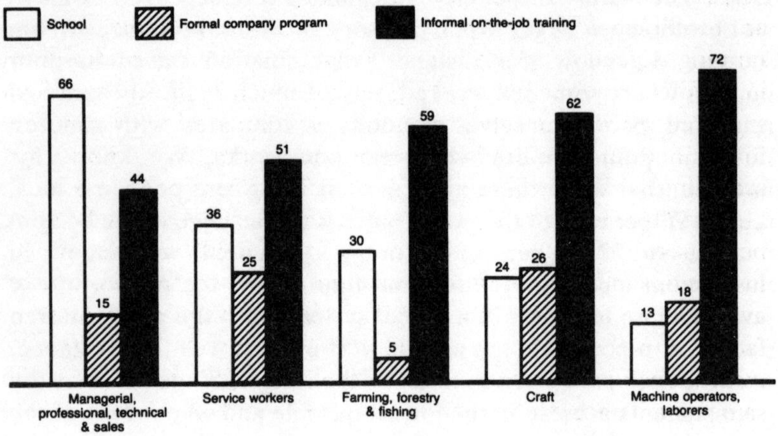

Source: Anthony P. Carnevale, American Society for Training and Development 1985. Based on data prepared by the Bureau of Labor Statistics.

Figure 2.3 Sources of retraining by occupational group

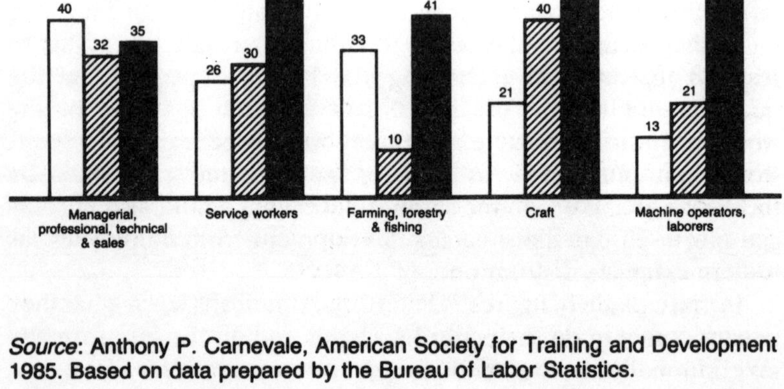

Source: Anthony P. Carnevale, American Society for Training and Development 1985. Based on data prepared by the Bureau of Labor Statistics.

professionals, technical and sales employees, and people in publicly regulated jobs. Formal employer training tends to be important for all employees except for those in "extractive" industries – farming, forestry, and fishing. Informal job training is important in all job categories but most important in blue-collar jobs. When surveyed about retraining, however, adults tend to emphasize formal and informal training in the workplace rather than formal schooling.

Workplace learning – formal and informal – provides substantial benefits to individuals in the form of increased earnings and to institutions in the form of increased productivity. Analysis of data available as far back as 1929, consistently shows that human factors are the major source of growth in individual earnings, institutional productivity, and national income. Moreover, the same data demonstrate clearly that "working smarter" – the ability of working teams to learn together – is the most significant among human factors in producing income and productivity growth. Analyses of economic growth through the 1980s, based on US Department of Commerce data, show similar patterns. Plant-level data are sparse but tend to corroborate national analysis. For instance, an analysis of 1983 census data shows that those who received informal training on their job improved their earnings by 5 per cent more than their peers. The effects of training on workplace productivity also appear powerful. For instance, after adjusting for inflation, the productivity returns to on-the-job training were 12.6 per cent for those who were college-educated and 19 per cent for those without college. A 1984 study found that 32 per cent of employees were more productive in the twelfth than they were in the third week of employment, suggesting improvements due to learning on the job.

Studies that map the sources of differences in the economic success of individuals are equally flattering to workplace learning. Earnings are largely a function of formal and informal learning on the job. Individuals tend to leverage their incomes by translating formal and informal learning on the job into higher wages. The best jobs are those that incorporate the most learning. Access to jobs with a high training and development content is the key determinant of lifetime economic success.

In spite of their importance, workplace learning structures are a dark corner in the nation's human resource development system. We know little about formal and informal learning on the job.

Consequently, the structures are not fully utilized as tools for expediting strategic change in employer institutions or for minimizing employee dislocations. The relationship between education and the productivity of American economic institutions and the earnings of individual employees is powerful, especially over the long term. In the short term, however, skill changes that are driven by technological and economic change impact first on the workplace. It is in the workplace that learning systems need to be responsive. Eventually, of course, incremental skill changes accumulate until they impact on the educational preparation for work. Sometimes the introduction of new technology requires an increase in the overall level of basic skills among the entry-level working population. At other times, specific skill changes in individual occupations can alter the necessary occupational preparation for work or create whole new occupations, as in the case of manufacturing engineering over the past fifteen to twenty years.

Ultimately, the education and pre-employment education and training system needs to be responsive to economic and technological changes over the longer term, while the employment-based learning system needs to respond in the very short-term if the competitive advantage of individual companies and whole economies is to be maintained.

PUBLIC POLICY

Federal, state, and local governments are making significant progress in reforming and reinvigorating the US education system. At the same time, however, there is little practical attention being paid to the quantity and quality of learning *in the workplace.* We have built substantial infrastructure for human resource development *outside* the workplace, but we have done nothing to encourage the quantity or the quality of retraining *on the job*.

Indeed, our tax system has created an investment structure that heavily favors machine investment in the workplace and discourages investments in employees. In the end, the current investment structure encourages an over-reliance on technology in employers' strategic planning, as well as underinvestment and eventual dislocation of human resources. Strategies for improving the responsiveness of workplace learning to economic and technological change are the missing link between the nation's human resource development system and the maintenance of competitive advantage.

Impediments to effective strategy for improving learning in the workplace are both political and economic. The national human resources lobby is made of public education and public job training institutions. As a result, when human resource issues arise, there is a natural temptation to use public infrastructure to resolve them. A second impediment to the development of a training system embedded in the workplace is the structure of the human resource policy-making system.

There are two policy structures in American government – one that deals with private employers and a second that is concerned with public institutions. Historically, the human resources policy system is heavily weighted towards the public side of the policy structure. The Labor and Human Resource Committee in the Senate and the Education and Labor Committee in the House largely operate through publicly appropriated delivery systems. The Departments of Education and Labor are also primarily responsive to public institutions outside the workplace. Moreover, these institutions tend to garner strong support from organized labor and an assortment of public institutions and demographic interest groups that derive upward mobility and a substantial share of their employment and income from the public sector.

Economic policy systems include Ways and Means and the Finance Committees in the Congress, as well as the Treasury Department, the Council of Economic Advisors, and some other departments, such as the Departments of Defense and Transportation, and the Executive Administration. These institutions tend to be responsive to business concerns and to deliver services through market-based tax incentives.

Historically, these two policy systems have focused on complementary but different sets of issues. The human resource development policy system, especially in the federal government, has tended to focus on those who did not share in the largess of the American economy. The economic policy system has tended to focus on economic institutions in the mainstream. Traditionally, the economic policy system has taken little interest in human resource issues as a lever for competitiveness and economic growth. This means that for business, our current difficulty is that questions surrounding the use of human resources as a lever for productivity and competitive advantage suggest a need for the inclusion of human resource issues in the economic policy structure.

Initial attempts on the part of the Finance and Ways and Means Committees to include human-resource-development tax policies have emerged in the context of the 1987 trade debate. The attempt to connect policies for dislocated workers to trade legislation is likely to continue outside the jurisdiction of the human resources policy structure. The effect, unfortunately, is to encourage a haphazard and uninformed debate outside this Committee and the Education and Labor Committee, where jurisdiction and expertise are more appropriately placed. If we are seriously to consider human resource policies connected to the workplace, we will need more cooperation between the two policy systems and the two sets of congressional committees.

The most serious impediment to crafting an expanded human resource policy in the context of the jobs and competitiveness debate, of course, is the oversized federal deficit. Until some progress is made in the deficit, it is unlikely that we will be able to expand policy in any arena.

The most direct approach toward improving the learning system in the workplace would be to enact some form of tax incentive to encourage more employer-based training. Such an incentive would encourage more responsive adaption to economic and technological change. An incentive for workplace training would also discourage dislocation, by putting human resource investment on a more equal playing field with machine investment. A training tax credit would encourage employers to respond to competitive challenges through human resource, as well as machine investment. Employers who utilize their human resources as a competitive resource would be less likely to allow technological investment alone to drive their competitive strategies.

A competitive strategy that relies on technology alone tends to encourage *dislocation.* And because technology and trained labor are compliments, an investment strategy that emphasizes technology and de-emphasizes training tends to result in more machines and fewer people who know how to use them. Moreover, as training investments become more apparent to employers, employers would be loath to lose training investments by firing employees during downturns or as a result of economic and technological change.

Many criticize the notion of a tax credit for employer-based training because they believe it would be simply a substitute for informal on-the-job training that already occurs. In my view, the formalization of informal on-the-job training would be a good thing. Much of informal on-the-job training is ineffective, inefficient, and unfairly distributed because of its informality.

Moreover, a tax credit for employer-based training would have important institutional effects. Currently, the human resource function is a relatively weak political institution inside the workplace. A tax credit would empower the human resource professional in the nation's employer institutions. In addition, the external authority of a tax credit would increase the visibility and strategic role of training in employer institutions.

A tax credit would provide a rallying point for the human resource development community. The current structure of employer-based training is highly decentralized and fractionalized in the separate employer institutions throughout the United States. There is no regulation, legislation, or institution that focuses the state of the art in employer-based training. Regulation is politically inconceivable. Even if it were possible, the harm it would do to the flexibility of American labor markets would probably exceed any positive effects from regulation. A tax credit would have several benefits. An employer tax credit for training would encourage employers and human resource professionals in the workplace to come together in order to enter into a dialogue with the government over the tax accounting and programmatic issues associated with the tax credit.

The tax credit would act as a focal point which would encourage the evaluation of programmatic effectiveness and professional development, which would in turn encourage the state-of-the art training to improve over time. Moreover, once infrastructure and some institutional cohesion becomes a reality in the employer-based training world, it would be a lot easier to talk about partnerships between employment training professions and public education and training institutions and their counterpart institutions in the workplace. Over the past twenty years, educators and public job trainers have attempted to make the connection with workplace training institutions with relatively little success, largely because their counterpart training and development professions in the workplace are not sufficiently organized or empowered to make successful partnerships possible. Moreover, for the first time, we would have in place public and private infrastructure that would be capable of providing a sequence of human resource development from pre-school to retirement.

In sum, a better understanding of training and development in the workplace would help education and training providers outside the workplace to develop practices that complement learning on the job. A better understanding of employer-based training would create stronger linkages between learning on and off the job and encourage a more cohesive lifelong sequence for job-related learning.

Absent the political will and resources for a tax credit, our best bet is the development of an institutional capability. A national Human Capital Institute would focus the state of the art in workplace training and allow for stronger public/private linkages. The facility would provide applied research and development (R&D) in various functional areas, including both supervisory and technical training. In addition, the facility would connect human resource development to broader strategic goals in employer institutions, such as quality, collaboration, adaption, the integration of technology and human capital, customization, globalization, and cost cutting. The facility's R&D agenda would also include a focus on issues associated with linkages and partnerships between employers and external education and training suppliers. Finally, the facility would attempt to connect human resource management strategies to particular industry groups.

THE BOTTOM LINE

The long view of economic history teaches us that people are the master economic resource. They are the master resource because they use their acquired skills and abilities as the catalytic agents that combine tangible elements and intangible ideas to make machinery and usable goods and services. In spite of that fact, there is a great temptation for employers and other leadership figures to ignore the long-term value of human investment. This is especially true in times such as these when investment capital is short and unemployment lines are still too long. Investment disincentives are especially strong for employers. In the short term, individual employers are faced with the prospect of losing their investment in people. Employees are mobile and machinery is not. When one employer invests in training and development, another can invest in wages and pirate employees at the completion of their training. Lastly, when jobs are in short supply, there is an equally great temptation to rely on a quantity of cheap labor rather than a quality few. Training disincentives are doubly strong for smaller employers, because their smaller staffs do not allow the economies of scale available to the training enterprise in large companies, and because they can least afford lost time off the job.

Although employers generally appreciate the longer-term yield of current investment in human resources, the press of daily business and the realities of the labor market encourage them to win their share of the nation's skilled workers through wage bidding and not through human resource development. We, as a nation of employers, have been going to the well for some time for skilled workers without replenishing the source of supply. As a result, the long term finally is arriving, as evidenced in a spate of statistics that suggest mounting skill shortages, reduced overall quality in the American labor force, shoddy workmanship, unsatisfactory maintenance, and wages which are not balanced by worker productivity. Further, attempts to improve productivity by increasing machine capital are proving costly and are resulting in protectionist resistance among current workers who are concerned for their own job security. Individual firms that once found it profitable to buy skilled workers by bidding up demand now find the price high, the supply short, and the quality low. What was good for individual employers has proven costly for all.

As a society, we will have to discover new mechanisms for employers to realize the longer-term benefits of employee training and human resource development. Public incentives that place investment in human resources at least on a par with investment in machinery will help. In the final analysis, resolution of the problem depends on the willingness of employers and our political leadership to look beyond the short-term economic dynamics that discourage human resource investment.

Commentary

Human Capital: A High-yield Investment

Arthur Cordell

AN OPTIMISTIC VIEW OF 2000+ FOR CANADA

We are now well into the early stages of the Information Revolution, which will dominate the life of mankind during the coming century. This far-reaching revolution, which is transforming our economy as well as our political, social, environmental, and cultural conditions, not only challenges the United States and other developed countries but also poses profound challenges to the future of the Canadian nation and all of its people. But the historical record of development – at least in Canada – gives promise for hope that it can be a leading country in the new revolution in which we are already deeply engaged.

A century and a half ago, as the industrial revolution began to gather momentum, first in Britain and Europe and later in the United States, Canada was regarded as something of a "poor relation" in the huge economic and social revolutions that were set in motion. It had emerged as a "basic resources" economy, with strong advantages in fish, fur, agriculture and lumber. Even the more advanced salients of Canada's development – in commerce, finance, insurance, transportation, and basic constituents of manufacturing – were believed to be essentially achievable only by key elements of "tutoring," foreign investment, skill and experience imports, and of course, knowledge and technology inflows from abroad.

Yet, in a more flexible, frontier-type society, absorption and deployment of productive resources on new frontiers of activity were remarkably rapid. The traditions of entrepreneurship and risk-taking in the big and open Canadian geography were powerful. The opportunities for deploying new knowledge and skills and venture capital to an underdeveloped country were luring and ultimately exceptionally rewarding for the successful. And internal responses to the new challenges were relatively quick and forward looking – for example, in educational development, in evolving trade policies, in governance and in inventiveness (and, even more, in adopting and adapting foreign inventiveness).

Through the turbulence of the latter half of the nineteenth century – and through the exceptionally tough and difficult decisions of trying to make an East–West country in the northern half of the Western Hemisphere – Canada struggled to achieve industrial progress. American "pull and push" was a strong underlying current compelling Canadian industrial progress; Canadians, very simply, found that they could not afford to retain a clear sovereignty for the country if lags and gaps with the United States became too large. The compulsive pace-setting impact of US industrial progress on Canada in the latter half of the nineteenth century and the early part of the twentieth century has perhaps never been fully understood or appreciated by Canadians.

The First World War impelled Canadian industrial advance more vigorously, and by the 1920s, Canada first began to think of itself in the terminology now generally used for high-income countries in todays's world – that is, an industrially advanced country. And when the first measurements were attempted to seek perspective on the relative levels of average standards of living, Canada clearly emerged near the top in such international rankings.

In the Depression of the 1930s, Canada's industrial progress faltered as a new generation of Canadians rediscovered that trade barriers – and other constraints on natural North–South economic and other linkages between Canada and the United States – had powerful adverse effects on Canadian welfare.

But in the context of the re-creation of much more open economic and financial relationships after the Second World War, the Canadian economy blossomed into a highly advanced state of industrial maturity. This maturity was buttressed by exceptionally strong demand and price trends for most of Canada's basic natural resources, as well as by an unanticipated burst of growth in its varied service industries. In turn, because of Canada's relatively cold climate, large geography, generally sparse population, demographic changes (especially urban growth and high immigration), and the heavy capital-intensity of many of its industries, new capital investment (and new applied technology) gave a strong boost to overall growth.

In the early 1970s, the incredible conjuncture of favorable growth factors began to run out of steam – that is, the vast array of factors helping to generate both resource and industrial growth in Canada. This was by no means a purely internal phenomenon. It took place within the context of a general slowing of the whole world economy, particularly the US economy, and also in the context of the extraordinary intensification of numerous new salients of international manufacturing competitiveness.

For at least a full decade, Canadian concerns could not really cope with the underlying realities of a world that was changing from an "old industrial revolution" to a "new information revolution." There were many words, but limited understanding.

Even by the 1960s, there were numerous institutional initiatives and much "wordsmithing" about knowledge, science, and technology – including such new ventures as the Science Secretariat of the Privy Council, the Science Council of Canada, the Ministry of State for Science and Technology, new technology-oriented federal and provincial institutions, incentives, grants, etc. But the real essence of the new information technology revolution has largely escaped (or at least has had a delayed response from) Canadian governments as well as such institutions as large corporations, unions, educational institutions, and many professional bodies.

Most major Canadian institutions are still continuing to react to, rather than to lead, technological change in today's information technology revolution.

The leadership that provides an optimistic scenario for Canada's future into the twenty-first century does not come very much from well-established institutions, either government or private. It is flowing out of flexible new organizations – many that are small, new, and medium-sized – that have a great capacity for innovativeness, flexibility, and adaptability. It is taking place in a crucible in which failure is quickly doomed and in which success is quickly rewarded. If "small is beautiful," it is truly because it is a marvelous arena in which experimentation can flourish, without the overburden of "cultures" or "bureaucracies" or too many "traditions." Creation and self-renewal are the ultimate sources of survival, not only in the tough world of pitiless competition, but also in the world of new and unlimited opportunities for new product and new process technologies. (Incidentally, a growing body of evidence on current and prospective world economic development would assign a much heavier weight to the importance of new product technologies than to that of new process technologies.)

An optimistic view of Canada's development potentials into the twenty-first century must first recognize that there are very major constraints on an effective Canadian breakthrough. Second, it must sense that there are powerful bases for believing that Canada can once again achieve the "catch-up" to outstanding "world class" that it in fact achieved between the mid-nineteenth century and the mid-twentieth century.

In conclusion, if we are to achieve this "world class" standing in a competitive global economy, we must first overcome the following ten constraints:

1 too much attention to natural resource industries;
2 too much attention to mature manufacturing industries;
3 too much attention to government influence and direction of economic, scientific, and other progress;
4 too much sensitivity to powerful new international manufacturing competition;
5 too little attention to service industry development (both domestically and internationally);
6 too little attention to the potential of new and smaller companies – especially in information technology and related fields (plus in the international, as well as domestic arenas);
7 serious neglect of fundamental rehabilitation in the new information-technology revolution environment to the critical field of "learning in and for the workplace";
8 too much emphasis in government and private politics and in human attitudes on preserving something like the present rather than in moving to a very different kind of future (above all, this applies to technology, and to the serious institutional barriers to technological change);
9 inadequate attention to how very important social and cultural goals can be accommodated in a "transforming society" (danger of cliffs); and
10 coping with absolutely fundamental demographic changes – the "graying" of Canada.

Chapter 3

Education for a Changing World

Erik Solem

ANTICIPATING A CHANGING WORLD

From most indicators available to us it seems that, by now, people in the developed world in general are finally becoming interested in the future. This is a relatively new development which has something to do with the approaching Millennium.

The remaining, lingering, question in this respect is whether or not their interest is an adult one. Very often individuals may have one of two images in their minds, either a utopian image or a doom-laden – dystopian – version filled with the horrors of the year 2001. Neither is an adult image. It is important that we try and change this, collectively as well as individually.

The mature – or adult – attitude toward the future manifests itself in an interest in what may happen, whether this is highly probable or quite uncertain, because knowing it may help us take decisions for which we are responsible, here and now. We should remember that the future is much less far off than we think. A child of seven, say, who has just learned to read will be a teenager by the beginning of the Millennium. The time for understanding, planning and anticipating the future is now rather than later on.

What is the proper way of reflecting on the future? First, our purpose must be to identify powerful trends, i.e. those that are very difficult to influence, and link them to events and outcomes. Second, we must try to understand how the strategies of various actors, whom we must identify – say governments, social groups, firms, etc. – will impact on future developments.

This may sound easier than it really is. In this context it is important to distinguish between short-term phenomena which may (or may not) be incidental, and long-term trends, which for our purposes are likely to be much more significant. For example, in discussing the price of oil, we must distinguish between the long-term "real" price, which is based upon the development of substitute sources of energy such as shale oil, and whatever short-term price results from quick adjustments between limited supply and a not easily reduced level of demand. The distinction here is as subtle as it is important. In our example short-term prices may be above or below the long-term trend. In either case this may be significant for a number of reasons.

The example of oil is actually particularly germane as pertaining to efforts of anticipating future change. A preliminary study carried out by Interfutures (1979) stressed the fact that there are several possible kinds of an oil crisis and that particular importance should be attached to political crises caused by upheavals in one or more oil-producing countries or to difficulties in relations between oil-producing and oil-consuming countries. In fact, a major cause of the oil crises which followed their study was a political phenomenon, as they said it would be – the revolution in Iran. Whereas it could have occurred a little earlier or a little later, hence there was an element of uncertainty about the time of its appearance, this phenomenon was definitely within the range to which attention had been drawn. As such it is a good example of a successful attempt of anticipating a changing world. The price havoc which followed on the oil scene only illustrates the seriousness of the situation and the importance of the business of anticipating change and acting on it. The 1990 "Gulf" crisis serves to illustrate how perceptive the "Interfutures" thinking actually was.

"Interfutures" and, before it the Club of Rome, are only two of several significant groups which have been trying to draw the attention of private and public decision-makers to the necessity of properly anticipating change and on acting on it in time. Their goals have been to try to raise the awareness for the need for appropriate mechanisms of foresight to be developed and incorporated into future decisions of public and private bodies. This ongoing process is particularly important in the fields of education and training, where the goals for future developments, curricular designs, and new ways of handling change and complexity evolve.

Anyone who thinks about the future must learn to pick out those elements of current life which he or she sees as significant for the future, while discarding the others. One must learn to examine the alternatives and choose the soundest path. This is often harder than it would seem. However, there are some "pointers" to the future which could usefully be followed. More often than not there is relatively high consensus about the importance of these. The development of automation, for example, is one such "pointer." Others include the appearance of the first computers in motor vehicles, the appearance of industrial imports from such countries as South Korea and Singapore, the creation of branches by large banks throughout the world, and the "graying" of developed world populations. Other examples are just waiting to be properly identified.

We are often helped in this by existing organizations with a useful capacity to carry out such research. The United Nations is a good example. On 11 July 1987 it officially observed the "Day of the 5 billion," promoted as a day to contemplate a future in which the population will eventually reach 10.2 billion. Within one hour, nearly 10,000 persons are added to the total population of the world. Each week the equivalent of another Houston, Texas; each year another Mexico. The implications go much deeper than just numbers. There is general agreement that unless more is done to control population growth many of the advances of the twentieth century, such as falling death rates and rising incomes, could easily be reversed.

The present expansion of human settlement may in fact pose unprecedented environmental challenges. As an example, the clearing of tropical forests for new cropland is thought by some analysts to contribute to the gradual warming of the earth's atmosphere, a phenomenon otherwise known as the "greenhouse effect." Some go as far as to say that environmental degradation may lead to the demise of the human species. They say that our piecemeal remedial action must yield to broadly based environmental literacy and concerted efforts.

Now, the fact that we have reached 5 billion inhabitants means that we have managed to overcome the high mortality of the past. However, it also underscores the need for effective family planning worldwide. Again, the importance of education and training in these fields is paramount.

To stick to our example, UN officials work with at least three population scenarios, each of which shows the level at which the world population will stabilize under different circumstances.

Their middle-range projection, some 10.2 billion, assumes steady progress in bringing down global birthrates through education and family planning. So far, actual population growth has in fact corresponded to this middle range – despite some ups and downs. For example the unanticipated early success of China's controversial family planning program has been offset by recent information and "failures" elsewhere in the global system.

As we know, several developing countries have made significant progress in slowing their growth rate, which has raised the hope that they would be able to follow the industrialized countries. However, an increasing number of analysts are now concerned that several developing countries could be stuck in what they consider a "demographic trap," i.e. a situation where rapid growth simply outstrips the ability to advance socially and economically. An example would be Nigeria, whose population is expected to increase rapidly from 100 million to about 532 million before it levels off in the middle of the next century. The immediate implication of this anticipated change is that Nigeria would then have a population equivalent to the total of Africa today.

As in our example, it should be clear that enormous stress could be put on the world's natural systems. And in many parts of the world these systems are already deteriorating. In many parts of Latin America and Africa, for example, real incomes have fallen in recent years.

Whereas the declining living standards in rapid population-growth areas is no longer hypothetical but in fact taking place, the link between population and economic prosperity is still somewhat controversial. Clearly a growing population could boost a nation's economy, by providing a larger pool of workers, expanded markets for manufactured goods, etc., as seen in the cases of Europe and North America during the period of the industrial revolution. Today, however, things may be somewhat different in one or two important senses. The accelerated development of multiple rapid changes may in fact pose perils, unless we know how to anticipate such changes. Mankind is, in fact, entering a new phase – one which in historical terms may be characterized as the emergence of the "global society."

The emergence of nations took hundreds of years, but the global society is emerging in terms of years or (at most) a few decades. What happened over a period of, say, 500 years is now materializing within a time frame of 50 years or less. This phenomenon, and our seeming inability to cope with it all, is sometimes referred to as "future shock."

Now, how will we manage to live in a global society? How do we relate to and make use of the new institutions which must be built to deal with the emergence of this new form of civilization? How, in fact, do we learn to cope with the seemingly *continuous* need to anticipate and manage change?

First of all we must accept as a fact that everything depends upon everything else. Today's problems are almost exclusively a creation of such developments. Let us look at population again for a moment. We know that the world's population will likely double in the next 30–40 years. The labor force on the global level over the next two decades will increase by one billion people. What this means is that we shall have to *create* one billion new jobs over the next 20 years simply to keep unemployment at the present level.

An illustration of the population growth in "less developed" vs. "more developed" regions of the world is given in figure 3.1.

We can look further, at Bangladesh, for example, which today has some 90 million people and is expected to have nearly 150 million by the year 2020. Or we can see that Mexico, with its present population of some 70 million, is likely to see an increase to 116 million by the Millennium.

Figure 3.1 Population growth (1750–2100)

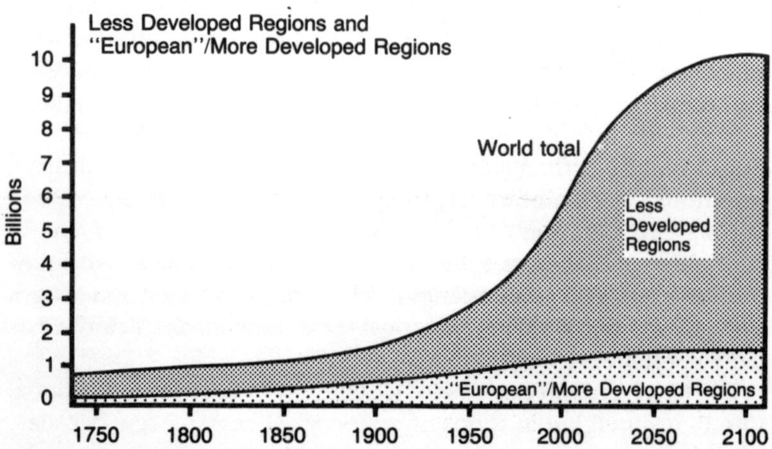

Source: Population Reference Bureau Inc.

These populations have to be fed. Many of their number aspire to the material possessions of people in the developed world – cars, refrigerators, television sets. What are the potential impacts on the environment of these aspirations? Developing world populations have to be properly trained and educated. Since population growth also means growth of human capital, it clearly means that there will have to be an increase in the number of professionals in the developing regions of the world.

Some have argued that a shift in the center of gravity in the world may be occurring. We know that in the past there was such a shift going from Europe to the United States, now perhaps going to Japan. In the future it is not inconceivable that such a shift could go further south. At any rate, in our attempt to anticipate a changing world, we must deal with such eventualities.

It is interesting in this context to look at the world's 10 largest cities, and to try to trace the changes of which we are talking (table 3.1).

Table 3.1 World's 10 largest cities (population in millions)

Rank	*1950*		*1985*		*2000*	
1	Greater New York	(12.4)	Tokyo/Yokohama	(18.8)	Mexico City	(25.8)
2	London	(10.4)	Mexico City	(17.3)	Sao Paulo	(23.97)
3	Rhein/Ruhr, West Germany	(6.9)	Sao Paulo, Brazil	(15.9)	Tokyo/Yokohama	(20.2)
4	Tokyo/Yokohama	(6.7)	Greater New York	(15.6)	Calcutta	(16.5)
5	Shanghai	(5.8)	Shanghai	(11.96)	Greater New York	(15.8)
6	Paris	(5.5)	Calcutta	(10.95)	Shanghai	(14.3)
7	Greater Buenos Aires	(5.3)	Greater Buenos Aires	(10.9)	Seoul	(13.8)
8	Chicago/N.W. Indiana	(5.0)	Rio de Janeiro	(10.4)	Rio de Janeiro	(13.3)
9	Moscow	(4.8)	London	(10.36)	Greater Buenos Aires	(13.2)
10	Calcutta	(4.7)	Seoul	(10.3)	London	(10.5)

Source: Population Reference Bureau Inc.

The increase in human capital combined with changes in population distribution on a worldwide basis would mean changes with which we have to cope. Another huge change will be the effects that the population–resources equation will have on the environment. We know, for example, that tropical rain forests are being depleted at a combined rate of an area similar to England and Wales each year. How much longer can this continue?

Also, the burning of fossil fuels creates carbon dioxide, which pollutes the global environment on an unprecedented scale. At present, there is roughly 17 per cent more carbon dioxide in the global atmosphere than existed prior to the industrial revolution. This level could reach 25 per cent before the Millennium. There are even projections which suggest an increase of some 60–70 per cent by the year 2030. Clearly, the climate in one country will depend on what is happening elsewhere on the globe.

Or let us look at agriculture. Agricultural land use in 1900 in the United States was some 24 acres per person. Today it is about eight acres. If this trend persists it could be down to 3 acres or less per person. This is not necessarily a disaster; one could even go down further, say, to one acre per person. However, when we take into account such additional variables as soil erosion, water shortage, etc., the picture which emerges could be a drastically changed one. In anticipating a changing world, all this must be taken into account.

In fact, when dealing with the environment, it is an unescapable fact that we – mankind – have tended to view it in a somewhat bizarre way. Currently we address environment as one issue

Figure 3.2 The environment as an issue among others

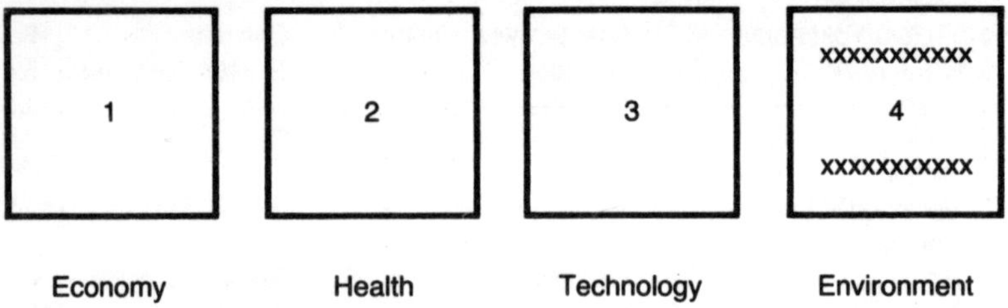

Figure 3.3 The environment as the context in which other issues arise

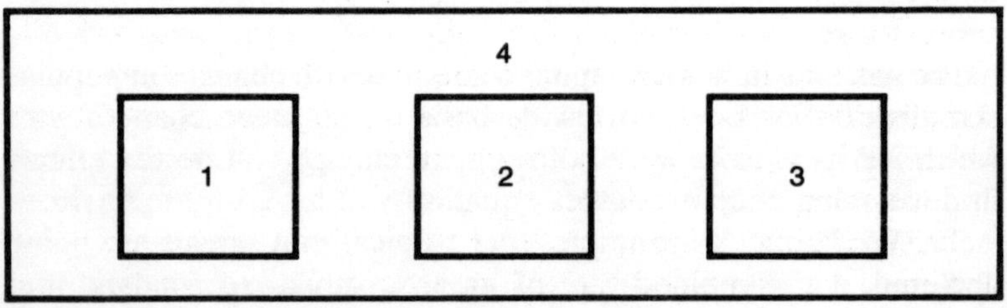

Figure 3.4 Education as the principal lever for preventive action

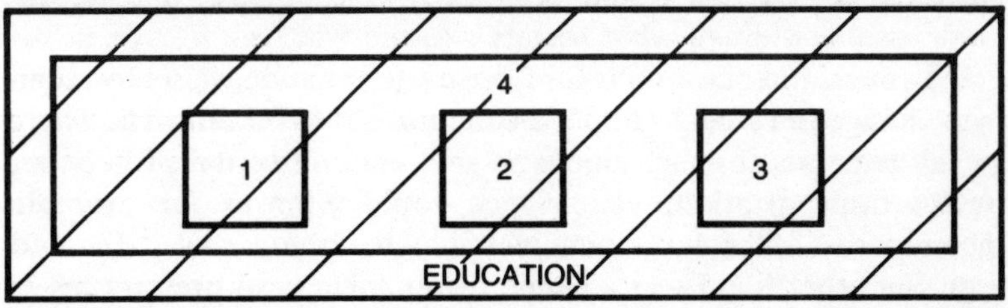

among others. Gail Stewart (1988) has used a technique called "optics" to show how this approach is too narrow (figures 3.2, 3.3, 3.4).

By shifting the focus we could arrive at a much more fruitful way of examining, assessing, and anticipating change.

This particular type of "optics" is often referred to as futures forecasting. It is no less than a revolution of the mind. Since it clearly defies any attempt at linear or "mechanical" thought process, it is – not surprisingly – viewed with alarm by some of the more doctrinaire or hierarchically minded individuals who presently hold power. It is fair to say that many of them are even opposed to this way of viewing the world. One reason is that it may threaten their authority. Another is simply likely to be related to a relative lack of understanding of what is taking place. Future shock, again.

Whatever the case might be, it is clear that a primary concern for all education and training, and particularly among adults, should be to break down such barriers to understanding as are often thrown up.

The work of those who think about the future is not only to try to pick out from the present those events that point to the future – a difficult enough task by itself – but also to marshal those facts, to see how they are linked, and whether they are likely to produce different futures. What may be of particular importance in this context is the possible change in values in the developed world in particular and how such changes are "factored into" our understanding. What kinds of changes are we talking about? Which values? Who is empowered through literacy and numeracy to lead in developing new directions?

This is a difficult area. However, such questions are inevitable and must be asked. Not to ask them is to restrict oneself to a linear view of the evolution of developed societies, for example, expressed solely in terms of, say, national income growth. Needless to say this would be a narrow, simplistic, and clearly inadmissable view of what society's future will be.

However, the question is far from easy. What do we really mean by a change in values? Here a distinction has to be drawn between social demands for such things as say, environmental protection, public transportation, etc., which could alter as for example incomes rise and fall, or new technologies become available and – on the other hand – at a deeper level changes in preferences in terms of political culture. Just look at the explosion of change in Eastern Europe. It is this deeper level of value change which is particularly important for us to understand. At least two central processes are involved, "cutting loose" – or liberating – and establishing new roots. The reference to a paradigm shift is, perhaps by now, seemingly as trite as it is highly relevant. There is really no better way of approaching this essential problem of changing concepts of the future, the key ones which will remain those of space, time, and image.

The form of cutting loose – or liberation – may take place through increased participation, independence of work, changes in the roles of men vs. women in society, and so on. Much of this is already taking place almost independently. The term paradigm shift also takes into account how people willingly wish to change the frame of reference, within which they operate. It is in the balance between, on the one side the family and on the other extreme the nation that new, often interesting forms of intermediate communities of human relationships will develop.

How fast such "new" values will take root and spread is harder to assess but that, too, is in the perspective. It is possible, for example, that such value changes could affect the middle classes more than other segments of the population. However, simultaneously new minorities could emerge, wanting either to adopt more divergent patterns of behavior or even express extreme points of view. The overriding question will be: is society then moving toward a new form of social fragmentation? If so, is this particular type of fragmentation superimposed upon earlier cleavages based upon already well known indicators, such as national income distribution? Or what are the new elements at play?

In the future, we shall be dealing with perhaps entirely *new* challenges which society has never encountered before. Two examples almost automatically spring to mind. One is the challenges of the applications of Artificial Intelligence and their socioeconomic impacts which are bound to be formidable. The other, perhaps equally large challenge to the future of society is the medium- to long-term impact of AIDS. Both are true future problems, both have to be encountered and dealt with in time. It is not too hard to imagine a world where new challenges, cleavages and almost entirely new social roles will spring up. We must be ready to deal with these types of problems through appropriate structures of understanding. The place to start this process of applying foresight is in education and training.

REFERENCES

Organization for Economic Cooperation and Development (1979) *Interfutures*: Research Project on The Future Development of Advanced Industrial Societies in Harmony With That of Developing Countries, First Report. Paris: OECD.

Solem, Erik (1986) "Foresight in Government: A Necessary but Rare Component", *Futures Canada*, Vol. 8, No. 1, Spring.

Stewart, G. (1988) "CANADIANS IN JUNE: The Summit, the Environment, and the Structures of Government, Some Reflections – Some Hope." Memo to Summit Decision Makers, Mimeo.

Commentary

Education for a Changing World

Frank Feather

We are succeeding magnificently at putting ourselves out of work. If we look beyond the immediate crises, which can at times be overwhelming, there is a possible future not often anticipated. We are racing at electronic speed – toward the "leisure society" which we have craved for the last 2,000 years. By 2001 the developed world will be a Fifth Wave Leisure Society and the "leisure ethic" will have replaced the "work ethic."

Beyond the Third Wave

For 30 years, Canada has been leading the world's developed economies into what Alvin Toffler dubbed the "Third Wave" post-industrial society. (The first two waves were agricultural and manufacturing economies respectively.)

In reality the so-called "Third Wave" may itself be divided into three sectors: (1) services, (2) information/knowledge, and (3) leisure/recreation. Since 1967 the service sector has increased at an average annual rate of 3.2 per cent, which compares to 0.9 per cent in the goods-producing sector. Almost 90 per cent of the increase in jobs since 1967 has occurred in the service sector, which now employs 71 per cent of the Canadian labor force (Economic Council of Canada, 1990).

The information (Fourth Wave) sector of the economy already provides about 40 per cent of Canada's jobs.

The Fifth Wave Leisure Society

The leisure sector (i.e. the emerging Fifth Wave) already provides 18 per cent of Canada's jobs – more than the declining manufacturing sector. Indeed, the leisure sector is the fastest growing sector of the Canadian economy in terms of job creation and will be the largest employer within 15 years. Perhaps the time has come to look at much more effective ways to interweave work, learning, and life. Perhaps, as Marilyn Ferguson said, "our pathology may (indeed) be our opportunity."

Beyond the Work Ethic

For a society which says it values the work ethic, I think we are all lying through our teeth. We place our real value in getting rid of work, in using science, technology, and knowledge to reduce human labor. We have moved from brawn to brains in producing wealth. Indeed, all the wealth ever created has come from new ideas. The so-called information society is nothing new.

The work ethic is based on the concept of paid work. But we are prepared to give up paid work in order that we can pursue education and enjoy more leisure – for which we pay handsomely! In other words we value them so much that we are happy to pay for them. We all prize leisure more than anything else.

With increased longevity, the rapid obsolescence of skills, and the negative impacts of unemployment, wouldn't it make much more sense to spread our education, work, and retirement over a lifetime. The current continuum, from front-end education, to thirty-plus years of work, to retirement, is no longer functional.

Toward a Leisure Ethic

We have inherited an ethic which placed too much faith in the work ethic. Leisure is no longer just for the affluent, the lazy, and the retired (who had earned it). Yet we still tend to envy the wealthy who do not "work." But what is "work"? While leisure is not "work," it is non-productive.

Leisure can provide the same personal satisfactions as work. Indeed, leisure can be defined as encompassing work – and you don't have to be a workaholic to reach that level of perception. Leisure now encompasses: work, hobbies, sports, social activities, education, community action and volunteerism. Sounds like life itself. Precisely! We are achieving what we have always craved – a quality life of leisure. We had better get ready!

The Economics of Leisure

Canadians are now spending $67 billion a year on recreation, education, and personal goods and services such as restaurants and hotels – a tenfold increase over the last 20 years. As a proportion of consumer spending, this has increased from 19 per cent to 25 per cent, and the trend will likely continue.

By the year 2000, our forecasts show that as much as 40 per cent of disposible income will be spent on living a leisureful life – a mammoth $1 trillion. (None of these figures include food, snacks, soft drinks, alcoholic beverages, or cigarettes.)

We already spend $15 billion in restaurants and hotels, $10 billion on recreation, sporting, and camping equipment, and $7 billion on education and cultural services. Yet, like "Alice," we are running so fast while standing still.

Challenges and Implications

This short commentary attempts to cast the "changing world" in a different light. It is based on over a thousand hours of research. In terms of jobs and economic activity, the trends of the Fifth Wave revolution are clear for anyone to see.

Still many of us remain wedded to a work-oriented society. As such, to manage, encourage, coerce, entice, or otherwise inveigle a person to work is considered an achievement. This thinking permeates our institutions. It conditions the way we govern ourselves.

Yet psychographic research shows that the five major status symbols over the next 15 years will be:

1 self-directed free time,
2 unity of work and play,
3 recognition as a creative person,
4 non-monetary rewards, and
5 social commitment.

Clearly, many managerial systems and incentives are out of sync with these changing values and attitudes.

The challenge to our governments, to the private sector, to labor, to educators, and to society at large is to embrace the Fifth Wave Leisure Society before it engulfs them. To further quote from *Alice*: "Cheshire Puss would you tell me please which way we ought to go from here?" The Puss answers, "That depends a good deal on where you want to get to."

REFERENCES

Economic Council of Canada (1990) *Good Jobs, Bad Jobs*. Ottawa: Supply and Services Canada.
Toffler, Alvin (1972) *Future Shock*. New York: Bantam Books.

Part II

Developing Resourceful Humans

Chapter 4

Wilted Flowers – The Demographic Imperative

Nicole Morgan

WILTED FLOWERS

Adult education took a beating when the baby boomers . . . were not adult. This rather obvious statement has major consequences for the first wave of baby boomers who have reached that crucial crossroads of adulthood when career opportunities fade but the thought remains that there are still choices somewhere, provided one takes the right approach and training. Considering the size of the baby-boom generation in Canada and the United States, this relatively well documented crisis of middle age is certain to assume the proportions of a massive crisis which to some extent will affect the entire work force. The result is an optimistic forecast of the future of adult education.

The search for another time around as well as the means to achieve it will be all the more acute because baby boomers (the generation born after the Second World War) are going through stressful changes in their working life:

The stress of constant changes, whether technological or economic

The classic pattern of one career in one or perhaps two companies is losing ground. Nothing seems stable any more and the fear of being left behind in a society more competitive than ever is enough to make even the most passive individual read the fine print of announcements about adult education in their local newspaper.

"Plateauing"

This feeling of insecurity is likely to be reinforced by the pervasiveness of plateauing within large organizations. This concept describes the unavoidable moment in a career when individuals will reach their highest levels and will have to change gears in order to adapt to a situation ill-fitted to the ideology of constant promotion. This usually leads to a form of anomie called demotivation, cynicism, or lack of loyalty, etc., which companies have started to experience.

The "Burnt-out Syndrome"

This third factor is linked to the preceeding one, and hits the high-flyers, the plateaued, and the insecure without distinction. There is a limit to the job-related stress that individuals can handle in a daily life compounded by traffic gridlock, debts, absurdity, and various kinds of drug abuse – legal or illegal. This leads also to anomie as well as the desire for a "cure."

But one could argue that these three factors alone are not really specific to a generation used to thinking that its existentialist experience is the navel of the world: drastic changes in wealth and job situation have been a daily experience of centuries for those who endured wars, famine, disease, and other calamities. Early plateauing was a feature for most employees in the first half of the century. And as far as stress, boredom, demotivation, and difficulties were concerned, some historical research will demonstrate that working conditions were much worse in the past.

What is new, nevertheless, is a very particular factor: our ancestors did not have any chance even to dream of other possibilities. Actualization of dreams took place in the heavens of religions and later in the promises of ever-beckoning futures. Exhausted workers of the nineteenth century dreamt about a life of choices and justice for their grandchildren, whom their children sent to school by droves. In other words the necessity of plain survival made it imperative to develop a culture of small adaptations, called traditions. It does not mean that innovators and conquerors did not exist. They did, to the extent that North American culture has its roots in the possibility for an individual to develop an empire from selling apples in the street. But somehow, the essential hope remained remote.

This absence of choice was comforting in many respects. One did not have to feel guilty at not moving up and there was, therefore, considerable pride in exercising whatever skill and trade were one's fate. Actually, the examples of heroes, such as the moneyed Rockefellers or the innovative Banting, offered enough reassurance that the mind was alive and irrepressible, that freedom existed somewhere and that fate was not absolute – without seriously disturbing those who did not live up to these expectations.

Nevertheless this fragile dialectic between an accepted fate and hopes has taken another turn with modern generations.

First, baby boomers stopped believing altogether in a redeeming heaven as well as a glorious future. All of a sudden one's individual life has become the melting pot of desires and pursuit of fulfillment and happiness. And no one counted any longer on grandchildren to carry the flame of an eternal hope. So much the better since a third of the boomers will remain childless.

Second, baby boomers now have the means to dream for themselves of choices that they would actually buy.

Social Security

Most developed countries, and Canada in particular, offer everyone a kind of absolute security net (welfare) which is not perfect but which deals with the most gripping fear: hunger for oneself and one's children. Also, thanks to the provisions of the old age pension and Social Security many of the baby-boom generation share the reassuring feeling that they will not be left absolutely financially deprived when old age strikes.

Assets and Savings

The flower children, symbols of a young generation in the midst of an adolescent crisis, have been blessed with an economic abundance in relatively peaceful times that no other generation in the world has ever had. The first cohorts of baby boomers have started to accumulate, as a group, quite a lot of wealth in assets and savings. (It is relative to the wealth of other generations. There is also little doubt that some have dropped out and will never catch up.) Citizens are also putting considerable amounts of money in savings of many kinds, mainly in Retirement Savings Plans and real estate. And as the boom grows older, it will benefit from a generous inheritance tax which will further the feeling of having enough security to open new horizons.

Two-career Families

A business association called two-career familes has widened the financial comfort zone one can enjoy when both spouses are working, as is the case for 80 per cent of the boomers. When there are no children on either side (in 30 per cent of the cases), disposable income becomes quite substantial.

And . . . dreams of other possibilities begin to surface as daily realities of working look grimmer and grimmer. One acknowledges having everything but not living accordingly. Time and fulfillment are missing and/or stress makes money taste bad.

This sets the scene for the entrance of what has always been "the engine of the 'Me Generation:'" the idea that choices of lifestyle and destiny are the highest form of civilization and are a right. The predominant belief of the 1960s was that everyone was a child of the world, able to choose whatever life one fancied. True, this idea has mellowed, but there is still a strong belief that one can model one's destiny or at least do something about it. This remains more than ever the backbone of the North American ideology to the point when "can" is understood as "must." Fat people can/must lose weight; miserable stalled middle-managers can/must do something for themselves; exhausted working mothers can/must opt for another lifestyle; very sick people can/must control their sufferings; arguing couples can/must work on their relationship, etc. What is actually striking in this ideology is the social impossibility for anyone just to live as time passes, adapting to whatever is one's lot, in other words to develop a set of traditions. Every single act or stage or state of life has the potential of becoming a problem and therefore of offering a solution which will solve it and which will depend entirely on the will of the individual.

This takes us back to the stresses of life in general and working life in particular as perceived as problems by a generation that persuades itself that none of the problems is destiny. Career choices can/must be made once more, especially at a time (the forties) when one has to contemplate and reflect on one's apparent destiny. The baby boomers will likely consider the first half of their lives as a necessary ordeal from which they should be born again. (A bit like their first marriage: a false start.) They will likely be far more inventive than their ancestors who in their forties dreamed simply of taking some well deserved retirement in order to live simply and quietly. Our "wilting flowers" have never been quiet (when fresh) and will never be. They will try to hurry and steer the normal course of events and make sure that choices of lifestyle are given to them before old age.

As a result of these many trends, *and provided developed economies do not commence a downward spiral* – which will reduce choices – the boomers shoud go massively in two directions, both connected with the idea of a second career and a second type of education. Indeed, Canada's Advisory Council on Adjustment (1989) states that we will change both careers and jobs many times throughout life.

At one end of the spectrum there will be frantic activity linked to adult education with the hope that one can give up one job for another with better rewards (in terms of money, freedom, and prestige). The phenomenon is being seen in the extraordinary surge toward aggressive entrepreneurship. Some jump from the boat outright, others take a part-time trial, others moonlight.

At the opposite end of the spectrum there will be a demand for phasing out, for leaving career-related stress entirely to find:

1 *a new approach to earning a living more compatible with other conflicting desires*. It finds its expression in the "Bed & Breakfast" phenomenon which allows baby boomers to get away from stressful cities, be their own bosses, as couples, in houses set in beautiful surroundings that could not be purchased otherwise. Women also are reinventing the cottage industry, which, they think, will give them some flexibility as well as taking them away from difficult large organizations.
2 *hobbies which one hopes will become full-time when retirement comes and in the meantime will carry enough weight to compensate for the hardship of competition on the job*. Job is then regarded as toil while philately, bird watching, or gardening grow to become the source of fulfilment through achievement. These hobbies have always been around except that when they are recaptured by the boom, they will take on a new intensity accompanied by high consumption.
3 *parallel skills that one dreams of developing to prove to oneself that one was not a failure*: such as becoming a writer which, we predict will become an obsession of the nineties. Autobiographies – this written version of acute narcissism – will become the novel of the end of this century.

4 *cultural craving and desire for meaning*, will characterize an aging generation which will develop an insatiable appetite for the past (history, genealogical trees), the mystic, the occult, philosophy, and the religious (another effect of age). Attendance at concert, plays, and other cultural events, which is nowadays declining, should revive enormously.

Within that perspective it is easy to predict that by teaching the skills of all of the above, adult education in any of these activities is going to become a soaring business which will open the doors to an amazing consumption of services. It will go from church basements to full-fledged courses in university going through a multitude of new schools, seminars, self-help groups, etc. It is likely that those universities that take the early train of offering well-adapted courses to adults will fare better and better, and one can foresee that there will be a substantial shortage of qualified professors and teachers within the next decade.

This does not mean that we are going back to an era of gentility and deeply rooted culture. For this trend will become the vehicle for may stresses – related, once again, to too many choices and the intense competitive feeling that one could fail in the search to look good in the eyes of one's peers.

New entrepreneurs will have to understand that nobody is one's own boss but that everyone depends on a market and on circumstances (luck, disease, etc.). Bird lovers will have to deal with drastic increases in prices in their field and gardeners, being baby boomers, will never experience the pleasure of the earth without trying to show off about it (e.g. writing a book on the beauty of not communicating with human beings). The stress related to the craving for culture was described in the 1930s by Herman Hesse (*The Glass Bead Game*). Everybody, in a dizzy way, will know a little bit of this and that. Fashion will dictate fascination for Pico de la Mirandola or Nietzsche followed by a rediscovery of Plotin. But nothing will be deep enough to connect these crumbs of culture to culture as a whole. Or it will be rooted in the real culture of our time, which is: panicky consumption.

REFERENCES

Advisory Council on Adjustment (1989) *Adjusting to Win* (report). Ottawa: Supply and Services Canada.

Commentary

Wilted Flowers – The Demographic Imperative: Contrasts and Connections

Elisabeth Gerver

COMMENT TO THE YEAR 2001: ONLY CONNECT?

Distant voices

The question in my title comes from the epigraph of E.M. Forster's *Howards End*, an early twentieth-century celebration of the values of what Northrop Frye called the educated imagination. Surely such a phrase comes from a voice too far away, both in time and in space, from Nicole Morgan's world of "panicky consumption?"

In Forster's novel, the protagonist, Margaret, is able to connect the world of money, which she inherits and into which she marries, with the world of the educated and civilized imagination – a world in which culture, art, music, and learning for its own sake combine with deeply felt responses to nature. The novel also attempts to connect normally opposed social classes with one another; tries to hold male and female values within a single moral vision; and urges, in phrasing that now sounds very outdated: "Only connect the prose and the passion, and both will be exalted." The plot depicts vividly the high price paid for such attempts, but the personal tragedies of the characters reinforce rather than undermine the imperative need for connection.

Is there a suggestion here of one way to achieve the remit which I have been given for this comment? I was asked to respond to Nicole Morgan with an optimistic vision, linked as much as possible to adult and continuing education. For me, what first emerged from her contribution was a sharp sense of contrast between a vision of the goals of society and of learning, in North America and in Europe. As I subsequently explored the contrasts, connections did begin to emerge. Both the contrasts and the connections are explored below.

There is, of course, no such thing as a "European" vision. Views of what constitutes Europe are currently changing to incorporate Mikhail Gorbachev's vision of a common European home. Even leaving aside the differences that exist between eastern and western Europe, however, there are profound differences within and among countries. There are ideological differences among the current governments of many European countries and, within the United Kingdom, between the views of the government and those of the majority of the electorate.

These differences are especially prominent in the world of the market economy as Nicole Morgan depicts it. For instance, the British government is highly committed to fostering as pure a market economy as possible. By contrast, the majority of people in Britain would prefer higher taxes with better public services than lower taxes but worse services, while 70 per cent say that the government should give a higher priority to environmental policy even if it means higher prices for some goods. This preference for a public policy of social justice and environmental protection is shared with probably most people throughout Europe.

Such assumptions distance Europe from Nicole Morgan's picture of North America. As she sees it, individuals' rewards for employment consist of money, freedom, and prestige; to that list most Europeans would add self-fulfillment and an opportunity to contribute to the life of the wider community. Moreover, Europeans live in a cultural milieu characterized by trends very different from those that Nicole Morgan depicts. She reports that attendance at cultural events is declining. In the United Kingdom and, I believe, throughout most of Europe, attendance at cultural events is increasing, perhaps most dramatically in that most elite of art forms, opera. Over the past ten years Scots have borrowed 14 per cent more books from public libraries, while in Denmark sales of magazines and journals have increased by about 20 per cent over the same period. In the United Kingdom new quality newspapers are being launched; and there have been significant increases in the numbers of local museums and art galleries, local arts festivals and outreach work by national companies in the performing arts.

Important contrasts between the two continents also appear in the motivations reported for adult learning. For Nicole Morgan, the initial impetus to return to learning arises from market-related forces: the "fear of being left behind in a society more competitive than ever," the "pervasiveness of plateauing within large organizations," and the "burnt out syndrome." By contrast, a recent study of the reasons why adults in Scotland returned to education and training identified the two most important motivations as "I thought it would help me in my job" and "the subject interested me;" among the purposes of returning, "personal interests/hobbies" ranked as equally important as "the job you were doing then," with all other purposes much less important.

Out of such contrasts, connections soon grew in my mind, but a problem of vocabulary emerged. The term "market-led" has a widely acknowledged meaning. But there is no comparable phrase referring to the complex of goals of adult education that include individual self-aggrandisement in the marketplace, individual self-development and the desire to contribute to the quality of life in the family and the wider community. To avoid lengthy phrasing in what follows, therefore, I shall use the term "value-led adult education" to refer to education that includes the full range of motivation; the term "market-led" will refer to learning experiences which are intended primarily to improve individual or corporate standing in the marketplace.

TESTING THE MARKET FOR LIFELONG LEARNING

As seen from Scotland, there are at least three connections between market-led and value-led adult education: an increasing demand for adult learning, a focus on the individual, and the development of more effective methods of quality control.

Increasing demand for adult learning

Over the past few years Scotland has seen a renaissance in demand for adult learning, a phenomenon which all available trends suggest will continue at least until 2001. Almost all forms of adult learning are expanding dramatically. Nearly five times as many adults are now studying in schools as was the case in 1984. The numbers of adults studying in further education colleges are now so substantial that in one region over 80 per cent of students in such colleges are adults. The numbers of adults enrolling for part-time degrees in Scottish universities (excluding the Open

University) increased by 193 per cent over the five-year period to 1986, while those studying full time rose by 38 per cent during the same period. Enhanced awareness of how training contributes to business development has increased employer-led training; to try to stimulate such developments further, the government is establishing employer-led local enterprise councils, responsible for training and development in their own areas. Adult education is playing an increasingly important role in trade unions and voluntary organizations, while enrollments in university and Workers Educational Association courses continue to flourish. There has been an eightfold increase in the number of open-learning courses available over the past eight years. And, as mentioned earlier, cultural life is flourishing. It appears as if adult education is, here as in North America, a "soaring business," as Nicole Morgan puts it.

The Scottish picture is not wholly bright. A recent report shows that, financially, British students over the age of 26 are considerably worse off than ordinary undergraduates, incurring heavy debts as a result of their study. Other reports point to the lack of employer interest in recruiting mature graduates, despite growing skills shortages. Informal adult education classes offered by local authorities in Scotland continue to decrease, as funding available for them declines. Fewer people who are qualified to enter university now can get places than was the case ten years ago. The only adult residential college has closed, at least for the time being, cutting back the options available for more disadvantaged adults.

Overall, however, expansion is likely to accelerate, driven both by economic as well as personal factors. Economically, growing skills shortages and a dramatic decline in the numbers of school leavers are focusing employers' minds on retraining their present staffs. As far as individuals are concerned, we know that the more education adults have, the more they want. Educational qualifications continue to rise in Scotland, so the healthy market in adult learning is likely to continue. Because adults learn for reasons that go beyond market imperatives, by 2001 there will be more highly educated people with more to contribute both to our economy and to the overall quality of life in Scotland.

The focus on individuals

A second connection between market forces and adult education is the extent to which both increasingly focus on discovering and meeting individual need. Political discussion about education in the UK often advocates educational vouchers (to enable individuals to undertake their education wherever and whenever it suits them rather than being confined to what the providers want to make available) or educational entitlements (to enable individuals to undertake their education wherever and whenever it suits them rather than being confined to what the providers want to make available). The political right favors vouchers because they would enable a market to develop, freed from the heavy hand of the state; the political left favors educational entitlements because they would allow individuals the right to learn. The outcome of either would be to empower individuals and to compel institutions to research need and to attempt to provide as attractively as possible for individual clients.

Even before either vouchers or entitlements become public policy, many institutions were researching the unmet needs and aspirations of potential learners. One straw in the wind, recognized by the Scottish Institute For Adult Continuing Education, is the Scottish study by Iain Macpherson, "Attracting New Students to Adult Education: the Learners' Point of View." He investigated students from groups which had traditionally been low participants in adult education. He concluded that individual students are highly attracted by precisely those elements of provision which are so far often undeveloped in Scotland, including free, small, locally based classes; flexible attendance patterns; childcare provision; cooperative and discussion-based learning methods; the breaking down of traditional tutor/student roles. In contrast to a market-led approach, he noted that "any provision attempting to attract low participant groups and incorporating the above elements requires appropriately high and consistent levels of resourcing".

While the focus on individuals leads to increased participation, then, it also raises in acute form a question about how far our societies wish merely to achieve the growth in adult learning that will almost automatically be achieved by market forces. Evidence is steadily accumulating that providing for mature and other non-traditional learners is more expensive than providing for younger adults from backgrounds which are already conducive to learning. Left to itself, the market-led model will not provide for those more expensive groups, whose well-being is a social and political rather than an economic necessity.

More generally, however, both market-led and value-led adult education share an interest in marketing to foster social expectations of lifelong learning. The use of strategic marketing approaches is new to many adult education providers in Scotland, but the past few years have seen an explosion in the numbers of marketing officers appointed by educational institutions as they compete with one another for students. The more careful shaping and targeting of education and training provision that results from such marketing will unquestionably benefit most potential adult learners, regardless of the purposes for which they study.

Quality Control

A third area in which the market-led approach connects with value-led adult education is the development of more sophisticated methods of quality control, including performance indicators. The market has traditionally measured its own performance by the bottom line. Until recently, publicly funded adult education has not been subject to as stringent methods of assessing its effectiveness. The British government is now insisting that all organizations which it funds should demonstrate their efficiency, economy, and effectiveness.

Research and development are also playing a more important part in the lives of educational institutions, analogously to the role that R&D have traditionally played in the market economy. It is significant that over the past three years Scottish research into the education and training of adults has moved up a gear. It now includes substantial investigations into opportunities for mature students, teaching and learning in continuing education, the training of part-time community education workers, the needs of mature entrants to higher and further education, returners to teaching, training women as managers, and the needs and aspirations of potential women returners. We have still not solved the problem of how most effectively to disseminate the findings and make them effective in practice, but staff development programs for adult educators throughout Scotland are now playing a far more important role in professional life than they did ten years ago.

All of these connections between market-led and value-led adult education have the potential to shape a future for lifelong learning that will empower adults to initiate change, to foster creativity, and to shape the future for their own ends. But the connections also pose daunting challenges for the future, where we shall have to make choices between goals that are often mutually exclusive.

NEW CHOICES

Some of the challenges with which the current growth of adult learning confronts us have been suggested above. Ironically, the contrast between the market-led and the value-led models of adult education is particularly acute in a time of growth, when a plethora of choice for most may be accompanied by the lack of means to make informed choices, decreased provision for the most disadvantaged, and insufficient attention to the long-term environmental effects of our present choices. I shall explore each of these challenges briefly below.

Educated Choice

By the term "educated choice" I mean the need for adults to be helped to make reasoned education and training choices based on accurate knowledge about the options available to them and the consequences of choosing any one option. It is now generally accepted in the United Kingdom that adult educational guidance is an essential component of any successful adult learning provision, in order to maximize the match between individual need and institutional provision.

In the market-led mass consumer society, consumers' associations have grown up to meet the need for informed consumer choice. It might be argued that, as we move toward a mass adult learning system, equivalent associations will develop in response to market needs. Such an assumption is overly optimistic. In contemporary mass learning societies, such as the United States or Denmark, such associations have not developed. On the other hand, where, as in Northern Ireland, an adult educational guidance system has developed with both public funding and private-sector sponsorship, individuals have been able to make informed decisions about the many options available; in turn, providers have shaped their provision to match as nearly as possible the demands that the service reflects back to them.

It is not chance that a developed adult educational guidance service exists in Northern Ireland, a small region where there is only a limited range of choices immediately available. The creation of such a service for the United Kingdom as a whole would be a formidable challenge, and the task will be made even more onerous by the coming of the single European market, when the range of education and training choices will increase dramatically. The setting up of local, national, and international structures to meet this need for adult educational guidance is one of the major challenges of the next decade, if the expansion of adult learning is to have maximum effect in the lives of individuals.

Equity

Some individuals are more equal than others in the choices available to them. There are many individuals for whom the market will always fail to provide, because their needs cannot be met at economically viable prices: the poor, the unemployed, the physically and mentally disabled. For them, access to existing provision requires additional expense which they are often unable to meet on their own. The expansion of adult learning to which Nicole Morgan points may even exacerbate their disadvantage. There is already evidence that the information rich tend to grow richer while the information poor become increasingly impoverished. How to intervene effectively to counteract this divisive process is one of the major policy issues for the coming decade.

Environment

Overriding all other considerations, however, is the need to educate both adults and children to take better care of our planet. Throughout Europe, both individuals and governments are increasingly concerned about the long-term ecological implications of market-led economies dependent on continued growth. The major challenge for the next decade may therefore be to move beyond market-led considerations and devise policies and structures to help to protect our long-term future, including educating people to consume less.

There has been a phenomenal growth of ecological movements in the United Kingdom: recently, membership of Friends of the Earth and of Greenpeace has more than tripled, while the British Green party polled 15 per cent of the popular vote in the recent European Parliament elections. This growing commitment to environmental issues has been paralleled by market-led interest in the new "green" consumerism. Relying solely on market-led interest in green issues, however, is unlikely in itself to avert worsening pollution and potential ecological disaster. How to save the planet when the major impetus of its economies is toward constant expansion is perhaps the most difficult and the most essential challenge for adult learning in the next decade.

BEYOND "PANICKY CONSUMPTION"

All these connections and challenges mean that adult education "is going to become a soaring business which will open the door to an amazing consumption of services," as Nicole Morgan sees. But the expansion of adult learning can also help to lead us toward a more equitable and ecologically aware society in which all individuals have the opportunity to make educated choices. Adult educators in Europe are greatly heartened by the many references to "lifelong learning" in the European Community's recently issued medium-term guidelines for education and training. But the challenges, the connections, and the contrasts of market-led and value-led adult education are likely to intensify, not diminish, as adult learning expands. Perhaps, in the end, Forster is not so distant from where we are going in the twenty-first century: "Truth, being alive, was not half way between anything. It was only to be found by continuous excursions into either realm, and though proportion is the final secret, to espouse it at the outset is to encourage sterility."

REFERENCES

Forster, E.M. (1910) *Howard's End*, New York: Putnam Publishing Place.

Chapter 5

Women, Work, and Learning

Linda MacDonald

> Men work from sun to sun
> But women's work is never done!

The message from technological change, however, is that there may be NO work for women in the future beyond the most menial and routine. From the traditional homemaker to the traditional secretary, teacher, or nurse, to the woman in the blue collar who punches the drill press as well as the time clock, women in all walks of life are finding that change is surrounding them and altering their place in society. The capabilities of the homemaker are replaced by the microwave oven, permanent press ready-made clothing, and even surrogate wombs. Office automation has replaced clerical support staff with a widening array of smart machines. Robots are telling blue-collar workers of both sexes that human labor is slow, costly and frequently inaccurate. Faced with a world where service is being performed by machines, women are finding that even their most basic roles are declared redundant.

Two questions arise from this situation: what has been the nature of women's learning and work in the past that has contributed to this situation? And what do women need to learn in order to have a place in the future world of work?

The increasing numbers of women in the paid labor force in the past ten years have been noteworthy not only for the fact that 54.5 per cent of Canadian women are now working or seeking work, but also for the concentration of these women in a very narrow range of occupations. This concentration has meant that 82 per cent of Canada's female labor force is in the service sector; that 78 per cent of all persons employed in clerical occupations, and 76 per cent of all persons in health-related occupations are women (Labour Canada 1983; Avebury Research Associates 1986).

The consequence of this over-specialization has been that women are extremely vulnerable to changes in demand or design of their work. Although there are some signs of change, declining school enrollments have meant a decreased demand for teachers, the single occupation which has contributed most of the women in the professional category. Microcomputers have eliminated thousands of jobs in the business world while at the same time widening the gap between the remaining low-level clerical jobs and entry-level management positions. Failure to make adjustments in career choices can doom women to sustained high unemployment and continued economic dependency. It is estimated that up to one million women in Canada may be unemployed in the 1990s unless women are more responsive to labour market demand (Menzies 1982; Phillips and Phillips 1983).

The capacity to respond to the demands of employers depends upon the kinds of learning in which women engage. The surge of women into white-collar clerical jobs has been as much in response to past labor market demand upon the reserve labor pool of middle-class educated women as to the exclusion of women from the traditional forms of productive work dominated by men. Because women were expected to have a short labor force attachment, employers were not apparently prepared to place a substantial investment in the training of this segment of the work force. This has meant that women have had to assume the full costs of their training and education themselves or with such public funding as is allocated to the training of women.

One priority for the public funding has been the training of clerical workers, both because of past demand and because of the relatively low expenditure required as compared with the heavy financial investment of most apprenticeship programs. In Canada, the two main sources of publicly funded training accessible to women have been the public schools, with their business education programs, and the programs funded by Canada Employment and Immigration.

These federally funded programs, operated by the provinces either directly or through the community college system, have until recently reinforced women's training for traditional jobs. With the implementation of Canada's National Training Act of 1979/1982, however, and the increasing impact of office automation, funding was shifted away from traditional programs to high-skill trades and technologies. In spite of a targeting of 30 per cent of training places for women, because of their lack of basic foundations in math and science women were unable to make the transition to this priority training. The result has been that both the number and proportion of women trainees declined in all areas of publicly funded institutional and industrial training (Henderson 1982).

On the other hand the self-selection process of the high school programs has made it easy for young women to participate in traditional job-preparation courses. In dropping out of math and science courses in favor of clerical training at this point in their education, however, they have locked themselves into a narrow career path, where short-term choices create long-term barriers. By placing this training within the public schools, the training system has assured employers of a large pool of cheap labor, each interchangeable with another as a result of the standardization of the training (Gaskell 1982).

While standardization has been most clearly evident in clerical training, it has also played a considerable role in other forms of women's learning, such as the spread of instructional manuals for elementary teachers as publishers strive to "teacher proof" their materials, and the emphasis in nursing education to follow prescribed procedures. Thus a major feature of women's learning for work has been the downplaying of initiative, independent judgment, and decision-making. The result has been the clustering of women in entry-level jobs, where little progress is made along a career path of increasing responsibility, and where career transitions from entry level to management have never been developed.

LEARNING AND THE JOB

One question which arises is whether women are, in fact, truly interested in accessing education and training. An explanation is that women have been socialized into thinking that education and training are not relevant to their lives because the greater part of their lives will be spent in the home. The evidence, however, shows that women's participation in post-secondary education has grown substantially in the last twenty years so that at present, women's enrollments in university education are just slightly in excess of their male counterparts. In fact, as they seek out occupational mobility, women have turned to university programs as a means of broadening their labor force participation. During the 1970s women, like men, showed an increased preference for degree programs in Business and Commerce (Belanger *et al.* 1982).

Not only have women considerably expanded their participation in the traditional forms of post-secondary education, but they lead men in their participation in many forms of continuing education. "One in Every Five: A Survey of Adult Education in Canada" (Devereaux 1985) indicated that the majority of participants in adult education (defined as all organized activities taken outside of a full-time program) are women, 56 per cent of the participants when self-selection, not referral, is the basis for participation. On average, 21 per cent of all women 17 years of age and over participated in adult education, with the highest participation group for either men or women being that of women 25 to 34 years of age, with a participation rate of 31 per cent. Twenty-nine per cent of women in the labor force participated in an adult education course, as compared with 21 per cent for men. Whether in or out of the labor force, the proportion of women who took a course exceeded the proportion of men.

It can be clearly seen that women place a high priority on learning and make considerable use of the opportunity, especially when they are able to take part without having to rely upon the sponsorship or referral of another agency or individual.

Another notable feature of women's participation in learning is that they are not as likely to be involved in job-related learning (39 per cent of participants) as are men. Only 34 per cent of the women respondents of the survey cited job-related reasons, such as improving their employment opportunities, as the purpose of their learning. An interpretation of this distinction can be very revealing of the nature of women's work roles and tasks.

Since much of women's work is routinized and offers little opportunity for advancement or growth in knowledge and skills (Kanter 1977), women may be using these learning opportunities in their non-work hours to provide challenge and enrichment in their lives. Additionally, some women may recognize and accept the dead-end nature of their jobs and that investment in job-related learning will pay no dividends (Meier 1983). For the woman who does take job-related learning courses, the focus on the job duties may have to be so narrow, in order for the employer to pay for the tuition, that she realizes such learning will never lead to career advancement.

The cost of learning may also be a deterrent for women's involvement in job-related learning. Only 14 per cent of women survey respondents had their tuition paid for by the employer, as compared with 35 per cent of men respondents. Even in the same occupation, men who undertook job-related learning were more likely than women to be funded by their employer.

The inequity of this subsidized learning is further augmented by the pay differential between the sexes. Overall, women's earnings are 61.5 per cent of men's (Labour Canada 1983). Thus for the seven out of ten women whose learning was paid for by themselves or out of total family income, this learning cost a higher proportion of their income. Indeed the case might be made that by paying for their own learning, women employees are in fact subsidizing the learning of their wealthier male colleagues.

Not only do employers leave to the individual woman the cost and responsibility for her initial learning for job preparation but they also expect the individual woman to bear the cost of her continuing professional development. This reluctance of employers to invest in on-the-job training for women has been justified on the basis of women's short-term labor force attachment, a conclusion not borne out by the large number of women now combining work with marriage and family responsibilities. Gaskell (1982) observes that because there is an assumption that women will not stay with the organization and become leaders, there is less need to control their learning. As a result, women are less likely to be in management training programs or other employer-sponsored training which would lead to senior positions.

The consequences of this lack of on-the-job training are high. Boothby (1986) has found that on-the-job training has the highest return of any kind of experience. The most important difference between men and women in work history is that women spend less time training on the job than do men, and this feature accounts for approximately 12 per cent of the wage gap between the sexes (Corcoran 1979).

INFORMAL WORKPLACE LEARNING

Even though the formal learning mechanisms of workplace learning may be unsympathethic to women, one could explore aspects of informal learning in the expectation that these might be more accessible to women. Informal learning does not require any expenditure of training budgets; can be carried on at an interpersonal level, a strength often attributed to women, and can provide access to employer-specific skills, the kind of training investment where employers are most likely to share in the costs.

Informal learning does not seem to be any more accessible to women than the formal kinds of learning on the job. Because of covert male values and attitudes, the information and skills of the informal learning network may be even more closed against women. In writing of women scientists, Cole (1981) attributed their lower publication record to their exclusion from the informal activities and the social networks of science that allow for full participation and growth and the generation of new ideas.

Informal learning which occurs as a part of formal learning opportunities on the job is an important part of the development of managerial skills. Training programs on the job serve as a mechanism by which managers can increase their contact with other managers, build important relationships crucial to career advancement, and share information (Harlan and Weiss 1982). Women's access to this kind of learning is hampered doubly, first by their low level of representation in managerial positions, and second by their more limited access to employer-sponsored training.

Informal learning is just as important to job performance and career success as formal education and occupational preparation. This informal learning may take place as hints and suggestions from colleagues, advice from a mentor, help from a predecessor. New jobs, even within the same employer, require new skills and behaviors, and these are acquired through informal networks that provide the necessary "how to" information (Harlan and Weiss 1982). Pesons whose background, experience, and values are similar are more readily assimilated into the informal learning network, and so for men, the experience is one of being brought into the network without any effort on their part. Women, on the other hand, report that they have to make a conscious effort to acquire the contacts and knowledge to become part of the informal learning environment (Harlan and Weiss 1982).

Not only is the informal learning system critical to the acculturation of managerial and professional workers, but it also makes a major contribution to the performance of support staff such as clerical workers. Group norms set the standard for the quantity and quality of work produced in a collective work setting such as a steno pool. The exceptionally capable worker who adjusts her work performance to fit the lower level of the group norms is learning not only the work climate and standards but is also learning the impact of peer pressure either to conform or to face isolation; and more significantly, is learning to devalue her exceptional status and to value conformity (Kolbenschlag 1981).

There is no doubt that informal learning in the workplace is a powerful and effective means for personal and professional development. Women have used informal learning in other settings such as consciousness raising groups to validate and extend their experience. Kolbenschlag (1981: 75) has noted that the woman who is able to support herself in work she enjoys gains an irreplaceable sense of competence, of self-validation, and social identity. It is the informal learning that creates the conditions and the source for both the enjoyment and the competence.

NEW PATTERNS FOR WORK AND LEARNING

For women to experience the workplace as a source of enjoyment and competence, there need to be changes in the nature of the work that women do, as well as in the ways that we women view ourselves and our work. A utilitarian approach to work is common to many women, as can be found in the claim that women work because they have to, out of economic necessity. The underlying implication is that if the economic necessity were removed, these women would not be in the paid labor force. Yet by limiting the work role to the utilitarian function, women miss out on other kinds of functions and rewards which work can provide: a sense of autonomy and transcendence of the limitations of oneself. Meaningful work can provide a source of creative fulfilment.

What blocks the development of this creativity and transcendence is the indisputable fact that much of women's work has been routinized and deskilled, with little or no opportunity for self-expression. Oakley observes:

> Women's work is typically work that requires little training, little in the way of mental initiative, and characteristically consists of interruptible short time-span tasks. It is often also described as caring work – work that promotes the welfare of others rather than the welfare and development of the worker herself.
>
> (Oakley 1981: 155)

Not only does the quality of women's work life need to be improved by providing opportunity for initiative and growth, so too does the quality of the non-work life. In place of the Type E Superwoman who is "Everything to Evervybody" (Braiker 1986), women have to give up their guilt-based control of the non-work environment and promote the integration of men into the reproductive work of the family while women themselves seek to play a meaningful part in the productive life of the workplace. Combined with these altered self-perceptions and changed roles there is also a recognition of the need for changes in how work is structured in the workplace. Instead of technological change leading to increased numbers of dead-end and deskilled jobs, this change can be managed to provide for the re-design of jobs for enrichment and growth. In place of electronic monitoring of narrow technical performance, the new technology could be used to redefine productivity and development from an individual to a group or team performance. Work in a group setting would include both formal and informal learning to function as part of the collaborative effort, as well as learning new skills in order to be able to switch functions and tasks with other group members (Hall and Associates 1986).

While much learning can be acquired on the job, for many women to make substantial career transitions they will have to undertake learning new content and new skills. Often this will mean a return to formal learning such as the community college or the university. For this learning and career transition to be successful, both employers and women must be prepared to make changes and concessions.

Women must begin to move away from traditional occupations and to seek training and employment in a wide and varied range of jobs. Work can no longer be defined as "men's work" and "women's work." If women, a large segment of the labor force, are to avoid a career of dependency, not only must they prepare for alternative forms of employment, but the unacknowledged barriers to these forms of employment must be overcome.

Employers too must make a contribution to these changes. In Canada, a national employer is responding to employment equity requirements by sponsoring on full salary a number of women as they study at university full time in order to make the move from clerical staff to management. Other employer-based options which support the career development of women also need to be explored. The most desirable approach would be part-time work combined with part-time learning.

Women are the greatest number of part-time learners. They are also the greatest proportion of part-time workers. But employers have been reluctant to invest in the training of these part-time workers, perceiving them to have a weak work attachment. The workers themselves have been almost as reluctant to invest in their own career development because the job opportunities at upper levels on a part-time basis are virtually non-existent. Both sets of assumptions are open to challenge and change, with both employers and learners able to benefit. The part-time worker who is also learning for career development may have a stronger work attachment arising from the opening of opportunity than the full-time worker who is experiencing alienation and frustration.

A policy of paid educational leave would be especially beneficial to women workers, since it would help to overcome the training differential that women experience. With equalized access to training opportunities and the staff development dollar, women would find themselves better situated to move out of the job ghettoes and into work which is capable of sustaining personal growth and creativity.

The goal of this learning and career transition is not to cast women in the mould of men. It is the passive acquiesence of women in the fragmented work structures and hierarchical patterns of power that has led to many of the present problems in the workplace, particularly for women. "More women the world over are coming to realize that educating women just to participate in and move up in the patriarchal and hierarchical structures will change nothing" (Fulton 1985: 22).

Women's learning must work to bring to the organization new forms of interaction and task design. This shift is itself a form of work since like other oppressed groups, women must not only free themselves from the internalized assumptions that limit and constrict their role and contribution, but they must also work to free, that is deprivilege, their male colleagues from their own distorted assumptions on the nature and quality of work relationships.

Two of these assumptions are of crucial importance to the full and equitable integration of women into the labor force. The first pertains to the concentration and use of power through authoritarian patterns of control and dominance, a use which must now be unlearned especially by those who have used such power to their personal aggrandizement. Leadership is being redefined to mean the distribution of power more broadly throughout the workplace with the implementation of matrix organizational design and shifting patterns of responsibility.

The second assumption calls into question the nature of work itself. Both women and men must learn to redesign their lives and activities so that all can accommodate the dual tasks of productive work and what is often called non-profit labor. It is no longer viable for male participation in capitalist economic structures to be used as an exemption from the responsibilities of personal maintenance and familial duties. The imposition of these responsibilities upon women solely has prevented women from realizing their full personal, economic and social potential. What women must learn is the confidence to bring these changes to the workplace with the understanding that this is the only way they can achieve equitable patterns of work and living.

Flexibility and collaboration are the primary features of the new patterns of learning and work. Shifting work groups, network lines of communication, and varigated job tasks appear on the horizon as promising strategies for organizing the workplace. These approaches seem especially attractive for enhancing the scope of women's participation at all levels and tasks. But these promises will not be realized if women do not take responsibility for action, recognizing that change will happen only through shared endeavour and positive assertion of women's right and obligation to name their world and their place in it.

REFERENCES

Adams, Jane (1983) *First Things First*. Toronto: Canadian Congress for Learning Opportunities for Women.

Agassi, J.B. (1982) *Comparing the Work Attitudes of Women and Men*. Lexington, MA: Lexington Books.

Avebury Research Associates (CGLOW) (1986). *Decade of Promise*. Toronto: Canadian Congress for Learning Opportunities for Women.

Belanger, R. (1982) Part-time Degree Students: Tomorrow's Majority? Ottawa: Statistics Canada.

Bennis, Warren and Burt, Nanus (1985) *Leaders: The Strategies for Taking Charge*. New York: Harper & Row.

Boothby, Daniel (1986) *Women Reentering the Labour Force and Training Programs*. Ottawa: Economic Council of Canada.

Braiker, Harriett (1986) *The Type E Woman: How to Overcome the Stress of Being Everything to Everybody*. New York: Dodd, Mead.

Cameron, Barbara (1984) "Labour Market Discrimination and Affirmative Action," in J.M. Vickers (ed.) *Taking Sex Into Account*. Ottawa: Carleton University Press.

Cole, Jonathan R. (1981) "Women in Science," *Scientific American*, July–August: 385–91.

Corcoran, Duncan (1979) "Work History, Labor Force Attachment, and Earnings Differences Between the Races and Sexes", *Journal of Human Resources* 14(1): 3–20.

Devereaux, M.S. (1985) *One in Every Five: A Survey of Adult Education in Canada*. Ottawa: Statistics Canada and Secretary of State Canada.

Employment and Immigration Canada (1983) *Learning A Living in Canada: The Report of the Skill Development Leave Task Force*. Ottawa: Supply and Services Canada.

Freire, Paulo (1970) *Pedagogy of the Oppressed*. New York: Continuium Publishing Corporation.

Fulton, E. Margaret (1985) "The UN Decade for Women: One Woman's Personal Assessment," *Women's Education des Femmes*. vol. 4, no. 2: 21–3.

Gaskell, Jane (1982) "Education and Job Opportunities for Women: Patterns of Enrolment and Economic Returns," in Naomi Henson, and D.E. Smith. (eds) *Women and the Canadian Labour Force*. Ottawa: Social Sciences and Humanities Research Council of Canada.

Gilligan, Carol (1980) *In a Different Voice*. Cambridge, MA: Harvard University Press.

Gregory, Judith (1983) "The Electronic Sweatshop" in J. Turner and L. Emery *Perspectives on Women in the 1980's*. Winnipeg: University of Manitoba Press.

Hall, Douglas T. and Associates (1986) *Career Development in Organizations*. San Francisco, CA: Jossey-Bass.

Harlan, Anne and Weiss, C.L. (1982) "Sex Differences in Factors Affecting Managerial Career Advancement," in Phyllis Wallace (ed.) *Women in the Workplace*. Boston, MA: Sunburn House.

Henderson, Heather (1982) *The National Training Prgram*. Toronto: Canadian Congress for Learning Opportunities for Women.

Jackson, Nancy S. (1986) "Who Gains From the New Skills Training?" *Women's Education des Femmes*, vol. 5, no. 2: 10–13.

Kanter, Rosabeth Moss (1977) *Men and Women of the Corporation*. New York: Basic Books.

Kolbenschlag, Madonna (1981) *Kiss Sleeping Beauty Good-bye*. New York: Bantam Books.

Labour Canada (1983) *Women in the Labour Force: Part I – Participation*. Ottawa: Supply and Services Canada.

Levine, J. and Emery, L. (1983). "Feminist Counselling: Approach or Technique?" in J. Turner and L. Emery *Perspectives on Women in the 1980's*. Winnipeg: University of Manitoba Press.

MacDonald, Linda A. (1985) *Training: For Self-sufficiency or Dependency*? Halifax: Canadian Congress for Learning Opportunities for Women.

Meier, Gretl S. (1983) *Worker Learning and Worktime Flexibility*. Detroit: W.E. Upjohn Institute for Employment Research.

Menzies, H. (1982) *Computers on the Job: Surviving Canada's Microcomputer Revolution*. Toronto: James Lorimer and Co.

Morgan, Gareth (1986) *Images of Organization*. Beverly Hills, CA: Sage Publications.

Neilsen, E.H. (1986) "Empowerment Strategies: Balancing Authorities," in Suresh Srivastva *Executive Power*. San Francisco: Jossey-Bass.

Oakley, Ann (1981) *Subject Women*. New York: Pantheon Books.

Phillips, Paul and Erin (1983) *Women and Work*. Toronto: James Lorimer and Company, 1983.

Ramsey, V.J. (1985) *Preparing Professional Women for the Future*. (Michigan Business Papers #67). Ann Arbor, MI: University of Michigan.

Rubensen, Kjell (1985) *Adult Education: The Economic Context*. Toronto: Canadian Association for Adult Education.

St. Peter, Christine (1986) "Old Skills, New Vision: Teaching Women To Make The Future", in *Educating for Change*. Toronto: Canadian Congress for Learning Opportunities for Women.

Schaeffer, R.G. and E.F. Lynton (1982) "Corporate Experiences in Improving Women's Job Opportunities" in Phyllis Wallace (ed.) *Women in the Workplace*. Boston, MA: Sunburn House.

Stager, David (1981) *The Federal Government Role in the Development of Highly Qualified Labour: A report to the Task Force on Labour Market Development, Canada Employment and Immigration*. Toronto: University of Toronto Press.

Statistics Canada (1987) *The Labour Force*. Ottawa: Supply and Services Canada.

Strober, S.H. (1982) "The MBA: Same Passport to Success For Men and Women" in Phyllis Wallace (ed.) *Women in the Workplace*. Boston, MA: Sunburn House.

Townson, Monica (1986) "Women and the *Canadian* Economy." Ottawa: Keynote Address to the Symposium on Women and the Economy, Canadian Advisory Council on the Status of Women, March 17, 1986.

Wallace, Phyllis (ed.) (1982) *Women in the Workplace*. Boston, MA: Sunburn House.

Whyte, Margaret (1983) *Women and the Labour Force: What Does the Future Hold?* Toronto: Canadian Congress for Learning Opportunities for Women.

Commentary

Women, Work and Learning

Linda Sweet

With the twenty-first century barely a decade away, the outlook for women both in and out of the work force has never been better. Rapidly escalating changes and improvements surrounding the role of women in our society are well in motion. The twenty-first century no longer holds mystery about the direction that women will be moving, only the speed in which they make their progress. While women's desire for equality of rights and opportunity has been an uphill struggle for centuries, efforts over the last ten to twenty years have brought about major changes in the quality of the lives of women. Even though significant advances have been made in family law, career choices and in movement toward equality of salary and opportunity, many women feel that for every two steps forward, a step backwards is taken. Progress has been greatly influenced by various political platforms and economical expansion and contraction pressures.

During the 1980s, women continued to do most of the caring, nurturing and cleaning in the home, regardless of whether they had employment outside the household. The abortion controversy has been a recurring nightmare, consisting of a dispute more about power than fetal rights. The suburban/city women benefited most in the 1980s while rural women often experienced uneven access of opportunity and of choice. In the 1980s women's salaries still consisted of only approximately 65 per cent of the income earned by men for equal work of equal value; and this income is being earned mainly at the lower end of the work force in education, politics, religion and social careers. Female "job ghettoes" in the service field are still very evident. In the 1980s, many rights of women became enshrined in legislation and political efforts generated greater impetus in forcing government, business and industry to provide equal opportunities for women in the work force. In the media it has been interesting to note that much of the debate has not been over whether women should or shouldn't be permitted to do . . . but over degrees of cost and inconvenience such changes would create when implemented.

In the 1980s women reached a new plateau in their push for economic, political, and social equality. Surveys have indicated that women have begun to feel better about themselves; women have been developing their skills for the work force, and women do expect things to be even better in the years to come. Recent studies have also found women far more optimistic than men, and women see major improvements to come. Women are more open to change and are beginning to be powerful enough to make significant improvements not only in their own lives but in the lives of others.

The final ten years of the twentieth century will hold few surprises because the patterns of change have already been set, the foundations established, and many of the milestones reached. There have been a number of very distinctive trends in progress in recent years; trends that are not only affecting the participation of women in the work force, but also wider participation in society. The 1990s will bring ongoing improvements for women and closure to many of women's present feminist concerns. Continued progress will be achieved through legislation and in funding support services. However, as in the past, this final decade will not be without its share of frustrations, inequalities, and setbacks.

Periodically, issues that had long been resolved will again be scrutinized and challenged. This will create regular reminders to women that constant vigilance is required, as a reversal in progress and in society's attitudes can be very subtle, yet can occur rapidly. Interest groups, both for and against equality, will fight strenuously to protect their objectives.

Trends that will profoundly influence women in the 1990s are the higher cost of living (which has created the need for the second income), the increase in litigation, and the growing impact of information from all areas of the media. Another trend has been the greater accessibility to, and an increase in women's support networks and crisis centers, which has assisted women in challenging domestic violence and in leaving unhappy marital situations for a new start for themselves and their children. Access to government support dollars, retraining programs, and litigation for employees as well as child support are trends that will also impact and greatly improve the quality of the lives of women in the 1990s.

The courts will also be playing a significant role in the interpretation of these rights and freedoms for women. In our rapidly changing world, new ethical questions and challenges will arise that will further complicate the legal rights and choices of women. Advancements in communication and information access, combined with the overloading of present transportation systems, will be a further catalyst in accelerating greater flexibility of work schedules, job sharing, and home assignments – which will in turn better suit the needs of working mothers.

Women will continue advancing into nontraditional areas of employment. Because some skilled trades and career choices will be more difficult to enter, women will either become more persistent and innovative or go outside the traditional system to gain the necessary skills and training and later return to positions at higher levels in their field. Greater opportunities for daycare in the workplace, new market services, alterations in present educational practices and innovative use of school facilities will further address the demands for increased child and family support services. In the coming decade, as women reach higher levels of employment and power in ever-increasing numbers, both in the government and in the private sector, they will not only be opening up opportunities for other women, but challenging present procedures, perceptions and expectations in the work place. At the same time women will be attracted to entrepreneurial ventures which offer greater flexibility in lifestyle options, and the potential for rapid skill development.

Over the next decade, women will progress to higher employment positions and be able to demand and create additional services from a widespread range of resource areas. The incidence of male chauvinism in the marketplace will proportionately decrease as it will not be tolerated when it results in loss of business dollars from women in the consumer and corporate areas. This will result in improved responses and attitudes toward women, from the copier repair "man" to the bank manager. The gap between male and female wage earners will lessen over the coming decade. With the aging work force, combined with the population decrease due to declining birthrates and natural calamities such as the AIDS epidemic, capable and qualified women will be sought after as serious candidates to fill the growing gaps in thc labor force. The trend toward increased worldwide competitiveness in the areas of manufacturing, services, and trade will be a powerful incentive for employers to choose the most capable candidates and not limit their choices solely to males.

In the 1990s, while continued progress and advances will be seen in the improved status of women, setbacks will continue to occur, but with little long-term impact. Hundreds of thousands of ordinary women will be continually challenging the system and winning their own "battles" at home and in their workplace. Through their collective and individual efforts, the evidence of real and lasting grassroots change will come. As in the past, legislation will continue to reflect and reinforce society's changes in attitudes and in values.

As it has been perceived in previous decades, as women's fight for self-determination for full equality continues over the coming decade at the pace as outlined, progress will continue to appear to be slow and labored. One must realize that the steady, uphill momentum toward equal opportunity and rights will not be fully realized over the next decade, but will continue to be an ongoing process, well into the twenty-first century. What is refreshing, however, is the rapid growth that third world women are making in "catching up" to the progress of women in the more advanced countries. Through the media, the work of female political leaders, relief workers, international networking conferences and access to technology and information, Third World women have and will continue to make significant strides in their awareness and quest for equality and opportunities. This rapid growth of feminism will continue to be the greatest achievement of women in the twentieth century.

In projecting an optimistic scenario of the place of women in society for the 1990s, projections have been based on patterns and developments that have already been in progress. A short-term view into the near future, based on trends to date, would be a very simplistic exercise based on present practices, unless one took into account some of the major, profound worldwide trends which will impact greatly upon our world societies, its priorities and subsequent decisions in the twenty-first century. Today's materialistic societies have continued to function following their traditional institutional structures in a rapidly eroding value system. In recent years it has become overwhelmingly apparent that the family, religions, and ideologies have been rapidly losing their power and no longer possess the control that they once had. The threats facing an ordered, productive and secure life are many.

Worldwide pollution, depletion of natural resources, extensive environmental damage, waste, inefficiences, bureaucratic ineptitude and short-sightedness pose major threats to our very health and survival on this earth in the twenty-first century. These, combined with overpopulation, world hunger, pressures from Third World refugees seeking improved living standards as well as massive Third World debts, have been overtaxing our world systems in recent years. All of these trends have also been drawing us nearer to a precipice of major disasters which threaten the economy, the environment and our social systems in the immediate future. We have been blindly living beyond our resources and on borrowed time – not only fiscally, but environmentally. Political instability, economic recessions and an increasingly competitive marketplace, chasing after the same dollars, all point to unsettling times and of a desperate need for innovation and change in our approach to the way we view ourselves, our institutions and our place in this world. Traditional, short-term, short-sighted solutions by governments, business, and industry are no longer going to be acceptable.

The challenges and successes of the twenty-first century will be greatly intertwined with the evolving role of women in our society. While women's political acceptance to full societal rights has been slow – it will be these very critical world threats and crises that threaten and jeopardize our very existence. These trends will act as a catalyst to propel women beyond "their issues" to their role as equal partners in meeting the organizational challenges and nurturing solutions of our world's peoples and their problems.

Together, men and women will begin pooling their talents to solve the problems the twenty-first century has in store for us. Such work would make the statistical counting of male/female percentages (wins and losses), as we have done in the past, seem mundane, trivial and wasteful effort in the light of the real work to be done. Women have gifts to offer our society: that of nurturers, watchdogs, and capable citizens. With their continuing education, retraining, and access to skill development opportunities over the coming decade, the longer vision of women in the future will see them not only as fulfilling their roles as care-givers, but as taking their place in leadership and decision making positions to act in accordance with what is globally right, as well as good for the well-being of our societies as a whole. This will include all men and women of all nationalities, regardless of age. The last decade of the twentieth century should offer smooth sailing in already charted waters. The twenty-first century will be the true test of the strength, resources, and problem-solving skills of both men and women, for all peoples of this earth.

Chapter 6

We Cannot Afford to Waste A Single Mind: Adult Literacy and Basic Education

Maurice Taylor

Recent reports by the Advisory Council on Adjustment, the Canadian Labour Market and Productivity Centre and the Economic Council of Canada attest to the fact that the influence of demographics, as well as economic and technical forces, pose challenges to our global community. An aging society, a knowledge-based economy, and the sophisticated skill requirements of the labor force require that new training strategies and partnerships be established. The concept of lifelong learning appears to be one of the key elements in any human resource development plan. But as training and educational opportunities continue to accelerate for the more professional sectors, it is equally important to consider the needs of the basic learner. In terms of resource development we cannot afford to waste a single mind. The purpose of this chapter is to examine the various facets of a vital constituency – adult literacy and basic education.

UNDERSTANDING WHAT LITERACY MEANS

Many attempts have been made to define and determine the extent of functional illiteracy in industrialized countries. The Canadian Business Task Force on Literacy (1988) indicated that there are currently a large number of definitions of literacy and illiteracy in use which correspond to many different contexts in which literacy related issues arise. For example, definitions often relate to the individual's ability to function within the business and societal context. Nesbitt (1987) maintains every study or commission involved in assessing literacy must struggle with its precise definition since no generally accepted definition of literacy yet exists. Literacy and illiteracy are rarely absolutes. Illiteracy does not necessarily mean "the complete absence of the ability to read" and literacy encompasses a broad spectrum of capabilities for which absolute attainment is difficult to achievc or infer. At the very basic level are the simple decoding skills and at a higher level are the skills involved in aesthetic appreciation and study. Literacy, then, is not a single skill but a set of complex information skills (Nesbitt 1987: 3).

Miller (1987) purports that there are two general types of literacy definitions:

1 conventional, involving simple reading and writing skills, and
2 functional, where a more complex set of skills and proficiencies is used as the standard.

At one end of the continuum is basic literacy, or what some authors refer to as conventional literacy. This is the stage at which a person's ability to read and write is limited to very simple tasks such as reading and writing one's name and address, recognizing and understanding social sight words, and writing simple sentences for communication purposes. Literacy is confined at this stage to simple "survival" skills of reading and writing. Harman (1987) defines conventional literacy as the ability to read and write and comprehend texts or familiar subjects and to understand whatever signs, labels, instructions, and directions are necessary to get along in one's environment.

As we move from conventional literacy we come to a stage known as functional literacy. Implied in the definition is a critical threshold which, once reached, enables a person to handle the tasks of everyday life with confidence and responsibility. The term "functional illiteracy" began to be used during the 1940s and 1950s to describe persons who were incapable of understanding written instructions necessary to accomplish tasks or functions. In particular the armed forces in North America used texts to distinguish Second World War trainees who needed additional educational training before they could comprehend military instructions. The conventional definition of literacy proved insufficient for making these distinctions.

Definitions of functional literacy depend on specific tasks, skills, or objectives thought necessary for the comprehension of a literate person. As various experts defined clusters of "needed" skills, definitions proliferated. These definitions became more complex as the technological and information needs of society increased. According to Hunter and Harman (1979: 9) functional literacy is

> the possession of skills perceived as necessary by particular persons and groups to fulfil their own self-determined objectives as family and community members, citizens, consumers, job holders, and members of social, religious and other associations of their choosing. This includes the ability to obtain information they want and to use that information for their own and others' well-being; the ability to read and write adequately to satisfy the requirements they set for themselves as being important for their own lives; the ability to deal positively with demands made on them by society; and the ability to solve the problems they face in their daily lives.
>
> (Hunter and Harman 1979: 9)

A recent Canadian study conducted by the Southam Press used the following definition: "the term illiterate refers both to adult Canadians who can barely read and write called 'basic illiterates' and also to those whose reading and writing and number skills are not sufficient to get by in everyday life called 'functional illiterates'." The study used an operational definition of literacy based on a series of tests of actual reading skills instead of educational attainment as a measure. Using the Southam study results, the functional illiteracy level of 4.5 million adult Canadians (24 per cent) is somewhat more than that which is derived by using the criterion of persons with less than grade 9 (21 per cent according to the 1981 Census). The Southam study showed that using the grade 9 criterion there are approximately 1.7 million who are wrongly labelled illiterate and a further 2.4 million who should be classified illiterate but who have levels of education of at least grade 9. (Canadian Business Task Force on Literacy 1988: 9).

Shortcomings of the Grade Level Equivalency Measure

Some researchers have attempted to define literacy by linking it to a grade level of performance. Harman (1987) reported that researchers have sought to identify a level that would form the benchmark of functionality and have variously proposed standards ranging from a fourth- to a twelfth-grade level. In Canada the grade level and equivalency measure has also been used. In the late 1970s organizations such as the Canadian Association for Adult Education considered the equivalent of at least the eighth grade of educational attainment necessary for functional literacy and Statistics Canada defined illiteracy as having less than Grade 9 education. (Thomas 1983; Calamai 1987). The unacceptability of this type of approach is highlighted by Kirsch and Guthrie (1977–8) who maintain that the average grade scores of eighth graders in Chicago range from 4.4 grade level in the lowest school to a median level of 10.5 in the best schools. Darling (1981) made an even stronger case for unacceptability by noting that of students registered for adult basic education in Kentucky, the median grade completed was 8.6 but the median tested reading level of entering students was 2.0.

As Nesbitt (1987) explains, studies involved in determining literacy have adopted a criterion measure of functional literacy, performance below which is judged to be functionally illiterate. But one of the serious problems with such a grade equivalency measure is the fluctuating standards for a given grade level. In a similar vein, Calamai (1987) reported that research also reveals that reading skills evaporate if unused for a lengthy period of time; a grade 9 education in the 1960s could have shrunk to a much lower reading level by today. Other studies have also found as much as a year's difference between the reading levels of Grade 9 students in different schools. Most experts are now rejecting this grade level approach to literacy.

Central Issues Related to Definitions of Literacy

Valentine (1986) has pointed out that much of the confusion surrounding the definitional problem derives from the fact that there is little agreement upon what skills comprise literacy. For example, which clusters of skills comprising reading and writing are essential? One can sidestep the issue of what skills comprise reading and writing and simply look at materials people are able to or unable to read and write. This, however, creates another problem of definition: literacy is being able to read and write which materials? Bormuth (1975) suggested that the list of materials will always differ from person to person and situation and therefore offers the definition of literacy as the ability to respond competently to real world reading tasks. Gutherie (1983) expands on this notion by noting that the reader's literacy depends on the context of the situation, not on a specific achievement level.

Bormuth (1975) also notes that there is no true definition of literacy. Rather, each definition must be designed for the purpose to which it is to be put to use, and its correctness may be judged only in terms of how well it serves that purpose. According to Lytle *et al.* (1986) the best definition, at least in terms of accurately reflecting the social and cultural nature of literacy, would be those that (1) emanate from individually defined goals and purposes and (2) view literacy as a process not a product. As Fingeret explains, "to establish a national set of standards for a concept that is relative in relation to time and culture will, to some extent, undermine efforts to develop literacy programs that are appropriate to the varying needs of adults in their social contexts" (1984: 9).

Because of the pluralism of values in industrialized countries a common operational definition may not be feasible, but as Thomas (1989) points out, there appears to be more or less general agreement on some of the underlying principles of adult literacy. First, grade level completion measures are inadequate for definitional purposes. Second there is a literacy continuum ranging from the mechanisms of learning how to decode and encode to the mature utilization of literacy skills and processes for informed action and aesthetic appreciation. Third, with a few exceptions, there is general agreement with the principle that literacy should be defined as the ability of individuals to function within a specific social economic or cultural context. Fourth, in an increasing technological and changing society, literacy thresholds are likely to be in a continuing state of flux.

It would appear that one uniform definition of adult literacy is not appropriate but, as Harman (1987) suggests, what is useful is a plethora of definitions, each appropriate for a specific community at a particular time. Within this framework such definitions would reflect environmental norms, expectations regarding literacy, and objective conditions. In other words functional literacy needs to be defined both for individuals and for communities.

THE SOURCE OF LEARNERS AND PROGRAMS IN ADULT LITERACY AND BASIC EDUCATION

The continual need to provide basic-skills education to adults comes primarily from two sources: native-born adults and immigrants and refugees. Native-born adults who can be classified as adult basic education (ABE) students can be divided into two categories. Mocker (1986) maintains that there are those who have developed some proficiency in the basic skills and who want to earn a high school equivalent degree. This group of learners have developed operative basic skills and now seek out expansion, specialization, and refinement. These are individuals who are ready to enter a General Educational Development (GED) program or grade 12 equivalency. The second category of native-born ABE students can be classified as what has been historically referred to as functionally illiterate. As discussed in the previous section these are individuals who have marginal skills in reading, writing, and mathematics. They are adults who find it difficult to cope with everyday tasks. Until a few years ago, the term ABE covered the grades normally associated with elementary schooling, that is, grades one through eight. More recently, the term has been expanded to cover the grade spectrum from one through twelve. Within this ABE range, the lower grade levels are designated for adult literacy training.

A second source of learners in adult literacy and basic education are the immigrants and refugees who have little or no understanding of English. According to Huyck and Bouvier (1983), over two-thirds of the refugees who have immigrated to the United States legally since 1975 have come from Southeast Asia. For the most part, the first wave of these refugees consisted of individuals who had been educated in their first language and who had previously worked for Western firms. Because most of these immigrants were highly motivated by the need to survive in a foreign land, this population was not difficult to recruit and teach in formal and traditional educational programs. But the more recent arrivals who have entered since 1980 generally have had little or no schooling, are semi-literate or non-literate in any language and never held a position in a Western setting (Longfield 1984). As Penfield (1986) maintains, there is growing evidence that this latter group of new refugees is encountering very serious adjustment problems in resettlement, in the acquisition of English oral and writing skills, and in obtaining employment. The 1987 Southam Literacy Survey, which defined functional literacy as the ability to read, write, and use numbers well enough to meet the demands of today's society, reported that large-scale immigration accounts for about one million of Canada's 4.5 million adult functional illiterates.

The literacy survey also confirmed high illiteracy among older immigrants. Nearly half of the immigrants who came to Canada at 30 years or older are functionally illiterate, double the rate among those who arrived at 19 or younger. Burnaby and Bell (1989) suggest that most Canadian ESL learners can be expected to be experienced in learning in formal educational settings and to have the knowledge and skills that are generally assumed to be the result of elementary and even, secondary schooling.

Adult Literacy and Basic Education Programs

In the industrialized countries, there are a great many literacy programs in numerous settings, using a multitude of curricula and varied instructional approaches, and catering to diverse groups. Thomas (1983) reported that the ABE professionals are inclined to use an eclectic approach based on adaptations and modifications of methods from various sources. She concluded that no single highly specialized method secured superior results in teaching illiterates. More recently, research at the Calgary Reading and Language Centre came to the same conclusion after directly comparing the Laubach phonetic approach with a whole language approach (Calamai 1987). Collectively, this experience provides proof of only one point – there is no one correct way, no best way to teach basic skills. As people – and the communities they live in – change, so too must the educational programs designed to meet their requirements.

As mentioned earlier, native born adults who can be classified as ABE students can be divided into two categories: those with marginal skills and those who have developed some proficiency in the basic skills. Both participate in various forms of ABE classes. Classes at the lower levels of prior ability are largely composed of minority-group adults, many of whom are school dropouts. Their participation in ABE is an attempt to break the cycle of poverty and disadvantage in which they find themselves, but it is often a frustrated attempt. They are constantly subject to pressures that conflict with regular participation, and family and friends are generally not actively supportive of their participation. Since the groups are usually heterogeneous, they are limited in providing meaningful support (Harman 1987).

Classes of ABE learners who have developed some proficiency in basic skills exhibit greater durability. This group is made up of people with higher ability and prior formal schooling. They are motivated to attend a program as a precondition to taking courses that lead to a high school equivalency certificate (GED) or grade 12 equivalency. Students view this certificate as important because it has some labor market value or provides entrance into further skill training.

Individually Based and Community-Based Programs

Much debate has taken place between two seemingly separate approaches to adult literacy and basic education – the individually based and community-based approaches. The individually based program seeks to equip the individual to function in the existing social system while maintaining a stance of political neutrality while the community-based program, through direct political action, seeks to empower groups of individuals to confront and change the status quo. In this type of program the social context in which learners reside becomes the central focus of instruction. Literacy in these programs refers not to mere reading and writing skills, but to the host of strategies which enable people to control their lives through collective action. Although the two approaches are often placed at opposite ends of an ideological continuum, as Snow (1986) explains, they contain some overlap. For example, "both serve to acculturate adults within a society; both include a pedagogy of skill development; both address an inequality of communicative competencies; both are concerned with issues of social mobility and social integration and both are partially or wholly committed to the goal of bettering individual situations within an ever-changing world" (Snow 1986: 344).

Latin American Approaches

Meritorious efforts have been made in the struggle against illiteracy throughout Latin America and the Caribbean. In 1980 Nicaragua launched a mass literacy campaign and at the same time organized post-literacy programs in order to consolidate and build upon the achievements of the initial campaigns. More than 500,000 persons, including 375,000 women, were taught to read and write in a very short period as a result of effective, decentralized organizational measures coordinated by teams operating at different levels, and the necessary financial resources being obtained through contributions from national and international bodies, and individual donations. In the Caribbean, the Jamaica Movement for the Advancement of Literacy attracted attention for its use of original approaches ranging from the advanced technology of the mass media to recourse to the traditions of folk music. The Movement was also noted for its work in establishing an infrastructure which had enabled the country to make an important methodological contribution to personal training, research, and evaluation. And, in Cuba, a vast program known as the Battle of the Sixth Grade, was undertaken by the Technical Workers' Collective for workers and peasants with a view to post-literacy instruction regarded as an essential factor in social change.

English as a Second Language Literacy Programs

In the developed nations, there has been an increasing awareness that a number of ESL learners have specific needs relating to the learning of literacy in English. Penfield (1986) reports that there are various approaches to ESL literacy instruction followed in adult education. Some basic-skills education programs delay ESL literacy training until a degree of oral proficiency has been achieved, while others integrate the teaching of all three skills of speaking, reading, and writing simultaneously (Ranard 1984). Although there is no available research on the strengths or limitations of the different approaches, experience suggests better achievement results when courses separate learners by literacy levels. In classes of students with various language proficiency levels, the demands are greater upon the non-literate ESL learner. Anxiety is heightened because such individuals are placed at such a great disadvantage in comparison with other students.

Penfield (1986) maintains that there is some research evidence to suggest that non-literate, unschooled, limited, English-proficient adults encounter difficulty acquiring both a second language and initial literacy in a classroom setting. In a study of refugees in Canada, D'Anglejan (1984) compared the successful and unsuccessful adult learner. The investigation revealed that low levels of schooling, marginal literacy, or illiteracy and high levels of anxiety characterized the unsuccessful adult learner. She also found that unsuccessful learners tended to be from rural backgrounds and consequently had difficulty adjusting to urban conditions. Those who had failed to acquire the second language had experienced very little contact with native speakers of that language. Although their primary contact with the language was in the classroom, it had been treated as an academic subjcct rather than a meaningful tool for students to accomplish tasks in their own lives. D'Anglejan reported that "those with little or no schooling, may be accustomed to acquiring important skills and knowledge in settings very different from classrooms where active participation in tasks and tacit observation of the performance of others are the privileged modes of learning" (1984: 22).

As Penfield (1986) suggests, based on such evidence language learning for such a population may result in higher success rates if it were to take place in non-academic, non-formal settings based more precisely on refugees' needs. One approach may be to relate employment and ESL literacy acquisition.

WORKPLACE LITERACY RESEARCH

Rush, *et al.* (1986) define workplace literacy as the ability competently to read required work related materials. The definition derived from Kirsch and Guthrie (1977–8) proposed that functional literacy be defined according to the demands of specific situations in terms of competency in reading alone, but more recent research has included listening, speaking, and writing. By definition functional literacy varies according to individual demands of divergent roles, settings, and materials. Therefore workplace literacy competencies comprise a subset of functional literacy.

Specific Literacy Demands

The work of Sticht and various colleagues has been the most current research conducted in the area of specific literacy demands for individual occupations. Within the military environment, they have focused on determining the literacy demands of jobs, determining the relationship between literacy ability and job ability, developing reliable and valid testing procedures for matching individuals with jobs and developing ways of restructuring materials to reduce the literacy demands. Research has also been conducted to distinguish between the two dominant uses of reading in occupational settings: reading to-do-tasks and reading to-learn-tasks (Sticht 1975, 1978). They differ in that the former is used to accomplish work while the latter involves retention of information for later use.

In translating this concept into practice, Mikulecky, *et al.* (1987) have advocated learning activities that simulate literacy requirements on jobs. They suggest that learners must have opportunities to use the types of reading comprehension required on jobs including:

1 Reading to accomplish a task: once the job is completed, the information can be and usually is forgotten;
2 Reading to learn: information which must be retained for later use; and
3 Reading to access: examining material to determine its use for a task.

Research on specific literacy demands for individual occupations in the civilian sector has tended to be minimal. Some of the areas of investigation have included literacy requirements necessary to hold different occupations, reading demands of the plumbing trade and clerical positions, and communication competencies required for future business people. (Moe *et al.* 1979; Chang 1983; Spicer 1975). In criticizing these studies, Jacob and Crandall (1979) stated that it is important to observe and interview more than one representative of a job, and to use appropriate instruments to examine the difficulty of reading materials in order to create a valid profile of the reading demands of that occupation and the strategies which individuals in those jobs use to fulfill those demands. It has been recommended that the procedure should involve interviews with individuals in the actual environment where the reading is done, observation for verification and the use of more than a formula to determine the difficulty of reading materials.

Occupational Reading

Kenter (1986) claims that as the workplace becomes complicated, requiring higher specialized skills and training, the definition of illiteracy will have to be broadened to include those who cannot meet the new workplace requirements. Current estimates of occupational demands for literacy indicate that over 90 per cent of occupations call for some reading and writing (Mikulecky 1982). Further, 70 per cent of occupations require reading at a grade

9–12 level. Only 15 per cent of occupations require reading levels below the grade 9 level (Mikulecky 1984). Researchers have found the average workplacc rcquires not only the ability to read, write, and compute but also the ability to use those skills in problem-solving situations. The average worker must read and skim a wide variety of materials to solve problems and make decisions. This is in contrast to the school environment where the student is reading primarily to gain literal facts.

Mikulecky (1982) reported that most jobs require about two hours of reading per day, ranging between a grade 10 and grade 12 level. Even blue-collar workers were reading about 97 minutes per day; these employees were reading forms, directions, order forms and printouts. A retail or clerical worker was found to read about three hours daily. Most categories of workers in fact read more than most students. Only 2 per cent of occupations examined required no reading or writing (Mikulecky 1987). These findings concur with the research of Rush *et al.* (1986), Taylor (1989), and other civilian and military settings. Though having a wealth of background knowledge on a topic can tend to effectively lower reading difficulty levels, the heaviest job-related reading is performed by new workers least likely to have the wealth of background experience.

Writing and Other Competencies

Diehl (1980) reported that in examining the tasks of occupational writing, 65 per cent involved completing simple forms or preparing brief memoranda. Writing tasks were repeated enough for workers to master the most complex forms. Memoranda were simple, concise, and relatively easy to write. Diehl suggested that further research may show that writing competencies required for successful job performance are simple, and unrelated to the writing tasks observed in schools.

The nature of listening competencies required at work has received little attention from researchers. Sticht (1975), however, described studies which show that military personnel learn equally well through listening or reading and noted that it is possible for such personnel to learn from tape recordings played at accelerated rates. A general sense of the importance of listening skills in occupational settings can be inferred from studies of adults in general.

The uses to which literacy and related competencies are put on the job appear to be more complex than typical uses of literacy in schools. The vast majority of school-related reading is reading to learn factual materials, while a comparable majority of job-related reading is for problem-solving and making applications. In addition the literacy strategies associated with high job performance ratings are primarily higher level metacognitive strategies involving monitoring, focusing, and managing information. Researchers are now pointing out that formal settings in educational institutions may not serve the hard-to-reach adults. More and more companies, unions, and industries are beginning to offer remedial literacy training. As Hull and Sechler (1987) suggest, industry-based education programs may increasingly become the setting for adults to begin or continue the development of basic literacy skills.

Implications

With the event of International Literacy Year in 1990 adult literacy and basic education were highlighted. Along with this awareness, certain issues have been brought to center stage. In developed nations there is a growing understanding that there are two types of adults who lack basic literacy skills. There are those who can barely read and write and there are those who cannot read and write well enough to meet the increasing demands of our society. These learners require different types of methods. Providers are recognizing that effective basic literacy training needs to be integrated with functional uses of literacy. Another concern is that the decision by individuals to participate in a basic education program appears to be a matter of personal choice. Individuals most in need of such programs may not recognize the advantages of participation, or recognizing the advantages, may be embarrassed to admit their inability because of the stigma of illiteracy. Therefore the provision of widespread publicity and information on adult illiteracy must continue in order to increase further public awareness and understanding of the problem. A third issue is the need for expanding training facilities for literacy personnel. As literacy partnerships between business, industry, and governments continue to grow in order to meet the basic skill needs of entry-level and dislocated workers, different types of teaching methodologies and curriculum are required. Learning how better to connect basic skills and literacy development to job training will be important teaching skills in the future. To avoid wasting a single mind we must greet this challenge now.

REFERENCES

Bormuth, J. (1975) "Reading literacy: Its definition and assessment," in J.B. Carroll and J.S. Chall (eds), *Toward a literate society*, New York: McGraw-Hill.

Burnaby, B. and Bell, J. (1989) "The Role of Literacy in Methods of Teaching English as a Second Language," in M.C. Taylor and J.A. Draper (eds) *Adult Literacy Perspectives*. Toronto: Culture Concepts Inc.

Calamai, P. (1987) *Broken Words*. Toronto: Southam Inc.

Canadian Business Task Force on Literacy (1988) *Measuring The Costs of Illiteracy in Canada*. Toronto: Woods Gordon.

Chang, K.L. (1983) *Reading demands of the plumbing trade*. Unpublished master's thesis, University of Calgary, Calgary, Alberta.

D'Anglejan, A. (1984) "Learning the Language," *Language and Society*, 13, (Spring), 21–4.

Darling, S. (1981) *Final Report: Jefferson County Adult Reading Project*. Department of Adult and Continuing Education, Jefferson County Board of Education, Louiseville, KY.

Diehl, W.A. (1980) *Functional literacy as a variable construct: An examination of attitudes, behaviors and strategies related to occupational literacy*. Unpublished doctoral dissertation, Indiana University at Bloomington, Bloomington, IN.

Fingeret, A. (1984) *Adult Literacy Education: Current and Future Directions*. Columbus, OH: ERIC Clearinghouse on Adult, Career, and Vocational Education, Ohio State University.

Gutherie, J. (1983) "Equilibrium of literacy," *Journal of Reading*, 26, 668–70.

Harman, D. (1987) *Illiteracy: A National Dilemma*. New York: Cambridge Book Company.

Hull, W. and Sechler, J. (1987) *Adult Literacy: Skills for the American Workforce*. Columbus, OH: The National Center for Research in Vocational Education.

Hunter, C. and Harman, D. (1979) *Adult Illiteracy in the United States:* A Report to the Ford Foundation. New York: McGraw-Hill.

Huyck, E., and Bouvier, L. (1983) "Demography of Refugees," *The Annals of the American Academy of Social Sciences*, 467, 39–61.

Jacob, E. and Crandall, J. (1979) *Job-Related Literacy*. Bloomington, IN: Center for Applied Linguistics.

Kenter, P. (1986) "The Three R's, Reading, Risk and Responsibility," *Occupational Health and Safety Canada*, 3, 4, pp. 24–30.

Kirsch, I. and Guthrie, J. (1977–8). "The concept of measurement of functional literacy," *Reading Research Quarterly*, 13, 485–507.

Longfield, D. (1984) *Teaching English as a Language to Adults*. Paper presented at the National Conference on Adult Literacy, Washington, DC, (June).

Lytle, S., Marmor, T., and Penner, F. (1986) *Literacy Theory in Practice*. Philadelphia, PA: Graduate School of Education, University of Pennsylvania.

Mikulecky, L. (1982) "Job literacy: The relationship between school preparation and workplace actuality," *Reading Research Quarterly*, 17, 400–19.

Mikulecky, L. (1984) "Effective Literacy Training Programs for Adults in Business and Municipal Employment," in J. Orasanu (ed.) *A Decade of Reading Research: Implications for Practice*. Hillsdale, NJ: Lawrence Erlbaum Associates.

Mikulecky, L. (1987) The Status of Literacy in our Society. *Research in Literacy: Merging Perspectives*. Thirty-sixth Yearbook of the National Reading Conference. (eds) J. Readance and S. Baldwin. Rochester, NY.

Mikulecky, L. and Ehlinger, J. (1986) The influence of metacognitive aspects of literacy on job performance of electronic technicians. *Journal of Reading Behaviour*, 18, 41–62.

Mikulecky, L., Ehlinger, J., and Meenan, A. (1987) *Training for Job Literacy Demands*. Institute for the Study of Adult Literacy, The Pennsylvania State University.

Miller, P. (1987) *Adult Literacy, Issues, Programs and Options*. Education and Public Welfare Division. Congressional Research Service.

Mocker, D.W. (1986) *Adult Basic Education in the United States*. Paper presented at the Sixth International Seminar on the Education of Adults, University of Surrey.

Moe, A., Rush, T., & Storlie, R. (1979) *The Literacy Requirements of a Licensed Practical Nurse*. Department of Education, Purdue University.

Nesbitt, P. (1987) *Literacy in Canada*: A Research Report. Toronto: The Creative Research Group Limited.

Penfield, J. (1986) "ESL Literacy and the New Refugees," *Adult Literacy and Basic Education*, 10(1), 47–57.

Ranard, D. (1984) "ESL Literacy: Questions and Issues," *TESOL Newsletter*, 18(2), 20.

Rush, R.T., Moe, A. and Storlie, R. (1986) *Occupational Literacy Education*. Delaware: International Reading Association.

Snow, B. (1986) "The Ends and Means of Adult Literacy," *Proceedings from the 1986 Adult Education Research Conference*. Syracuse, NY: Syracuse University.

Spicer, C. (1975) "The identification of communication competencies required by future business persons," paper presented at the International Communication Association Conference, Chicago, IL.

Sticht, T. (1975) *Reading for Working* VA: Human Resources Research Organization.

Sticht, T. (1978) *Literacy and Vocational Competence* Occasional Paper No. 39. Columbus, OH: The National Center for Research in Vocational Education.

Taylor, M. (1989) *Occupational Literacy*. Ottawa: Algonquin College of Applied Arts and Technology.

Thomas, A. (1983) *Adult Illiteracy in Canada*. Occasional Paper No. 42, Ottawa: Canadian Commission for UNESCO.

Thomas, A. (1989) "Definitions and Evolution of the Concepts," in M.C. Taylor and J.A. Draper (eds), *Adult Literacy Perspectives*. Toronto: Culture Concepts Inc.

Valentine, T. (1986) "Adult Functional Literacy as a Goal of Instruction," *Adult Education Quarterly*, 36(2), 108–13.

Commentary

We Cannot Afford to Waste a Single Mind

Stuart Smith

There is nothing new in the idea that human beings learn throughout life. A hallmark of our species is the rapidity with which individuals adapt to change and learn from experience – at all ages.

There is also nothing new in the notion that formal learning experiences need to be structured for people in their adult years, irrespective of what schooling they may have received in childhood. Throughout most of the world, formal adult education has for years been required to impart basic skills which, were it not for poverty, would have been acquired in the early years of school. In the advanced countries, some adult programs are intended to make up for basic schooling deficiencies, but adult education more often aims at broadening personal horizons, refurbishing and updating skills, or supplementing what has been learned earlier. Both on-the-job training and formal educational programs have long been widespread and popular.

What *is* new in adult education, particularly in the industrialized countries, is not the concept but the *degree* to which it will now occupy the time and attention of every person. Formal adult learning experiences are now not only among the most *desirable* of human activities, but are becoming *economically* essential, both to individuals and to national economies.

Powerful forces are driving advanced economies to specialize in production of those goods and services that are based on the newest available knowledge. On the one hand, there is the rapidly increasing availability of new knowledge, accelerated by the microprocessor. On the other, there is the relentless move of standardized industries to lower wage countries so that the products and services offered in the advanced world need to contain large amounts of new knowledge. Advanced countries hope that their ability to produce such knowledge will constitute a major comparative advantage, given that they can draw on long traditions of research and education.

For industries, all of this means that rapid changes will be the new reality from now on. Since knowledge advances so quickly, all products and all skills will have a short "shelf life." This, in turn, means that people will have to change jobs, and even careers, as the years pass. Even within a given job, new knowledge and new skills will be needed repeatedly during a working lifetime. Yet it is not only individuals, but entire economies, that will suffer unless there are programs to retrain people or upgrade their skills. Only with such continuing education can successive generations of goods and services be competitively produced.

Aside from the economic imperative, there is another reason why adult education is now more important than ever. As automation reduces the hours of work, and as people live longer, individuals will find ways to occupy increasing amounts of discretionary time. What values and satisfactions will motivate people and what activities will give meaning to their lives? Chief among these values, after love, may well turn out to be learning, in all its forms. Education, associated with the joy of self-improvement and the development of the individual, is one of the few human activities of lasting importance, ranking over the long run well ahead of the pursuit of pleasure or power.

So, for both economic prosperity and for personal satisfaction, our society is coming to recognize and value lifelong learning. Where adult education is concerned, we know that both public and corporate policy lags behind the perceptiveness and practice of individual citizens. We must not delay much longer the policies that truly respond to the current knowledge and technology explosion. We will be a Learning Society – or a stagnant one.

Chapter 7

Learning in Communities

Stephen Brookfield

It is an educational truism, but nonetheless significant for all that, that much of the most significant learning people undertake occurs outside of formal educational institutions. In adulthood, this is especially the case, given that participation in formal educational activities is not mandated by local and national governments. In studies of adults' significant personal learning – that learning which entails changes in adults' self-concepts as a result of critical reflection on the values, assumptions, and norms underlying their thoughts and actions – learners very rarely report participation in formal educational activities as a prompt to such learning (Brookfield 1988). In investigations of learners' self-reported learning projects (Tough 1979; Brookfield 1984) participation in formal educational programs assumes very little significance. Studies of successful self-directed learning (Brookfield 1981; Thiel 1984; Danis and Tremblay 1985) reveal how such learners firmly and consistently place their conduct of learning activities within the framework of community groups, voluntary associations, and informal learning networks.

In this chapter one dimension of learning in communities is discussed – political learning. The range of learning activities, domains, and dimensions which fall under the heading of "learning in communities" is enormous and includes learning within intimate relationships, learning at the workplace, recreational learning, and learning through mass media of communication as well as political learning. Political learning is chosen because it is concerned with how adults make sense of, and act within, political and community structures. Political learning occurs when people become aware of the pervasiveness of issues of power and control in all spheres of human interactions, and when they work to create and alter different patterns (autocratic or democratic) of interaction. A major context within which such learning occurs is the media. The mass media of communication play a crucial role in framing our views of the world and in defining the context within which we define what we see as significant issues and important problems, particularly in the political realm. For educators concerned to help adults become critically aware of how institutions transmit the values of dominant groups within their cultures, the media comprise a focus of crucial interest (Brookfield 1986).

POLITICAL LEARNING

Power is all pervasive. It exists in personal relationships, in the distribution of wealth, in institutional forms such as military and police forces and in economic processes. As the International League for Social Commitment in Adult Education (1986) states, power relationships often work "through hidden cultural processes that make people believe that violence and poverty are inevitable or even their own fault." Political learning occurs when people become aware of the pervasiveness of issues of power and control in all spheres of human interactions and when they work to create and alter different patterns (autocratic, democratic) of interaction. It involves intellectual analysis, critical reflection and action in the world. It can take place in widely varying settings and at different levels of involvement.

Political learning is not necessarily about the stuff of politics as it is formally defined; for example, the workings of the constitution, the separation of powers, the arguments surrounding proportional representation, how bills are passed through congress or parliament. Rather, it is becoming aware of how hierarchies of power and status infuse all personal and group relations. It is realizing that patterns of dominance and submission become etched into the ground rules of relationships, unless constant and determined attempts to prevent this happening are made by those involved. It is knowing that stereotyping, discriminating, propogandizing and deceiving (both oneself and others) are endemic to relationships and interactions on personal, community and national levels. It is working in concert with others to change organizational structures, unquestioned values and habitual patterns of interaction. It is making explicit the connection between change in one's personal life, and the need to press for often controversial and deep seated structural changes in the institutions in which that life is embedded. And it is working collectively with others to bring about such a change.

On the level of personal relationships, political learning is seen dramatically in the changing nature of male–female relationships. The women's movement of the last twenty years has prompted an enormous amount of political learning in men and women. First, women have become aware of the oppressive lines woven into the fabric of their relationships with men, a powerful piece of learning in itself. Second, they have summoned the courage to confront their male friends, lovers, and colleagues with these inequities, stereotypes and false expectations. Third, those men able to consider altering fundamentally the structure of expectations each partner has in a relationship, have undergone a significant perspective change. Fourth, in the act of renegotiating the expectations in a relationship, both partners have probably learned to communicate more honestly. They will also have become better at accepting criticism offered by the other.

This learning may be observed in external behaviors such as a reversal of traditional roles where the man stays at home to take care of childrearing and housekeeping and the woman is the chief source of household income. Almost as dramatic is the situation where decisions regarding moving residence are made as much on the basis of the woman's job as they are on the man's work situation. More prosaically, decisions to do with the division of household tasks where both partners are working full time are political. The man's assumption that women are natural cooks may be equalled in its falsity only by the woman's belief that men are natural carpenters, electricians, or plumbers. When these assumptions are challenged, and contradicted in practice, then political learning is taking place. When sexual roles and expectations are challenged and deliberately ignored, this is an act of critical reflection on a personal level.

It is through their involvement in some form of community action that many adults who think of themselves as political creatures acquire their political knowledge and skills. Boggs (1984) writes of the "nationwide mosaic of citizen study and action groups" which emerged in the 1980s. These have formed in response to events such as initiatives to establish hazardous nuclear and toxic waste disposal sites; proposals to build highways, nuclear power plants and high voltage power lines; efforts to convert recreational land to commercial use; foreclosures on family owned farms; and plans to close down factories in single industry communities. These groups have some form of organizational structure, though they are outside of the formal political system. They cut across class, ethnic, and regional lines, and are not specific to communities or areas.

As is evident from these examples, most community action efforts arise out of residents perceiving some kind of threat to their community. Armstrong's (1972) conceptualization of community action notes:

1 that community action manifests itself in a specific, ad hoc fashion,
2 that it devotes its resources and energies to a particular issue, and
3 that community action groups take their name from the problem they seek to address.

Almost every reader of this book will probably at some time have been involved in a community action initiative in which community members came together to achieve some desired change in their neighborhoods. These groups are not established for educational purposes, but significant political learning undoubtedly occurs through members' participation. People acquire knowledge, change behaviors, develop skills, realize insights, change attitudes, and alter their self-concepts as a result of participation in community action.

Armstrong and Davies acknowledge that even though members organize to achieve purposeful community change "the amount of attitude change which occurs or political awareness which grows up is a major by-product" (1977: 153). Wright (1980) offers the concept of community learning to describe that learning which occurs as adults attempt to improve their communities. Paterson's (1985) study of six social action programs records a process of action learning in which four processes are evident: becoming aware of one's individual problem, understanding that this problem can only be understood in a social context, analysing the problem's causes, and joining with others in collective action to create a new reality. This phasic transition from awareness to understanding to analysis and finally to action is a political exemplification of the processes of critical reflection.

Analysing the learning of those involved in community action is complex since five interconnecting and overlapping domains are often involved; knowledge acquisition, skill development, behavior change, alteration to one's self-image, attitudinal change and insight realization. None of these is a discrete and separate domain. For example, behavior change will sometimes follow altering one's self-concept (as would be the case with people whose experiences had led them to see themselves as advocates for their communities rather than silent minorities). At other times trying out new behaviors might precede a change in self-concept (as would be the case with people who had been forced to speak at public tribunals on behalf of their causes or communities and who now saw themselves as leaders rather than followers). Taking an example of a community action initiative might help to illustrate the kinds of learning this involves.

A group of residents in a New York apartment block have suffered from poor maintenance for several years. Water supply has been irregular, the heating is erratic during the winter months, the cockroaches run rampant and the external facade of the building is crumbling so that blocks of masonry fall regularly to the ground threatening passers-by. In short, a typical Manhattan residence. The residents have complained to each other regularly and intermittently to the agency which owns and runs the building. However, since the rents are controlled by city ordinances they are much lower than the going market rate. This has served to mollify residents who could console themselves with the thought that their building services might be inadequate but their rent was artificially low. As a result of new legislation at city, state, and federal level, however, these rent control laws have just been abolished and the building residents have all received written notice that in two months' time they will be subject to a 300 per cent rent increase, with no accompanying agreement to improve the building's condition.

The prospect of paying a vastly increased rent for the same poor level of services and maintenance galvanizes the tenants into action. A group of them decide to hold a public meeting to discuss these developments and explore possible responses. At this meeting those attending decide to form a tenants' association as a way to document their grievances and present these complaints to their governing agency. They locate and scrutinize the new rent control legislation and compare its provisions with their agency's intentions. They decide which repairs and improvements the agency is legally impelled to undertake before raising their rents, and what legal sanctions are open to them if it refuses to comply with these. They compile and present a report to the agency and enlist the support of their local assemblyman on their behalf. They cultivate contacts on the neighborhood newspaper and in the local TV and radio news stations, trying all the time to make their efforts the focus of a news story.

While waiting for the agency's response to their petition the residents form a committee to determine how those repairs and improvements the agency is not legally impelled to make might be accomplished through voluntary action of tenants. They hold a street fair, establish a building improvements fund, and compile a resource index of the skills possessed by different building residents which would be useful to repairs and improvements projects. They also consult the offices of the city administration to find out what grants are available for citizen sponsored, voluntary neighborhood improvement projects.

Irrespective of the outcomes of this fictional example of community action, a great deal of critical political learning has already taken place. Using the five categories mentioned earlier, this learning might be identified as follows:

1 *Knowledge Acquisition*: the residents have acquired legalistic knowledge on three levels. First, they have acquired information about the specific leglislation relating to rent control. Second, they have learned to decode the jargon and legalistic phraseology endemic to building legislation. They have been able to translate technical terminology into specific actions relating to their building and to make connections between general legal rules and their own personal circumstances. Third, and perhaps most importantly, they have learned how to negotiate official channels of communication so that the system of storing public information is now accessible to them.

2 *Skill Development*: many residents will have developed or refined various skills during this project. The broad categories include interpersonal skills (personnel management, understanding and managing group dynamics, cultivating contacts in the media), organizational skills (committee formation and management, planning future action, prioritizing, arranging a street fair), administrative skills (compiling a skills index, report writing) inquiry skills (finding out about grants), financial management

(establishing a building improvements fund, dealing with profits from the street fair) and public relations skills (publicizing the original meeting to form the tenants organization, trying to use media coverage to their advantage, advertizing the street fair).

3 *Behavior Change*: no predefined performance objectives will have been set by residents as evidence that learning has taken place. They are too concerned with achieving some change in their neighborhood for this to be the case. Nonetheless, there will probably have been many instances for people to behave in ways which they had previously never considered, or dismissed as "not for us." In any action initiative such as the one described there will need to be many opportunities for residents to voice their concerns and explore common issues. People who have never previously thought of themselves as public speakers will have to say their pieces in public. People who have never considered themselves especially articulate will have to explain their reasons for and against proposals which affect them directly and about which they feel passionate. People unused to dealing with elected officials or media representatives in an assertive manner will find themselves doing just this because they feel so strongly about their cause. In a host of ways, then, residents will be experimenting with behaviors (sometimes unwillingly) with which they are unfamiliar. To make a contribution to a public meeting, and to find out not only that one can do this, but also that people listen with attention and sometimes approval, is an act of learning with powerful outcomes.

4 *Alteration to Self-Image*: as a result of participating in community action projects people may alter how they think about themselves. Those who previously felt they had a divine right to be leaders of any project in which they were involved, might find cause to doubt their presumed authority. Those who previously saw themselves as passive followers might find that they had come to view themselves as initiators. Those who excused their non-participation in projects as a result of their supposed introverted nature, might realize extrovert elements in their personalities. Those who thought of themselves as operating in narrowly defined skill areas (such as being "practical" people at ease with machines rather than abstract ideas) and being unsuited to others (such as being able to argue for ideas in public) may come to redefine themselves in ways which might alter significantly their future actions.

5 *Insight Realization*: this domain is the most complicated of all

to explore. It involves a number of sophisticated mental operations in which attitudinal change, conceptual learning, abstract thought, inductive inference and reflection on experience are involved. It is the area in which political learning as defined earlier is most likely to take place. This learning will most probably have as its focus the discrepancies and ambiguities of trying to operate according to democratic principles when contextual variables distort their realization. Examples of theory-practice discrepancies in the realm of democratic action are legion, and neophyte activists very quickly become aware of the troubling need to balance expediency with philosophical purity. Those becoming involved in community action will be aware of a range of ethical dilemmas generated by philosophy–practice anomalies. A concrete example of this might be the decision as to whether committee members who are self-centered, obstructive, and insistent on pursuing their own private agendas to the disregard of group concerns, might "accidentally" be left off the mailing list for an important decision-making meeting.

Another ambiguity might be caused by the obvious desirability of forming informal caucuses prior to formal committee meetings, so that lobbying for preferred policies can be made in advance, thus smoothing the passage of a decision. Such caucuses contradict the democratic principle of openness, but most "democratic" bodies rely upon them for reasons of organizational effectiveness. Yet another dilemma is posed regarding the point at which further discussion of a decision is ruled out of order by the chairperson, and whether or not the committee members choose to ignore this. The "means–ends" question inevitably and irrevocably imprints itself on the minds of any group which is trying to effect some kind of change. Do the ultimate ends of justice or equity justify intermediate dissimulation, outright lying, suppression of embarrassing information or the bypassing of formal committee procedures? In the abstract world of democratic theory or civic education it is easy to condemn all such apparently sharp practices. In the ambiguous, distorted world of political in-fighting, with all its opportunity for self-deception, hidden agendas, concealed motives and ego-aggrandizement, such moral certainty may be a luxury one can sometimes ill afford. In experiencing and grappling with the resolution of such dilemmas, discrepancies, and ambiguities people undertake some highly significant political learning.

The foregoing discussion makes it clear that political learning is something which happens experientially; indeed, in personal relationships, interculturally, and at a neighborhood level it is practically impossible not to undertake some kind of reflection upon political aspects of these environments. It is probably the case, however, that those involved in the examples described will not be aware of the political dimension to their reflections. Most probably they are unlikely to conceptualize their activities as political learning. Political learning as described is not restricted to those who watch television programs such as the *MacNeil-Lehrer Report*, *Nightline*, *Weekend World* or *Panorama*. It is a daily reality for many adults as they reflect upon the societal forces, structures and individuals who exercise power over their lives. Such powers include the power to decide whether people stay in work and are thereby able to feed, clothe and shelter themselves and their families; the power to declare that people should consider themselves to be at war with another country; the power to alter the physical face of people's communities; and the power to frame, pass and enforce laws which govern the behavior, expression of ideas, and artistic creations of citizens.

Political learning is evident whenever people notice, and begin to ponder, the discrepancies and inequities among groups in their societies. Questioning the basis on which individuals, groups and systems exercise these powers over one's life is the beginning of political learning. Making connections between personal crises and broader political happenings, is at the heart of critical reflection on the political world. Imagining alternative ways in which power and wealth could be distributed, and structures organized, is a major prompt for collective political action. Helping people to ask awkward questions about the rightness of, and justifications for, their actions, is the focus of critical helping.

FOSTERING POLITICAL LEARNING: CONNECTING THE PERSONAL AND POLITICAL

One fundamental purpose of fostering political learning is to help adults feel a sense of personal connection to wider happenings. Kretovics (1985: 56) writes of the need to develop critical literacy in people so that they have "the necessary tools and skills to make sense of the social relations, material conditions, and cultural milieus in which they exist and their relationship to the wider society and dominant rationality." Such critical literacy includes forms of political and media literacy, not just the ability to read and write. Those involved in developing these kinds of literacy will be "providing students not merely with functional skills, but with the conceptual tools necessary to critique and engage society along with its inequalities and injustices" (Kretovics 1985: 51).

Political learners make explicit the connections between the personal and the political in their lives. They are aware that individual crises often reflect wider social changes. They know that what might initially be regarded as an idiosyncratic, wholly personal tragedy (divorce, dying of AIDS, unemployment, drug abuse) is frequently a problem shared by large numbers of people. One of the best expressions of this linkage of personal difficulties and broader political forces is that undertaken by C. Wright Mills in *The Sociological Imagination*. Mills explored the connections between what he termed private troubles (such as unemployment or divorce) and public issues (broad social, political, and economic changes). Private troubles occur in the context of our individual lives and are seen as wholly idiosyncratic by those affected by them. There may be no awareness of a causal connection between a personal tragedy and broader socioeconomic trends or political changes. Hence, unemployment or divorce might be seen as serendipitous happenings or as the result of personal inadequacies.

Private troubles are, however, social products. Mills writes that "inside a marriage a man and a woman may experience personal troubles, but when the divorce rate during the first four years of marriage is 250 out of every 1,000 attempts, this is an indication of a structural issue having to do with the institution of marriage and the family and other institutions that bear upon them" (Mills 1959: 9). Through political learning we become aware that individual biographies are partly social products and that values, beliefs and behavioral norms are culturally produced. From this awareness springs an understanding that changes in individual lives are often inextricably linked to alterations in wider political structures. In *Mass Society and Liberal Education* Mills declared that the task of educators was to help people understand how their individual biographies were constructed by broader social and political forces. Realizing this would be a liberating experience. When people saw that private problems were reflective of some wider dislocation or contradiction in social structures and political arrangements, then they would realize that collective action was sometimes necessary to deal with what they had thought to be individual problems. Instead of an individual feeling overwhelmed by mass society and immobilized by personal difficulties she or he would realize that "what he thinks and feels to be personal troubles are very often not only that but problems shared by others and indeed not subject to solution by any one individual but only by modifications of the structure of the groups in which he lives and sometimes the structure of the entire society" (Mills 1954: 14).

We can see in the spread of AIDS how the most private of tragedies has become an activator of collective political action in the gay community in particular. Although the aids virus attacks heterosexuals (especially intraveneous drug users) it has generally been associated with a homosexual lifestyle. Because of the condemnation of the values and actions of this sub-culture by the dominant culture, very little public money was initially made available for research into how to combat the virus. Through plays such as Larry Kramer's *The Normal Heart* the connection between a friend or lover dying of AIDS, the absence of media attention devoted to the disease and the lack of government funding for research on this, especially in the 1980s, has been made explicit. A debate has been raging recently in the New York City school system regarding the teaching of sex education classes in which homosexual activity and the contracting of AIDS are discussed. Gay activists across the country are pressing for increased governmental funds to be made available for research on an antidote to the virus, and the media are beginning to cover demonstrations and marches held to highlight this issue. The gay community has realized that only by mobilizing for collective action will the political changes needed to relieve personal traumas be achieved.

Other writers have explored this connection between private troubles and public issues. Keddie notes how helping professionals who view their clients as "disadvantaged" are often guilty of "a severing of the connections between the political nature of social problems and the individual who presents problems which, if they are severe enough or sufficiently troublesome to others, will be dealt with as individual problems by the social worker, the police, the remedial teacher" (1980: 87). To Wexler, academic social science "makes us content with the present, portraying it as natural and inevitable" (1983: 2). As an alternative to this Sullivan (1984) proposes a critical psychology which "would provide a critical interpretation of what is happening within people within the context of wider social structures". He argues that if psychologists seek to understand individual biographies as being partly framed by social forces, then they will seek ways to help clients change their lives in beneficial ways. Fay outlines the task of critical psychologists as being to help people "to understand themselves in their situation as the product of certain inherent contradictions in their social order, contradictions which they can remove by taking an appropriate course of action to change this social order" (1975: 97). Critical sociology, in Hansen's view, helps people to recognize that "the biography of our own life cannot be understood until the many relationships it involves are understood, until the economic and social conditions in which we grew are fathomed" (1976: 231).

The women's movement offers a good illustration of how perceiving the connection between personal troubles and political forces leads to political as well as individual change. In her study of women's collectives Hart writes that "only through an intersubjective recognition of shared experience can previously simply private and idiosyncratic feelings be validated as subjective experiences of a general impersonal, objective context of repression" (1985: 124). Mezirow views this activity of "relating one's discontent to similar experiences of others or to public issues – recognizing that one's problem is shared and not exclusively a private matter" (1981: 7) as an important stage in the perspective transformation experienced by women who re-enter college after a period of raising families. Through their creation of support and consciousness-raising groups, women have become aware that what they had perceived as individual difficulties and purely personal traumas are, in fact, problematic situations experienced by many. Within women's groups the emphasis is on articulating one's own and others' experiences and envisioning a way of life different from that currently lived. Participants engage in "creating their own knowledge" (Spender 1980), in "speaking for themselves" (Gayfer 1980) and in "re-visioning themselves" (Callaway 1981). Thompson's (1983) descriptions of women's learning groups emphasizes the collaborative questioning of prevailing, predominantly male, modes of knowledge, the generation of alternative perspectives and frameworks of interpretation, and the collective attempt to create new ways of thinking and living.

Some of these new ways of thinking and living are local, such as creating a neighborhood women's center or a refuge for battered wives. Others involve challenges to social structures such as educational institutions or the occupational sector, where law has mandated against discrimination based on sex. Women have also been successful in challenging cultural mores regarding sexual stereotypes and expectations of innate capacities of women and men. They have initiated a heated public debate on what are acceptable forms of artistic representation of sexual eroticism, particularly where eroticism is linked to violence visited on helpless, submissive women. In the creation of legislation regarding equal opportunities at work and in education, and in the establishment of organizations such as Planned Parenthood of America, women have viewed political action within the wider society as inextricably connected to individual liberation.

Evidence of adults undertaking political learning is one of the chief things we look for when assessing the democratic health of a society. Encouraging the kind of debunking skepticism involved in political learning often brings people into conflict with established norms, laws and institutions. Official definitions of social order, dominant values and normative behavior are perpetrated by those in positions of power and authority. To question the legitimacy of such official definitions (for example, it is the duty of a populace to fight war whenever the government decrees this) can be interpreted by those in authority as an intrinsically subversive activity. In fact the opposite is true. At the heart of democratic processes, particularly in representative democracies such as the United States, there must be a willingness and an ability on the part of citizens to subject their elected representatives, the policies they enact, and the justifications they provide for those policies, to a continuous critical scrutiny. In complex, industrial societies, where the onset of the computer age has made possible governmental surveillance to an unprecedented extent, the power of elected representatives and security agencies can only be held in check by an informed populace watching their actions carefully. In this regard a freedom of information act through which security and surveillance agency activities can be scrutinized and publicly challenged, is an institutionalized form of critical thinking in a democracy.

In socio-political terms, political learning entails the habit and ability of asking awkward questions. Questions such as "why are nearly all faculty at my college white, and nearly all the service staff black or hispanic?" Questions such as "how can a government condemn other countries' shipments of arms to a nation as wrong, when we're doing the same thing secretly?" Questions such as "Why is a group of people challenging the government in one country labelled 'freedom fighters' while a group doing the same thing in another country is labelled 'terrorists' by our government?" Being critically alert also means being able to make connections between personal circumstances (such as the closing of a local health facility, a farm foreclosure, or the appearance of more streetpeople in a town) and broader political happenings (cutting health services budgets, the removal of farm subsidies, adopting "community mental health" policies and the consequent reduction in residential places for the mentally ill). It means being able to question the accuracy of politicians' justifications for what is just (such as requiring citizens to fight for a war a government has declared) and what is necessary (such as using millions of dollars to build a new defense system). It means questioning the validity of any claims for universal truth such as "build this weapons system and the world will be safe from war forever".

For the continued health of a democracy, helping adults become political learners should be a fundamental concern of educators, trainers, community workers, social activists, counselors, therapists, and others in the helping professions. Only if adults' powers of political analysis and reflection are nurtured will a truly responsive democracy flourish. In this regard not to encourage the development of critical political capacities is inherently antidemocratic. Far from political learning being some kind of cognitive guerilla terrorism destructive of democracy, it is only through such learning that citizens can hold their elected representatives publicly accountable for their actions. Without citizens who are in the habit of asking awkward questions, governments will be more likely to feel justified in keeping secret actions which they would prefer not to be public. Political learning does not imply a negative pessimism or disrespect for democratic processes; it only implies a disrespect for those who ignore such processes.

REFERENCES

Armstrong, R. (1972) "Towards the Study of Community Action," *Adult Education*, 45 (1), 21–6.

Armstrong, R. and Davies, C.T. (1977) "Community Action, Pressure groups and Education," *Adult Education*, 50 (3), 149–54.

Boggs, D. (1984) "Citizen Groups: Their Significance for Adult Education," in R. Hoghielm (ed.). *Rekindling Commitment in Adult Education*. Stockholm; Department of Educational Research, Stockholm Institute of Education.
Brookfield, S.D. (1981) "Independent Adult Learning," *Studies in Adult Education*, 13 (1), 15–27.
Brookfield, S.D. (1984) *Adult Learners, Adult Education and the Community*. New York: Teachers College Press.
Brookfield, S.D. (1986) "Media Power and the Development of Media Literacy: An Adult Educational Interpretation," *Harvard Educational Review*, 56 (2), 150–70.
Brookfield, S.D. (1988) "Significant Personal Learning," in, D. Boud and V. Griffin (eds), *Understanding Adults' Learning: From the Learner's Perspective*. London: Kogan Page.
Callaway, H. (1981) "Women's Perspectives: Research as Re-vision," *Convergence*, 14 (4), 34–43.
Danis, C. and Tremblay, N. (1985) "Critical Analysis of Adult Learning Principles from a Self-Directed Learner's Perspective," *Proceedings of the Adult Education Research Conference*, No. 26. Tempe, Arizona, AZ: Arizona State University.
Fay, B. (1975) *Social Theory and Social Practice*. London: Allen & Unwin.
Gayfer, M. (1980) "Women Speaking and Learning for Ourselves," *Convergence*, 13 (1–2), 1–13.
Hansen, D.A. (1976) *An Invitation to Critical Sociology: Involvement, Criticism, Exploration*. New York: The Free Press.
Hart, M. (1985) "Thematization of Power, the Search for Common Interests and Self-Reflection: Towards a Comprehensive Concept of Emancipatory Education," *International Journal of Lifelong Education*, 4 (2), 119–34.
International League for Social Commitment in Adult Education (1986) "The Art of the Oppressed: Learning About Power and Powerlessness," Announcement of Third Annual Conference, Folkhighschool Bergen, Netherlands, June 28–July 3, 1987.
Keddie, N. (1980) "Adult Education: An Ideology of Individualism," in J.L. Thompson (ed.) *Adult Education for a Change*. London: Hutchinson.
Kretovics, J.R. (1985) "Critical Literacy: Challenging the Assumptions of the Mainstream," *Journal of Education*, 167 (2), 50–62.
Mezirow, J. (1981) "A Critical Theory of Adult Learning and Education," *Adult Education*, 32 (1), 3–27.
Mills, C.W. (1954) *Mass Society and Liberal Education*. Chicago: Center for the Study of Liberal Education for Adults.
Mills, C.W. (1959) *The Sociological Imagination*. Oxford: Oxford University Press.
Paterson, J.W. (1985) "Learning in Social Action Settings: Implications for Program development." Unpublished doctoral dissertation, Department of Higher and Adult Education, Teachers College, Columbia University.

Spender, D. (1980) "Learning to Create Our Own Knowledge," *Convergence*, 13 (1–2), 14–23.

Sullivan, E. (1984) *A Critical Psychology: Interpretation of the Personal World*. New York: Plenum Press.

Thiel, J.P. (1984) "Successful Self-Directed Learners' Learning Styles," *Proceedings of the Adult Education Research Conference*, No. 25. Raleigh: North Carolina State University.

Thompson, J.L. (1983) *Learning Liberation: Women's Response to Men's Education*. London: Croom Helm.

Tough, A.M. (1979) *The Adult's Learning Projects*. Austin, TX: Learning Concepts Ltd.

Wexler, P. (1983) *Critical Social Psychology*. London; Routledge and Kegan Paul.

Wright, J. (1980) "Community Learning: A Frontier for Adult Education," in R.D. Boyd, J.W. Apps and Associates. *Redefining the Discipline of Adult Education*. San Francisco, CA: Jossey-Bass.

Commentary

Furthering Learning in Communities

Teresa MacNeil

Brookfield limits the very broad concept of learning in community settings to the more specific notion of "political learning." By doing so he places at least some restriction on an immense area of informal adult education. Despite the effort to set it apart, political learning is a concept which itself encompasses far too many dimensions to be easily described. Yet, it is a useful and significant concept. It reawakens images of democratic participation. It challenges agents of change (including adult educators) to be facilitators of the greatest possible amount of learning as they assist groups who contend with various forms of intrusion upon their democratic rights. It suggests that social, cultural, and economic contexts are the media out of which individual problems arise and where they can be solved.

One of the greatest difficulties with the idea of political learning is its potential to be a threat to established systems. As Brookfield suggests: it involves attention to hierarchies of power and status, and to the ways they "infuse all personal and group relations." Presumably, the more who know of such forces, the greater is the threat. And even more threatening are actions to contend with those forces. The suggestion that political learning might become an established facet of adult education practice is quite impractical when one considers that it must do so with the consent of the "hierarchies of power and status."

The idea of political learning is a fundamental notion for adult educators who work to further social movements. Brookfield's reference to the women's movement is one example of the importance of building a strong learning component into strategies to alter relationships between women and society. Little change can be realized until new behaviors are demonstrated by both men and women to reflect their assumptions about the place of women in society. Such new behaviors are invariably the product of learning. And so it is with all social movements: where primary assumptions have to be changed about the place of particular groups or individuals in society, measures to achieve such change must necessarily focus on learning. Such requirement for profound change in social relationships is bound to be resisted by those who are most powerful in society. Public support for political learning in that kind of setting will not come easily.

The situation is somewhat different for those who assist special interest groups to achieve short-term goals through political action. Their efforts are less likely to be resisted because the purpose is to achieve relatively minor structural change. But their efforts are also less likely to be treated as a prime opportunity for learning. For them it is a matter of helping groups to expediently win a point, such as a change in a zoning by-law, or an improved system of fire protection.

The importance of Brookfield's message is that the critical reasons why citizens act to change circumstances are also critical opportunities for adult learning. Although it is likely that the actions which involve people most personally will have the most remarkable learning outcomes, that should not preclude the prospect of looking for substantial learning benefits from all types of political action efforts. While the reason for attending to learning is less urgent in the case of short-term, single-issue efforts, these can also contribute to the development of a more vigilant citizenry.

Brookfield referred to citizen groups founded to study and act upon issues which cut across such conventional dividing lines as social class and geographic boundaries. This is a basic feature of current and, undoubtedly, of future political action groups. It is a reason to be optimistic about the prospect of treating political learning as an important dimension of adult education. More and more, global communications systems make it possible for large numbers of people to be alert to take action on situations which reduce their chances of being part of a life-supporting world. Consequently, many networks of people assemble, for example, around the Brundtland Report to study its estimate of the future of the world's physical environment and to act on its particular suggestions. Taken together, activists working on environmental issues alone number in the millions, and are located throughout the world. Probably the most engaging feature of political learning is that it is issue-bound. It transcends conventional limits and permits the development of unique, new alliances.

Attention to the world's physical environment is but one example of an issue which prompts citizens to organize on many levels. Whether it be as local as a town's sewage system, as regional as the spraying of insecticides, or as global as the thinning of the ozone layer, there are individuals and groups who have reason to learn about ways to stop abusing their natural surroundings. Enabling such learning is an enterprise which challenges adult educators to be alert to the dominant issues and to assist those who would study and act on them.

Being alert to the dominant issues is a relatively simple matter. It primarily means paying attention to social and economic trends and listening to voices of concern. In 1985 the Canadian Association for Adult education signalled its interest in political learning by issuing a "Declaration on Citizenship and Adult Learning." That action, in turn, lead the Association to listen to voices of concern through a series of conferences. The product was a set of seven issues which form the basis of the Association's current program. They include Adult Literacy, Learning our Culture, Learning and the World of Work, Local Economic Development, Peace Education, Women and Learning. Through its listening device came this not-surprising set of concerns.

It is quite another, and much more difficult, matter to locate and to assist those who would study and act upon those issues. That takes precise and discriminating listening devices; and it takes especially fine response mechanisms. It takes very skillful practitioners who would work among those who seek to achieve profound change. Ideally, it calls for practitioners who will assist the process of political learning. The Adult Education Association could and did play an effective role in alerting those who cherish social justice and who value a truly democratic system. But the work of fostering the achievement of these ideals is remarkably the work of individual practitioners whose purview may be as local or as global as the purview of the organization that formed around the particular concern.

Brookfield gave some direction to those who would be effective practitioners in relation to political learning. He referred to five interconnecting domains within the process of political learning: knowledge acquisition, skill development, behavior change, alteration of one's self image, and insight realization. With the possible exception of the impact on one's self image, these are the same aspects which are generally associated with learning. More important than identifying these domains is the task of ensuring that political learning does in fact take place. The opportunities for political learning are among the richest of all learning opportunities. Since virtually every aspect of life is being profoundly challenged by change – home, family, job, church, party politics, marketplace, school – the prospect of learning through the home, family, etc. is indeed bright. The major question for adult educators is not one of whether there is a place for political learning. Rather, it is the extent to which political learning can be part of their professional endeavor.

Brookfield expressed enthusiasm about the importance of having an informed and vigilant populace to watch the actions of government. He regards the ability to ask awkward questions as a significant indicator of a population's vigilance. And he suggests that the "helping professions" should be concerned about assisting adults to become political learners "for the continued health of a democracy". He conveys no suggestion of doubt about the extent to which political learning should be part of the adult educator's professional endeavor. Taken in terms of the benefit to be gained by society, by individuals and by the professional adult educator one would not argue with Mr. Brookfield. The open question is the extent to which society values and is willing to pay the cost of having an informed and vigilant populace.

If society does treasure the goal of having a well-informed and vigilant populace, then there is nothing to stop those who would foster political learning. It becomes a matter of having both the seekers of change, and those from the "helping professions" take every opportunity to make sense of the events which shape and sometimes interfere with their freedom. It also implies that there will be a reward for being involved in activities which are directed toward structural change. But will the occupants of established positions choose to reward those who seek structural change? This surely is the question which makes the difference between political learning being an informal activity which is entirely voluntary in nature (including voluntary helping agents), and political learning which is a publicly recognized, non-formal learning enterprise where there is systematic support for both the learners and the agents who foster their political learning. It is the difference between a publicly sanctioned effort and a private, informal, and at least, mildly subversive one.

Much has been written and said over the past twenty years about the role of informal adult education. It is with a large measure of pride that promoters of lifelong learning refer to the very extensive number of learner-initiated projects which have no direct connection with formal learning systems. Although there is room to argue, these examples are presented as evidence that the youth-oriented formal system has worked; that adults are able to learn on their own without support of elaborate educational formalities. Those informal individual learning projects have two features which distinguish them from examples of political learning: they do not normally require group activity, and they do not normally challenge the *status quo*. Consequently they can be easily applauded because they imply no particular cost to society; indeed they suggest enrichment of society. But is society quite so ready to acknowledge that political action should be supported as a way to ensure that the populace is well-informed and vigilant? Is society willing to provide financial support for adult educators (or other helping professions) to supply high-quality services to groups engaged in study of and action on political issues? And if the answer to those questions is negative, would the helping professions be prepared to provide their services in the interests of political learning without being paid?

Among the negative features of informal systems of learning is that they can be as poor or as rich as those who engage in them are economically capable of paying the cost. As such they provide no hope of equity for persons or groups of limited means. Thus, those whose freedom is most threatened are likely to least afford to engage in political learning.

Perhaps as we look at the impressive range and importance of issues which call for a vigilant and informed populace, we might look forward to an era when society will so value political learning that it will choose to pay for it. Then adult educators will be able to sharpen and apply their competencies to ensure rich returns both for the individual learners and for society. Perhaps such an era is near. After all, we witness more and more facets of knowledge being developed through research and through new courses of study. Perhaps the business of promoting greater political sensitivity can become a socially acceptable way of ensuring that our political systems are keeping pace with the issues which engage the concern of the population. Perhaps we will grow to the point where citizenship education becomes a lifelong effort for which society will absorb the cost of having it be as rich in learning as it is most surely capable of being.

Chapter 8

Continuing Education and Unemployment

Derek Portwood

In the United Kingdom, the responses of the Department of Employment Services to high rates of unemployment have in the past centered on a broad definition of continuing education. This has further advanced the development of continuing education in relation to socioeconomic changes. Outreach, recruitment, educational guidance, funding, and working with other agencies have consequently become prominent issues along with questions over appropriate forms of curriculum, pedagogy, and assessment.

Continuing education and unemployment through the agencies of colleges and unemployed people clearly affect the perceptions, policies, and practices of each other. This reciprocal and pragmatic relationship is explored in the following, particularly in respect of higher education institutions, using material from case studies of Wolverhampton and other published educational literature. Among the main issues raised in the following Centre for Unemployment Studies, Wolverhampton Polytechnic Case Study, are the relation of continuing education to the employment prospects of the unemployed, the formation of new political and industrial alliances, the need for a review of educational and social values, and the development of corporate strategies on employment and unemployment.

High rates of unemployment have elicited a variety of government responses at national and local levels. In the United Kingdom, the Manpower Services Commission (MSC) has devised and administered most of these, including a wide range of training schemes. Only in the past few years, have the Department of Employment Services (DES) and its agencies initiated educational and training programs to meet industrial demands over skill shortages, work adaptability and updating of technical and professional skills and to combat the negative social consequences of prolonged high levels of unemployment. The programs have been based on a broad definition of continuing education which goes beyond the traditional work of extramural departments and must be widely based in each educational institution.[1]

Unemployment, however, is only one indicator of broad socio-economic changes. Technological and demographic changes and growing demands, at all age levels, for occupational credentialism, personal development, and leisure fulfillment had already given continuing education increased social and educational significance. The snag for continuing education is that it responded to these other changes on the assumption of full employment. Hence, while its modes of part-time study and short courses suit the needs of unemployed people, especially when they are subject to state benefit regulations over availability for work, its values and organization are neither tuned to, nor equipped for, the new context of mass unemployment. Large numbers of unemployed people have little prospect of finding permanent employment and their often unfavorable experience of schooling and present disadvantaged circumstances are challenging the priorities of continuing education. Outreach, recruitment, educational guidance, funding, and working with other agencies now need to become prominent educational issues, not least in the higher education sector.

Under its Replan initiative, DES turned in 1984 to national educational agencies, especially the National Institute of Adult Continuing Education (NIACE), the Unit for the Development of Adult and Continuing Education (UDACE), and the Further Education Unit (FEU), for answers to these issues[2] as well as for the development of appropriate forms of curriculum, pedagogy, and assessment. At college level, the response to unemployment was focused initially on the traditional providers of adult education, although further education colleges soon became involved because of mounting demands for basic academic qualifications and low-level, skill-based courses. Institutions of higher education, which were generally not involved substantially in continuing education, remained largely unaffected until this situation faced them with local political demands and the need to exploit new sources of funding and develop new areas of work. Their involvement led to widespread interest in access courses, distance learning, open colleges and new emphases in staff development. In 1991, as Western economies moved into recession once again, the long-term adjustment leverage of continuing education initiatives took on renewed importance.

Unemployment, therefore, is now high on the educational agenda; but what have the colleges and unemployed adults made of it all? Educational literature has left the topic relatively unexplored, preferring to concentrate on the problems of school leavers and criticisms of youth training schemes. For example, the *Times Higher Education Supplement*, over the period March 1984–July 1985, when the DES Replan program was launched and developed, gave scant attention to the subject of adult unemployment, referring instead to youth unemployment in 88 per cent of its 48 reports on unemployment. Other educational publications either neglect the subject or reflect a similar interest in youth unemployment. Even *Adult Education*, from September 1981 to June 1985, had only ten items on the subject. For information and insights, recourse is needed to case studies. The example of Wolverhampton is used because of the availability of comprehensive and detailed information, but this needs to be supplemented from other projects, strategies, and initiatives to gain a full picture.

The key question is what is the nature, shape, style, and outcome of the relationship between continuing education and unemployment. Early evidence suggests that continuing education is being affected more extensively and radically by unemployment than the other way round. However, it is important to view the relationship as a two-way process if only to understand what will motivate adult educators to review and reform their values and practices. If they cannot positively affect unemployment, why should they trouble themselves? The relationship, therefore, needs to be regarded as reciprocal and pragmatic. This does not deny that the core determining factor of unemployment is the state of international and national political economies, but it indicates that within that framework colleges and unemployed adults mutually affect each other's perceptions, policies, and practices. Clearly there are inhibitions to full dialogue and involvement from both sides but I will argue that it is still sufficient to affect the future shape and direction of both education, including the higher education sector, and wider social policies and values.[3]

Broadly, unemployment affects continuing education because it creates a new constituency, questions its definitions and orientations, demands that its provisions and strategies be developed, and seeks a review of its values. In turn, continuing education affects unemployment because it relates education and employment prospects, helps to resource the unemployed, equips the providers of education for the unemployed, and develops new political and industrial formations and strategies. Some of these effects may currently be more potential than actual and local rather than national.

Unemployment affects continuing education, first, by creating a new constituency. This is far larger and more socially and educationally heterogeneous than the conventional adult education population. In the Wolverhampton case study, where the unemployment rate was 20 per cent, the estimate was a potential demand from 40,000 adults; however, this was far from being tapped. Following a large-scale publicity campaign in the summer of 1984, only 3,000 of this grouping (7.5 per cent) enrolled in courses, and this group consisted mainly of young, female, and educationally qualified persons. This is the customary social profile of further and adult education students and effectively comments on the limited success of the campaign. Older students, particularly men aged 25–44, were heavily underrepresented.[4] Other analyses report that disabled persons and ex-offenders are also difficult groups to attract.

The problem in Wolverhampton was that, despite the publicity campaign, two-thirds of unemployed people were unaware of what was available and in any case did not see education as relevant to their particular circumstances. They rated welfare benefits, housing, and health far higher in their priorities than education and then only considered it if it was practical, skill-based, and vocational. Their image of colleges as another version of school did not help.

Higher education institutions appear to have a special problem recruiting local people because they tend to hold rarified views of such institutions and find them forbidding. Developing access courses, engaging in outreach work and helping unemployment groups to gain resources from DES are ways in which Wolverhampton Polytechnic has tried to overcome this. This engagement in community work, particularly the formation of a network of unemployed workers' groups, has received recognition in the form of research grants from FEU and the EEC under its Second Programme to Combat Poverty. The outcomes have been the creation of self-learning groups which run courses of their own choice on their own premises with teaching inputs from college staff and the representation of these groups on policymaking bodies in the education service. This and other research conducted by the Centre for Unemployment Studies has affected the colleges' pedagogic practices, curriculum content, and structure and staff development programs. A similar outcome occurred in Glasgow where the involvement of higher education in the community led to a rethink of what constitutes appropriate academic behavior.

However, the remarkable diversity of the unemployed population requires full mobilization and utilization of all educational resources. In Wolverhampton, this has taken the form of proposed tertiary reorganization coupled with the development of borough-wide educational information and guidance services. The next planned stage is a regional open educational network linking all colleges in the tertiary sector and stimulating collaboration between the colleges and with industry, the media, and local authorities.

Thus an educational strategy is evolving which, while recognizing the special needs of unemployed people, attempts to cover the whole population. Wolverhampton Polytechnic, through the creation of specialized units and secondment of staff, has sought to research and develop a variety of initiatives within this strategy.[5] As in the case of Glasgow, this entails deep involvement in the policymaking structures of the Borough Council, and Polytechnic staff now service, and in three instances chair, the subcommittees of the Local Education Activities (LEA). More generally, the Education Campaign revealed that the most difficult problem for the colleges is to counter the pervading sense of depression and lack of self-confidence among unemployed people, especially when this is linked to their doubts about the valence of continuing education. It seems that a primary consideration is to challenge popular stereotypes of continuing education, often firmly held by unemployed people. This has led in Wolverhampton to a revision of publicity materials, the introduction of promotional events in the main shopping center, and the opening of an Education Shop for information and advice in the town center.

Second, unemployment challenges the colleges' definitions of and orientations to continuing education. Nationally, considerable variations exist over whom it is for, what it should attempt to achieve, and how it should approach the assessment of potential students. There is no agreement, for instance, over the starting age of continuing education. A tertiary system would suggest post-16, whereas adult colleges vary between 18, 19 and post-21. This is significant for unemployed people, who frequently have more than one person unemployed in their households (an incidence of two in five of unemployed people in Wolverhampton) because often these are fathers and their unemployed teenage sons or daughters. Should one be included and the other excluded? In Wolverhampton both an Adult and Further Education College found themselves heavily impeded in their work with unemployed people by the traditional age range of their students. Unemployment compelled them to cooperate with and learn from each other as a preliminary to becoming a post-16 Community College. This is one manifestation of the changing balance between initial and continuing education where unemployment is playing a crucial role. The response in Wolverhampton is the creation of a Post-16 Education Committee, which has policymaking and budgeting functions.

Multiple unemployment in households also means that educational provision needs to cater for collective as well as individual needs. This frequently extends to neighborhoods. Unemployed people may think that the repair of their damaged social networks and family relationships are far more important than acquisition of new knowledge and skills for themselves individually. An FEU-funded project at Wolverhampton Polytechnic is currently examining how colleges can recruit and train community leaders.

The implications for curriculum development are considerable. According to many surveys on what unemployed people want, courses need to be far more practical and vocational, and while this appears to be happening in many cases, universities may experience difficulties because of the liberal emphasis of their continuing education. Educational provisions also need to be more finely tuned to the specific requirements of "target" groups (e.g. ethnic minorities, disabled people, women, and older redundant male workers). Probably this also means that colleges will have to be far more outgoing, empathetic and collaborative with other agencies, particularly in the voluntary sector. Perhaps on this score, analyses of the role of colleges, especially in the higher education sector, usually start with recommendations for fundamental change in institutional attitudes and propose programs of staff development to achieve it.

Among areas of attitudinal change are the status of continuing education and institutional isolation. At Wolverhampton Polytechnic these have been seen as going hand-in-glove. Hence, the creation of a cross-faculty unit to promote continuing education throughout the Polytechnic is itself intended to be the precursor to a regional open educational network of all colleges. Education for unemployed people must cross institutional boundaries if outreach, publicity, information systems, and educational guidance services are to become effective. Wolverhampton Council has taken this process one stage further. In order to provide comprehensive and integrated services to meet the totality of needs of unemployed people, the education department is engaging in local community developments with the housing and social services departments. Continuing education is being challenged to contribute to this policy. On a less ambitious scale, the varied curriculum demands of unemployed people call for pooling or interchange of resources, credit transfer arrangements, and new forms of access and accreditation. Wolverhampton Polytechnic and other higher education institutions are proposing or beginning to franchise parts of their courses to other colleges partly as a response to this need. Reports from Open Colleges indicate that they may be specially meaningful for the educational needs of unemployed people.

Finally, the scale and scope of unemployment and, perhaps most of all, the status of unemployed people question educational and social values. Bryant (1983) observes that long-term unemployment confers negative master status of powerlessness upon those subjected to it. Despite the government's conception of education as a remedy for economic and social ills, it is doubtful that it can radically affect the status of unemployed people. The problem is not the colleges' inability to guarantee job outcomes for their students or even to do much about their employability. Rather it lies in social evaluations based on paid employment. The social disadvantage of unemployment is primarily tied to having no access to a positively valued source of income. State benefits are not viewed in this light. Thus the issue is greater than that posed by a work ethic and embraces the waged-work system and the allocation and distribution of jobs.

Continuing education's contribution to these questions of political economy must necessarily be severely limited, although it can raise awareness of the issue through seminars and conferences.[6] However, any review of the underpinning value system means that continuing education must reconsider its support of several of its features. These go back to notions of full employment and especially the measurement of social status and its attendant income by occupational achievement, which itself is strongly determined by educational attainment. This whole process is individualized and related to notions of occupational career which implies progress and permanence. However, mass unemployment strikes at the heart of established views of full employment and is much more likely to be the outcome of change in occupational structures rather than the consequence of personal characteristics of those who are made redundant. It also undermines the permanence of occupational positions and structures. Thus, even in occupational terms, continuing education must address the issue of serial employment or recurring unemployment and become more clearly related to general quality of life as well as narrow occupational success. Assuming that the system of paid work remains, one solution would be an interlocking system of "paid" education which has similar status outcomes to that of employment. In a word, unemployment necessitates that continuing education is treated as a positively valued end in itself as well as a means to positively valued employment and its students should be rewarded financially.

Another means of reversing the negative social valuation of the income of unemployed people is to give them financial resources to develop their own educational and training initiatives. An experiment in Wolverhampton, funded by Replan, has led two small groups to expand their activities and numbers beyond the capacity of their existing premises. They are also attracting middle-aged men and women. Their own control of resources is enabling them to learn social responsibility and financial management. It also boosts their confidence and they now engage in their own advocacy, particularly with the Local Authority. This experiment challenges, of course, the providers' ethos of continuing education and this questions the value system within continuing education itself.

Ultimately, of course, these considerations demand a revision of the social meaning of work and the relationship of education to it. While this sets a task for educational philosophers, it also draws continuing education into political debate over unemployment. Perhaps it can be justly claimed that education has had little hand in creating unemployment but it cannot avoid reinterpreting societal values which govern many of the human effects of unemployment. Unemployment thereby compels continuing education to undertake its paradoxical function of conserving and transmitting social values while simultaneously transforming them. This gives a fairly clear remit to researchers and scholars in higher education but still leaves unclear how teachers and administrators will translate that revision into action.

The starting point appears to be how college staff of all grades approach, regard, and treat unemployed people. This involves personal respect and institutional significance for what is provided for them. Colleges are not helped when controlling bodies suggest that they should fund this work from other profitable educational activity. Such uncertainties over funding mean that it tends to be sporadic and piecemeal but even in this uncoordinated and undeveloped state it is still pertinent to ask how continuing education in its turn affects unemployed people.

The importance of the socioeconomic context of this issue becomes immediately apparent because the most pressing task facing colleges is how to maximize the employment prospects of unemployed people. Usually this has been interpreted as improving their employability through developing job-seeking and job application techniques as well as equipping them with a range of validated skills and academic credentials. The hope is that this will restore self-confidence and provide an alternative time-structure to their lives. However, the question of the job outcomes of this activity cannot be neglected. The reality of the limitations of the labor market could render much of this educational effort futile. Indeed, the prevalence of part-time, temporary, and low-paid job vacancies could mean that students become over-educated and suffer frustration as a result. Even where higher-ranked skill shortages exist, the question is whether colleges are aware of them and are able to equip unemployed people to fill them.[7] Thus the claim of colleges to enhance "employability" may hinge on the problem of employment for what?

However, colleges are becoming increasingly mindful of these pitfalls and are beginning to tackle the harder question of their own capacity to assist in the creation of jobs. This may vary from sponsoring to actually undertaking industrial production (e.g. Sheffield's Centre for Product Development Technological Resource).[8] If only for their own survival, institutions of higher education are strengthening their links with industry and commerce. This may occasionally be at the level of liaison with major firms, or creating science/technology parks and educational/industrial consortia but almost universally is in the sphere of fostering small businesses. In itself this indicates their increasing involvement in their local economy.

The emphasis though is not academic but pragmatic. An overriding consideration is to attract external funding. Consequently MSC and the European Economic Community Social Fund have been approached with numerous innovative training schemes, particularly for heavily disadvantaged groups (e.g. the disabled and ethnic minorities) which often contain high proportions of long-term unemployed people.

The fact of job shortages, however, means that other coping strategies are required as well. A little-explored area is that of how to resource unemployed people on a collective basis. Unemployment is often socially clustered and communities as well as individuals suffer. Colleges may respond through supplying a range of services to unemployed workers' centers or through actively developing self-learning, mutually supportive groups of unemployed people through leadership training and briefing. This requires appropriate forms of curriculum and also instruments of evaluation. The FEU and the action-oriented research programs of individual colleges seem to be addressing such issues and one manifestation is the trend toward modularizing courses and thereby developing associate studentships and credit transfer arrangements.

Helping the unemployed to be resourceful cannot be achieved, however, without reequipping and reorienting the educational providers. This involves making teaching and administrative staff sensitive to the needs of unemployed people especially at the point of initial contact. A more deeply rooted problem is pedagogy. Questions over student participation and self-learning techniques arise and professional commitment is especially important because much of the work with unemployed adults carries few extrinsic career rewards. Most of it is based on hand-to-mouth funding and neither involves high-status knowledge nor "normal" working conditions. The need for flexibility in time-tabling and the use of premises away from university and polytechnic campuses, raises issues for the trade unions and professional organizations of both non-academic and academic staff. The dilemmas over working conditions and pay are compounded by those which professional staff experience over their own sets of values. It has already been noted that these are posited on assumptions of full employment and that social mobility is possible through occupational advancement. But what happens when their students have never worked (22 per cent of the unemployed in Wolverhampton) and have little likelihood of doing so in the immediate future? What can be the level of contact and communication when the teacher's set of values does not correspond with the experience of realistic possible life-chances of the student? The staff development program of Replan is beginning to address at least some of the less knotty of these problems but the larger task lies in the hands of those engaged in initial and in-service training of all manner of professional workers. Published literature indicates that this re-equipping and reorienting of professionals is at an early and rudimentary stage.

Continuing education also influences unemployment by affecting public attitudes to it. Here its action-oriented research function and its relation to mass media are crucial. Both Instructional TV and British Broadcasting Corporation TV have become specially interested in countering myths, false images, and stereotypes of unemployed people. They seek assistance from the colleges and especially academic researchers on unemployment. However, few research units on unemployment exist in higher education institutions and most of these are small segments of units devoted to other subjects including industrial relations, local government, and urban policy studies.

The flow of published material is consequently sporadic and disjointed. Most journals contain few contributions, and even those which publish widely on the subject (e.g. *Sociological Review*) tend to do so more by accident than design. The signs are, however, that the topicality of unemployment is becoming increasingly recognised through Conference themes and through invitations for articles to debate the issue in journals (e.g. *Social Policy and Administration*). These developments, of course, directly affect a limited audience but may contribute to a broader awareness of the effects of unemployment and the policy and practical issues these raise. Clearly this does not constitute a counter-ideology of unemployment (Sheffield City Council 1983) but even these developments, as is shown in Wolverhampton, can initiate corporate strategies to combat unemployment at the Local Authority level.

It is in these spheres of local government that a few institutions of higher education (e.g. Wolverhampton, Newcastle, and Lancashire Polytechnics) are beginning to affect unemployment, particularly through their research activity, leadership of local initiatives and continuing education programs. Perhaps their most significant contribution is to stimulate and support new political and industrial alliances and formations. The realization of their own community role and the need to tackle local economic and social problems mean that they have had to cross educational, industrial, and political divides. The connecting links appear to be mainly in the spheres of technical and professional training and combating the social disadvantages experienced by local groups. The concepts of open college and industrial/educational consortia and an evolving policy to second specialist staff to the Local Authority to design, organize, develop, and monitor its own unemployment initiatives are illustrations of this tendency.[9] The public sector alignment of polytechnics give them a special role in these local strategies and initiatives. More broadly, it has been noted that this process of collaboration is becoming apparent between state departments; between central and local government; and between government, educational institutions and major non-government organizations. One manifestation was the announcement of DES to set up a national standing committee on continuing education across the binary line.

It is clear from this analysis that the relationship between continuing education and unemployment is reciprocal and multidimensional. It covers ethical, practical, political, economic, and ideological factors, although the emphasis is pragmatic. Within continuing education itself, this calls for reorientations, realignments and revised priorities and practices, especially at the levels of intercollegiate, community, and industrial relationships. Among unemployed people it may mean revision of their images and views of education, a fuller role in their own educational development and a more willing and wider use of educational provision.

In summary, continuing education and unemployment are critically related. Although tightly constrained by socioeconomic conditions and political priorities, together they raise questions over the scale and distribution of educational resources and the orientation, content and implementation of educational and social values. Continuing education may help to formulate a counter-ideology of unemployment or, more probably, a reinterpretation of the concept of full employment, while unemployment may help to reformulate the character, constituency and practice of continuing education. Inevitably their developing relationship will lead to the evolution of an educational strategy for the unemployed at local and national levels. In turn, this will stimulate the development of corporate strategies on employment and unemployment, and thereby will contribute to reshaping general social attitudes, policies and values.

NOTES

1 Its importance has been acknowledged in the Green Paper on 'Development of Higher Education into the 1990s' (HMSO), e.g. "the Government agrees with the UGC and the NAB that the provision of continuing education should be one of the principal parts of higher education's work" (para 4.1). However, the seriousness of the government's intention to implement this declaration has been widely questioned, e.g. at the SRHE/THES Conference on the Green Paper, 9 July 1985 – see typescripts of main speeches published by SRHE (undated).
2 These are the focus of various developments and research projects, e.g. on experiential learning, educational guidance systems and curriculum models for unemployed adult students. FEU has taken a prominent lead in this respect but is strongly supported by investigations carried out by UDACE and the field operations of Replan.
3 This approach goes beyond that of Rose (1985), who stresses socio-economic forces but ignores the role of education in that context.
4 This confirms Tolley's observation that, even for those in employment, the colleges devote little more than 1 per cent of their teaching and other resources to those in mid-career (Rodcrick in Titmus 1985: 14).
5 Units include those of the Center For Unemployment Studies, Unit for Industrial and Commercial Collaboration, Small Business Unit, Micro-Computer and Business Systems Centre, West Midlands Industrial Study Unit, Trades Union Study Center and the Media Centre. Seconded staff are working on the development of storage and retrieval information systems, educational guidance systems for the Borough and coordination of developments in tertiary reorganization in Wolverhampton.
6 These may be sponsored by single institutions (e.g. at Wolverhampton in February 1984, see Portwood and Cheeseman 1984) or by national associations (e.g. Polytechnic Association of Continuing Education Annual Conference in Cardiff, March 1986) or through Replan-sponsored events at local, regional, and national levels.
7 Academic approval and validation procedures may not help when DES and CNAA are involved. New courses often need two years' "lead time" before becoming operational and by then the occupational

opportunity may have been lost. If colleges are to respond quickly to labor market intelligence, approval and validation procedures need to be reviewed.

8 Another example is to use academic expertise for commercial expansion as in the case of Wolverhampton Polytechnic's collaborative project with MSC, DES and local industry on "Information Technology For Profit."

9 M. Richardson, "Policy, Obligation and Right" (Titmus 1985: 79), observes that "realistic developing continuing education policies are likely to be inter-departmental (and) consortial arrangements of a variety of kinds, bringing together the resources of institutions across the binary line and linking the interests of local and central government."

REFERENCES

Advisory Council for Adult and Continuing Education (1979) "Towards Continuing Education: a discussion paper" Leicester: ACACE.

—— (1982) "Continuing Education: from policies to practice" Leicester: ACACE.

Anthony, P.D. (1977) *The Ideology of Work* London: Tavistock.

Bryant, I.(1983) *The Educational Needs of Long-term Unemployed Adults.* Glasgow: Department of Adults and Continuing Education, University of Glasgow.

Burgess, T. (1985) "The organisation of continuing learning in higher education," in C. Titmus (1985) *Widening the Field: continuing education in higher education.* Guildford: SRHE & NFER – Nelson.

Charnley, A.H., McGivney, V.K. and Sims, D.J. (1985) *Education for the Adult Unemployed: some responses.* Leicester: NIACE.

Dickson, A., Callagher, J., Longden, B. and Bartlett, P. (1985) "Higher Education and the Community," *Higher Education Review*, 17, 49–58.

Fleetwood-Walker, P. and Toyne, P. (1985) "Jam today? The UGC and NAB Reports," in: C. Titmus (1985) *Widening the Field: continuing education in higher education.* Guildford: SRHE & NFER – Nelson.

Further Education Unit (1984) FEU Statement on the Provision of Education and Training for Adults, London.

Gorz, A. (1985) *Paths To Paradise.* London: Pluto.

Handy, C. (1984) *The Future of Work.* Oxford: Blackwell.

Hoggart, R., Stephens, M., Taylor, J. and Smethurst, R. (1983) *Continuing Education Within Universities and Polytechnics.* Leicester: ACACE.

Holmes, J. and Storrie, T.C. (1985) *Consett: a case study of education and unemployment.* London: FEU.

Howard, R. and Plante, C. (1984) "Report on the Counselling and Teaching Programme for the Long-Term Unemployed. "Wolverhampton: Centre for Unemployment Studies, Wolverhampton Polytechnic.

McDonald, J. (1984) *Education for Unemployed Adults: problems and good practice*. London: DES.

Munday, J. and Munday, S. (1983) "What the unemployed want?," *Adult Education*, 55, 334, 342.

National Advisory Body (1984) "Report of the Continuing Education Group," London.

Percy, K.A. and Lucas, S.M. (eds) (1980) *The Open College and Alternatives*. Lancaster.

Portwood, D. (1985a) *Colleges and Unemployed Adults*. Wolverhampton: Centre for Unemployment Studies, Wolverhampton Polytechnic.

—— (1985b) *Continuing Themes and Emerging Trends in Unemployment*. Wolverhampton: Centre for Unemployment Studies, Wolverhampton Polytechnic.

—— (1985c) "Careers and Redundancy," *Sociological Review*, 33, 449–68.

—— (1985d) *Local Authorities' Unemployment Strategies, Social Policy and Administration* (forthcoming).

Portwood, D. and Cheeseman, J.R. (1984) "Unemployment: proceedings of a one-day conference," February 1984, Centre for Unemployment Studies, Wolverhampton Polytechnic.

Portwood, D., Ryder, K., Williams, F. (1985) *Unemployment Studies: a literature search on unemployment in recent issues of journals and periodicals*. Wolverhampton: Centre for Unemployment Studies, Wolverhampton Polytechnic.

Roderick, G. (1985) "Provision and need for continuing education," in C. Titmus, (1985) *Widening the Field: continuing education in higher education*. Guildford: SRHE & NFER – Nelson.

Rose, M. (1985) *Re-working the Work Ethic*. London: Batsford.

Rumberger, R.W. (1984) "The growing imbalance between education and work," *Phi Delta Kappa*, 65, 342–6.

Sheffield City Council (1983) *Out of Work*: policy discussion note, 2 December.

Titmus, C. (1985) *Widening the Field: continuing education in higher education*. Guildford: SRHE and NFER – Nelson.

University Grants Committee (1984) Report of the Continuing Education Working Party. London: UGC.

Ward, K. (1983) "A university adult education project with the unemployed," *Studies in Adult Education*, 15, 74–84.

Watts, A.G. (1983) *Education, Unemployment and the Future of Work*. Milton Keynes: Open University Press.

Williams, S. (1985) *A Job To Live*. London: Penguin.

Willis, P. (1985) *The Social Condition of Youth in Wolverhampton in 1984*. Wolverhampton: MBC.

Wood, D. (1982) *Continuing Education in Polytechnics and Colleges* Nottingham: Department of Adult Education, University of Nottingham.

Commentary

Continuing Education and Unemployment

Dale Shuttleworth

Derek Portwood has provided a most inciteful analysis of the myriad of programs initiated by Britain's Manpower Services Commission and Department of Education and Science to deal with the problems of unemployment and under-employment in the post-industrial age. In particular, he addresses these social and economic realities through the perspective of continuing education.

Traditionally, continuing education provisions have attempted to respond to the needs of the intermittent or sessionally unemployed but the prospect of large-scale structural unemployment is a new phenomenon.

The author begins with an overview of a variety of strategies offered by educational institutions, which are focused primarily on the concerns of school leavers with little reference to the long-term employment needs of adults. Because traditional continuing education providers have not tended to be as much affected by the political fall-out from the unemployment crisis, they have been slow to react. However, as the true nature of long-term structural unemployment is better understood, it is beginning to shape the future direction of continuing education in the United Kingdom.

A whole new constituency of available learners has been identified whose service needs must be addressed at both the local and national levels. But many of these potential constituents do not see education as a priority if it is not directly related to employment skills and socioeconomic security. This has been particularly evident in strategies attempted by institutions of higher education.

What has been proposed is a comprehensive plan to involve

both colleges of further education and colleges of adult education. In both instances, these colleges must overcome the fragile self-confidence, depression, and sense of alienation many of the unemployed harbor toward institutions of formal education. Therefore, a neighborhood-based outreach approach, which recognizes individual differences and mobilizes local initiative, seems most appropriate. Such a community development process would involve local residents identifying their own needs and helping to mobilize educational resources to respond to these conditions. Another important issue is the sense of powerlessness which many unemployed, impoverished people feel concerning their future. It is obvious that feelings of social and psychological well-being must be part of any continuing education strategy to serve the unemployed.

Clearly, the question of financial support for such ventures must be answered. Such programs cannot operate on a user-pay basis. Only a large-scale infusion of funds from external sources, whether from governmental or commercial sectors, will suffice. However, what are the outcomes of raising the expectations of the unemployed if there still are not enough job opportunities in the marketplace?

Obviously, a completely new approach to continuing education provisions is required. This must include outreach, advocacy, community development, training in the workplace, job creation, and local economic development. The author poses the major dilemma that many continuing education providers do not currently understand, or are sensitive to: the needs of the unemployed. Nor is there sufficient community education going on to influence public attitudes and perceptions. The teaching methods and curriculum materials must be changed to enhance student participation and self-directed learning. There must be a working knowledge of community economic development and ways that continuing education can complement job-creation programs. Much more research and development must be undertaken by institutes of higher education to reflect conditions at the local level.

Derek Portwood has provided a valuable overview of existing practice, as well as an analysis of future trends which may affect the nature of continuing education provisions in impoverished areas. The point he makes throughout the chapter – continuing education can affect unemployment only if the reality of unemployment changes the nature of continuing education – is an extremely important premise to be used to reform education at the local and national levels.

Let us hope his article is read, understood, and acted upon by educational and governmental authorities.

Chapter 9

Higher Education Partnerships: Practices, Policies, and Problems

Gerard G. Gold and Ivan Charner

WHAT MAKES THE NEW PARTNERSHIPS DIFFERENT?

When we talk of partnerships (or collaboration) between higher education and other organizations, do we mean anything different from the exchanges of goods, services, and ideas with which we are already familiar?

In a world in which no individual or organization is self-sufficient, exchanges of one sort or another are the incessant ebb and flow of daily life. Universities purchase food, computers, books, and other goods from companies. Businesses hire college graduates as employees and faculty as consultants and may purchase licenses to university-owned research. Some unions negotiate faculty contracts while other unions represent different groups of college and university employees. Academics, employers, and employee representatives mix their interests while serving on boards of trustees and advisory committees. Colleges and businesses and associations, because they bring jobs and budgets with them, are sought by politicians and other citizen groups who want them to locate in one or another state or community. In thousands of ways all these people help themselves by helping others, exchanging a part of their time, energy, funds, or expertise for some resource provided by others.

Why then does the rhetoric of the new partnerships and of collaboration raise hopes and fears quite different in character from the emotions and expectations related to the routine purchasing, selling, and interacting that go on daily among the sectors of our society?

By new partnerships or collaboration we mean the joint ventures between higher education and other organizations (particularly the business sector) that are characterized by: voluntary institutional participation; multi-sector leadership, problem-solving, and performance-based orientation; shared or complementary interests; and shared responsibility for agenda planning and action. But is this new partnership just another name for patterns of institutional behavior that have been with us for a long time? Or are the patterns themselves changing and in the process forcing us to create new behaviors and new ideas to guide those behaviors?

First, we can readily admit that in many respects the future is but an extension of the past. Certainly in the United States, with its diversity of public and private colleges and universities, many of them founded and supported through close relationships with business and industry leaders, there has been little ideological basis for separation between the institutions of work and learning.

Nonetheless, the concepts of institutional collaboration and partnership do imply changes in both style and substance affecting these relationships in some basic ways. In style, projects we designate as partnerships and collaborations imply a greater degree of collegiality, openness, and commitment to shared values than would be typical of an exchange relationship. We do not use the term collaboration to describe a contract under which a company provides food services, maintenance services, or computer services to a college. But "collaboration" seems just the right word to describe a project to develop a new computer-assisted manufacturing process or to help employees learn English as a second language. Here both the college and a "partner" such as a union or a company assist in the effort. It is not collaboration when a company or a government agency contracts with a university to survey employee needs, conduct archeological assessments in advance of new road construction, or design the reorganization of a department or office. Yet "collaboration" seems to fit the situation when university and contractor, with or without external funding, work together on organizational effectiveness research, develop guidelines for employee needs surveys, and share personnel and task responsibilities in carrying through the work. The closer we look at the situations we call "partnerships" and those we do not regard that way, the more we see partnerships and collaboration as dominated by collegiality and shared responsibility across institutional boundaries in the performance of substantive tasks.

In substance, projects and programs we designate as partnerships and collaborations imply a breaking or at least a temporary minimizing of the boundaries that normally separate organizations. Rules regarding the sharing of information or the qualifications of certain personnel or the scheduling of certain activities are bent if not changed. The more rules that are bent and exceptions made, the greater we feel the influence of the collaborative style.

Style and substance merge. In this breaking of rules the participants experience, to varyng degrees, a sense of adventure and exhilaration. Collaboration and partnership become words that imply a feeling of synergy, of extra energy, and imagination applied to a problem.

Thus what we call collaborative activities are different. They create situations in which decision-making authority over the design and operation of certain missions and functions of an organization is shared with "outsiders." This threatened sharing of authority is what makes collaboration risky as well as challenging and exciting. The organization's norms of leadership and control are questioned. The job has to get done. The organization needs to prove itself, to show that it can do the job. But it cannot do the job by itself. The opportunity and responsibility must be shared. This dilemma strikes at the emotional and pragmatic gut of an organization. All the more reason, one concludes, that the benefits of partnership programs should far outweigh their costs.

Throughout this chapter examples of higher education partnership efforts are provided. The majority of these examples are taken from a group of projects which comprise the Education and the Economy Alliance, a program supported by the Fund for the Improvement of Postsecondary Education, US Department of Education. (For more information on any of these projects, contact the National Institute for Work and Learning.)

THREE CATEGORIES OF PARTNERSHIPS

Partnerships between postsecondary education institutions and work organizations directly challenge the ideal of the autonomous university or college. In the face of declining youth enrollments, growing control by public agencies and state legislatures, and increasing costs that cannot be passed on to consumers, post-secondary education institutions look to partnerships with corporations and unions as one way to help balance sources of revenues, political pressures, and student enrollments. From the model of faculty and institutional autonomy, the modern education institution shifts to a model of multiple power centers of students, government, business, labor, and other groups as external forces with faculty, administrators, and boards of trustees in higher education performing a balancing and integrating function at the hub of the postsecondary education enterprise.

Three Categories

Essentially partnerships and joint, or collaborative, activities involving post-secondary education institutions with employers, unions, professional associations, and other groups may be said to trade in three types of resources: ideas, wealth, and people. In well-planned projects these three resources reinforce one another. These three types of resources play dominant roles in three corresponding types of partnership activities (see Johnson 1984):

1 *Joint research partnerships* are built on the production and development of ideas and concepts. Basic and applied research potentially leading to new and profitable products can be a highly rewarding basis for education–business partnerships, especially in scientific and engineering fields.
2 *Economic development* can be defined as the creation of new wealth through the use of money, markets, manpower, materials, and management, the "five M's" of economic development theory.
3 *Human resource development* can be interpreted in either the more narrow, utilitarian, economic development sense of investing in people to make the most productive use of their talents or in the broader humanistic sense of enabling people to develop their individual talents for their own sake.

Each of these broad categories has many varied specific incarnations. Each category has its own sets of strategies for successful partnerships. Each has diverse programs and outcomes. Yet, the three can be related. Bridges can be built from one type of partnership, with its goals and programs, to the other two types of partnerships with their goals and programs. A joint research project, for example, can also be developed to train a new generation of researchers or to build the conceptual basis for a project with economic development implications.

Similarly, activities in these three areas can be pursued at various levels of cross-institutional involvement. Johnson (1984) describes three levels of interaction between academic and industrial (or business) organizations:

1 Least interdependent are academic activities oriented toward business. This level includes research centers and institutes established on a unilateral basis by post-secondary education institutions, publication and speaker programs oriented toward business audiences, and professional curricula serving business purposes.
2 Academic activities in cooperation with industry require more sharing of resources and responsibilities. These may include: personnel exchange programs, research consortia, contract research, adjunct faculty, advisory committees, cooperative education, extension services, consulting relationships, and development of industrial research parks and small business "incubator" facilities.
3 Academic/industrial partnerships are defined by Johnson (1984) to include such activities as cooperative research centers, joint planning and program councils, and cooperative entrepreneurial development projects.

The more specifically we describe a project the more difficult it becomes to categorize the project neatly by level of involvement.

The broad sweep of collaborative possibilities can be suggested, however, by the identification of some sub-categories of such projects. Closer examination of substantive topics possibly deserving of multi-sector attention also points to some of the problems inherent in the practice of partnership developments.

Research Partnerships

Corporate research tends to be skewed toward the development of marketable products. Academic research tends to pursue the goal of new knowledge regardless of its commercial value. Between these two main tendencies are many points of overlap and separation. Many ideas produced in universities enter public use and discourse through publications and teaching without ever becoming the basis for formal collaborative projects. And much of the thinking, research, and teaching in colleges and universities is shaped by major events and issues in the world outside. At the same time, each sector has its own separate culture where direct contact with outsiders may never occur.

Partnership activities, therefore, tend to favor those parts of their respective institutions having the most similar interests and methods and having the potential to provide mutual rewards. Inevitably this skewing of focus raises questions about the integrity of academic and professional practices, including the freedom to select topics, to pursue ideas wherever they seem to lead, to publish findings freely, to discuss research ideas with peers and students, and to move unhindered from one institution to another.

In recent years many of these "principles" have become negotiable because of the growing similarities between the roles of researchers in industry and those in academic settings. Theoretical knowledge in many technical fields is finding quick absorption into applied knowledge. Theory is being developed more rapidly under the pressure of challenges in product development. The closing gap between theory and practice in technical fields and even in many social science fields such as organizational leadership, decision-making, and political science is triggering an era of good feelings among corporations, unions, and universities that was largely unforeseen and even unwanted two decades ago.

Typical of these science and engineering research partnerships are:

1 Monsanto and Harvard University – research on biochemistry and biology in organogenics.
2 Bristol-Myers Company and Yale University – production of anticancer drugs.
3 The Standard Oil Company of Ohio and Stanford University, the University of Pennsylvania, Pennsylvania State University, the University of Illinois, and MIT – research on offshore engineering, crop genetics, and mining technology.

Corporate interest in state-of-the-art research in areas other than science and engineering has extended primarily to business-related specialized topics in organizational psychology (for insights into leadership and supervisory behavior), communications theory (for command and control systems used in defense and multinational corporations), and general management theory. *In Search of Excellence* (Peters 1982) and other landmark studies, for example, have been the result of joint research projects initiated by either university faculty or management consulting firms. In these business research projects as in the sciences, partnership projects and the opportunities they bring for individual involvement tend to be limited to the elite public and private research universities (Peters 1982).

Not yet a widespread occurrence but with the potential to reach into a wider range of colleges and universities are examples of research on topics of regional and community interest involving colleges and universities with regional and local constituencies. Here business sponsorship tends to emphasize analysis of regional economic, demographic, and political trends on the one hand, or the development of research programs closely linked to industries (for example, ceramics, or automobiles, or construction) with a strong presence in the region.

Labor unions have had almost no role thus far in these research partnerships, with some very modest exceptions involving state universities with strong programs of labor studies or industrial relations. Professional engineering and scientific associations have played a modest yet important role in raising corporate attention to concerns such as the shortages of engineering faculty and in encouraging the development of education–corporate partnerships through reports, publications, presentations at annual meetings, and the formation of associations dedicated to cooperative education.

What appears to be lacking in these research partnerships is serious attention to potentially controversial areas in which corporate performance in matters affecting the public welfare might be subjected to public criticism. Issues such as disposal of chemical wastes, affirmative action, occupational safety, health and environment, plant closings and worker displacement, and investment in overseas production facilities may affect corporate profits and products in direct, occasionally spectacular ways. Yet corporations, or unions for that matter, tend not to seek out joint research projects on these issues. Foundations, government, and public interest groups tend to be the sponsors of college and university research on these topics.

Opportunities for research partnerships also are directly affected by national and state laws dealing with tax, antitrust, and patent policies. Fears of antitrust prosecution have inhibited the formation of industrial consortia sponsoring university research projects in the past. The financial value of a research project differs if it is treated as a philanthropic contribution from a corporate foundation than if it is treated as a depreciable or tax creditable investment in corporate research facilities. In recent years some of the main legal barriers to partnership programs have been removed in the United States. With those barriers eliminated, some of the advantages of campus-based research environments, especially for consortia-type research, have emerged. The more open-ended, exploratory atmosphere of the campus, the greater credibility associated with research findings produced in the "neutral" campus environment, and easier access to inexpensive yet highly motivated student research assistants all favor collaborative campus-based projects once negative factors are removed.

In sum, joint research partnerships encourage participation in a relatively narrow band of intellectual topics and appeal to individuals who are committed to a specific scientific or engineering research topic. Such persons may also be relatively sympathetic to corporate interests in developing products based on the research. Researchers – whether employed by corporations or universities – who are involved in topics of public controversy or topics far removed from product development seem to be less likely to become participants in education–business research partnership projects.

Economic Development Partnerships

Partnerships between higher education and business for economic development are changing and increasing (Doyle and Brisson 1985). Economic development partnerships have three faces:

1 *Community development* refers to planning and implementing projects and programs to improve the economic and social qualities of life in a whole community or geographic area. Gains in individual or institutional wealth are assumed to contribute to overall public welfare. A new college campus, a new office of a government agency or of a private employer, a new factory, a new museum, or the upgrading or expansion of these, are actively sought and developed by public and private interests for the additional jobs, tax revenues, and consumer spending they can be expected to bring to a community and region. Part of this expected value may be more indirect: for example, the expectation that the presence of one organization may attract others, whether as suppliers, competitors, or simply as neighbors constituting a core for economic growth. The Economics Education Project of

the Highlander Research and Education Center in the state of Tennessee is an example of a new partnership for community development. The project is developing a participatory research and education process to enable residents of rural Appalachian communities to deal with the impacts of the changing economy on the economic and social qualities of their communities. Models of new partnerships between local higher education institutions and grassroots community groups have been developed. A new economics curriculum for local community development is also being developed.

2 *Institutional development* involves a more self-serving analysis and utilization of the organization's own resources. In recent years, for example, colleges and universities have more carefully analyzed their real estate holdings and other real estate parcels in their vicinities. Reflecting on the successes of Silicon Valley near Stanford University in California, the Route 128 corridor near the research and engineering schools of the Boston area in Massachusetts, and the Research Tirangle in North Carolina's university research center, colleges and universities are placing new and higher values on their regional investments, their faculty, and their physical resources. Even universities that do not aspire to national status are more aware of the attractions of the campus research environment for businesses involved in knowledge production. Institutional development involves new ways of identifying the tangible and intangible assets of the institution and finding ways to capitalize those assets and market them to potential partners. An example of a partnership for institutional development is the Model CAD/CAM Training Center at the Milwaukee Area Technical College in Wisconsin. The CAD/CAM Training Center offers software and training materials in "Computer Integrated Manufacturing" for retraining industrial workers. As part of the Center, a microcomputer-based CAD system was developed. The system has been sold to educational institutions and a dealership network has been established.

3 *Business development* includes elements of both community and institutional development. The aim here is to grow new enterprises or to assist older ones. Sponsoring entrepreneurial "incubator" centers and venture capital funds for small businesses, or organizing small business assistance centers (perhaps with state or federal government funding) may have community development as a

primary purpose and institutional development as a secondary purpose. The method chosen is clearly that of improving the chances of business owners to achieve product development and marketing success. This is in some contrast to the emphasis of community development on building an infrastructure of public services and core employers which supplies the economic "yeast" for self-generating growth. And it is also in contrast to the emphasis of institutional development on the comparatively narrow self-interest of a specific organization. The Small Business Incubator Project of Portland Community College, Oregon, or the Northwest Enterprise Centre (Thunder Bay, Ontario) are examples of partnerships for business development. In addition to offering low-cost rental space to small business, these projects provide support services, classes, seminars, and professional consultations to the prospective entrepreneurs. Businesses can remain in the incubators during their developmental periods.

Education–work partnerships can be used to generate development projects, or partnerships can be nurtured and generated as a result of effective economic development projects.

As with research partnerships, economic development projects frequently depend on government funding or tax policies as a sometimes active and sometimes silent partner. Interest-subsidized revenue bonds, for example, may be more easily justified in public policy rhetoric if a university or similar non-profit research organization is a sponsor of a project and is likely to be a major beneficiary of the public subsidy. Urban Development Action Grants (UDAG), Community Development Block Grants (CDBG), and other direct payments from governmental programs can be used as incentives for collaborative projects in the United States. Similarly in Canada and the United Kingdom special partnership programs exist through the Labor Force Strategy of Employment and Immigration Canada and through Manpower Services and Open Tech in the United Kingdom. The US, federal and state training funds from vocational education and Department of Labor training programs are used in many states to build programs of job training partnerships among community colleges, employers, unions, and other community-based education and training organizations. Some states, Massachusetts and Pennsylvania, for example, have created state-funded programs which require matching contributions and collaborative agreements between employers and education institutions before state financial support is provided. Finally, the largest incentives for college partnerships with employers and unions may be through tax-financed student grants, loan guarantees, and subsidized tuition rates at public institutions.

The incentives for economic development partnerships are many and varied. Full understanding of these varied incentives, of the financial savings that can be built into programs serving different institutional and community needs, and of the ways programs can be marketed to different audiences in business, labor, and the public sector can be an important factor in determining the success of partnership programs.

Human Resource Development

The life of every working adult is a kind of informal partnership between education and work institutions. A career with a steady flow of income is the implied reward that follows from educational preparation. Individuals must draw the connections by making career choices, selecting educational programs, earning income to pay for education, searching out a first and successive jobs, learning on the job, and using the career advancement network to move from position to position.

Many corporations have their recruiters. Colleges have their placement offices and cooperative education programs, as well as their continuing education programs. Nonetheless, collaborative partnerships for career development are as underdeveloped and as open to innovative possibilities as are the research and economic development programs currently attracting leadership attention. Gradually, employer, union, and education leaders are recognizing opportunities for programs that formalize explicit relationships between performance at work and performance in education.

Put in terms of career progression, human resource development partnerships can be categorized as:

1 Entry-level preparation and orientation;
2 Technical skill development and maintenance;
3 Career transition preparation and skill enhancement; and
4 Career completion.

Entry-level Preparation and Orientation

Instructional programs at most colleges and universities are dedicated primarily to preparing young students for their first major transition from education to work. Whether the goals of study be liberal arts, sciences, engineering, technician skills, legal or medical studies, few students would attend undergraduate, graduate, or professional degree programs without career preparation as a primary motivation. At first glance, education institutions ought to be expert in understanding and shaping the subtle and complex relationships between intellectual training, skill training, and career transition planning.

In recent years entry-level preparation by post-secondary education institutions has come to include remedial education in basic skills presumed to have been taught during elementary and secondary education. Some corporations and unions have contracted with post-secondary education institutions to provide basic skill training to their employees or to develop basic skills curricula for adult learners. The English Language Training for the Workplace Program of Arizona State University provides English-as-a-Second-Language training to employees of Honeywell's Large Computer Products Division. The program uses an innovative "functional" approach to language training. The curriculum deals with language in a comprehensive way including grammar, pronunciation/intonation, spelling, communication strategies, style, and culture. The aspects of language skills are always presented with content drawn from the work environment at Honeywell.

In other instances, universities and colleges have become involved in collaborative projects with employers, local governments, unions, and others to improve the effectiveness of elementary and secondary education. Sharing responsibility for the design and effectiveness of the entire education system may lead to new ways of incorporating the traditional liberal arts core of the undergraduate curriculum into pre-occupational training. In many communities, making these changes from the traditional role and content of post-secondary education institutions has required collaborative business–academic leadership. Indeed some corporations are finding with profound technological and workplace innovation that a number of their valued employees lack even the basic literacy and numeracy skills to take on new roles. In Canada companies such as the Weston Bakeries have started major workplace literacy programs.

Technical Skill Development and Maintenance

These have long been a higher education function. These activities range from the summer executive seminars for alumni and corporate top managers to the skill training of associate degree or certificate programs. The rapidly growing training function within corporations is the catalyst for greater use of contract training and long-term "retainer" training relationships. Employment-based tuition assistance programs have become a mainstay of many continuing education programs at nearby colleges and universities. On the basis of these two sources of employer funding – training and tuition assistance – specific degree and non-degree programs can be developed. The Special Technician Training Program of Rio Salado Community College in the US state of Arizona has trained production line workers of Motorola, Inc. in electronic and semiconductor technology. Participants are given paid leave for one year with all tuition costs covered by the company. The community college has designed a one-year Associate in Applied Science degree program with courses held five days a week for eight hours a day. Upon completion, participants are placed in electronic technician and semiconductor processor positions within Motorola. The contract between Motorola and the community college includes provision of a training center, technical equipment, and cooperative education experiences for students.

Career Transition

Similarly, collaborative opportunities abound in the development of programs and research supporting the career transitions of adult workers and of retiring workers. Whether these transitions are initiated voluntarily or involuntarily by the individual, employers are assuming more responsibility than has been the case historically for the financing and planning of personnel changes. An outplacement industry of consultants is being created first by difficult economic conditions and second by a fundamental restructuring of the "social contract" between employer and employee. As researchers, as consultants, and as traditional providers of career counseling and training, post-secondary education institutions still have much to learn about the educational needs of adults facing occupational and economic transitions. But their position is no different from that of employers, unions, professional associations, and adults themselves who are also moving quickly into uncharted territory. With these uncertain times and the anxieties of many workers is coming a strong compulsion for lifelong learning: the need to have multiple skills and experiences simply to make career change less risky. Better understanding of the dynamics of career change can itself be a basis for the development of partnership programs.

Summary

Collaborative partnerships between post-secondary education institutions and work institutions are essentially of three types: research partnerships intended to produce and develop ideas; economic partnerships intended to produce and develop wealth; and human resource partnerships intended to develop people. Within each of these categories are many different opportunities for substantive projects linking education and work institutions. But the likelihood of actual project initiation and the scale of resources allocated to specific activities are influenced by many factors and problems. Collaborative activities tend to develop around substantive issues where common interests are strongest. These common interests may engage only small aspects of the collaborating institutions. Moving beyond the margins of prestigious areas of collaboration requires persistent creativity, persuasion, and solid performance.

WHO COLLABORATES?

Who participates in collaborative projects? Each partnership activity has a ripple effect on the politics and personalities of the institutions involved. One must ask in each case not only if the respective organizations benefit, but also who else benefits.

Some understanding of the organizational conditions for collaboration is essential to an understanding of who collaborates and who benefits from collaboration. The basic factors involved can be described from four perspectives:

1 The perspective of organization mission: Are the style and substance of the collaborative program consistent with the organization's sense of its own identity?
2 The locus of the initiative within the organization: What are the effects on those involved and those not involved?
3 The level of leadership directly responsible for the collaborative initiative: what powers of position and resources are brought to bear in support of the program?
4 The depth of institutional involvement in the program: are the activities restricted legitimately to a small corner of the organization or are the opportunities and rewards widely distributed?

Effects of Mission

An organization's mission, its sense of main purposes, has much to do with the projects it selects for collaborative programs, the types and size of resources devoted to these programs, and the selection of people to be involved. Computer firms prefer programs and projects that advance the sophistication, quality, uses, and reputations of computers. Insurance firms also look to ways of enhancing their products, including economic and community development activities that enhance the value of real estate properties in their investment portfolios. Labor-intensive businesses and labor unions seek ways of enhancing the quality of the labor force, particularly as it affects the quality of entry-level workers, supervisors, managers, or skilled labor. The Honeywell English Language Training Program and the Motorola Special Technician Training Program are examples of how an organization's mission determines the nature of the partnerships entered into with institutions of higher education.

Similarly the missions of education institutions establish the direction of their partnership interests. Research universities such as Yale, Harvard, Rutgers, Oxford, Cambridge, McGill and Queens, look primarily for partnerships which enhance their reputations as innovators on the cutting edge of new knowledge in fields such as pharmaceuticals, business organization, or ceramics. Other universities, such as University of Waterloo, Johns Hopkins, and University of Leciester, and colleges (or other departments at the same institutions) seek partnerships which enhance their reputations as innovators in applied research and producers of quality professional workers. Liberal arts colleges seek partnerships enhancing their view of the world, seeing themselves as producers of creative managers and pre-professionals. Community colleges draw on their several missions: as providers of lifelong learning to adults entering new careers, as produers of quality entry-level technical workers, as providers of remedial learning to employees lacking skills, and as sources of technical assistance to local small businesses.

The Education Bridges to Options in High Technology Employment project of San Diego State University (CA), the College of Staten Island (NY) Upper Division Bachelor of Science in Nursing (BSN) project, and the School for New Learning graduate program of DePaul University (IL), are examples of how the mission of the education institution can dictate the nature of its partnerships. The San Diego State University project offers retraining and updating in biotechnology and analytical chemistry to mid-career scientists for professional development and career enhancement. The project responds to the school's mission of serving the expanding high-technology industrial community in San Diego County. The College of Staten Island project provides a means for working nurses to have access to and progress toward the bachelor's degree. The program responds to the college's mission of meeting the educational needs of working adults and the human resource needs of the health and social service deliverers in New York City. The DePaul University project directly responds to the School for New Learning's mission of offering innovative experiential liberal arts programs to working adults. This Master of Arts program integrates skills and perspectives of the liberal arts with individually tailored programs of study in various professional areas.

Thus, an organization's mission in many direct and subtle ways stereotypes the reputations of the people who work for it, both enhancing and restricting the opportunities available to them for collaborative action. Even so, the experience of American colleges, universities, corporations, and unions over the past few years appears to indicate that all these institutions have seriously undervalued the resources they bring to the partnership negotiating table and underestimated the variety of profitable opportunities for collaboration among education and work organizations.

Employer organizations and unions tend to undervalue the

learning that occurs daily on the job. Consequently they often neglect ways of improving workplaces as learning environments. Work organizations are only beginning to understand that the spirit of self-initiated learning and problem-solving can be nurtured and combined with techniques of training and formal instruction as important aspects of business success. As workplaces become better organized as learning environments they will also become more attractive partners for colleges and universities trying to show connections between theory and practice.

Similarly, post-secondary education organizations have not viewed themselves as the owners of franchises on important aspects of research, knowledge, and instruction. Organizations are established and maintained only at great cost. Once established, their presence tends to ward off the estblishment of similar organizations. State boards of higher education may explicitly limit competition by preventing other institutions from developing competing programs.

Businesses and labor organizations have long appreciated the power of such "franchise" positions. Unlike large and wealthy corporations able to seek out information and expertise anywhere in the nation or world, the typical employer, union, or student must look closer to home. Education institutions, while thoroughly experienced in exploiting their geographic proximity to high school graduates, are frequently naive in exploiting that same proximity to other organizations.

The language arts faculty need not be of national stature in order to provide top quality instruction tailored to the needs of nearby managers and industrial workers. The economics department can develop a strong reputation locally as a source of regional economic data and analysis without expecting to compete with major university researchers in the pages of professional journals. The mathematics, science, business, and language departments, by paying more attention to the economic and demographic characteristics of the region's employers, may be able to develop special expertise in areas of research, scholarship, and instruction that will bring national or international fame while also attending to matters of immediate import in the region. These opportunities and possibilities are inherent in almost every collaborative relationship.

Serious development of education–work partnerships should strengthen the diversity of post-secondary institutions. Better understanding not only of their own strengths and weaknesses as isolated institutions but also of the strengths and weaknesses of the communities, regions, and other organizations within their reach should result in more sophisticated understanding of organizational missions and identities. This deeper understanding should lead in turn to more creative uses of joint ventures between education and work organizations. For example, a nation's elite research universities can work more actively to capitalize on their "franchise" resources of expertise and prestige (including joint research projects, research park and real estate developments, community action programs, and even summer sports camps). Other educators following these examples will come to see the opportunities for partnerships that can be found in their own backyards.

Locus in the Organization

At first blush, the problem of location within a given organization of a partnership project or program must appear obvious. Of course a new genetic engineering partnership program will involve a few key academic departments and one or more of the few firms with expertise in that field. And of couse the new automotive technician program sponsored by the local automobile dealers' association will benefit the automotive specialists.

Programs in each of the three categories of partnership activities tend inevitably to benefit those responsible for organizing and directing the programs. Publicity, possibly prestige, job security, and professional opportunities may accompany the project.

But the location of a program can work in opposite directions. Most partnership efforts are small, tentative explorations of new ways to provide services, solve organizational problems, or develop credibility and trust across organizations. Ventures that have the blessing of high university and corporate officials may be viewed suspiciously or merely negligently if not given appropriate attention and resources. Ventures lacking higher endorsements face all kinds of obstacles of attitude and administrative practice unless the entire organization is accustomed to the nurturing of innovative programs. Such innovation-nurturing organizations are rare.

In this broad analysis, therefore, location of a partnership program activity can elicit two types of effects: rewards or difficulties. In either case a special entrepreneurial outlook will be required on the part of the individuals responsible for the project or program.

Over the years most faculty have learned to live with the fact that certain specializations and professions have greater opportunities than others for external consulting and the income and visibility that such activity provides. Within departments accommodations are made for the star performers. To the extent that these activities bring additional funds, students, research opportunities, and prestige to the institution, the faculty and departments involved often find ways to claim special rights and treatment in dealing with other department and campus administrators. Depending in large part on the mix of personalities, the internal politics can be either ferocious or diplomatic.

Collaborative activities of a low-key nature, small in scope and involving only a few faculty, can have much the same impact within a college or university as a consulting relationship. But the relationship takes on a different quality and significance once an official institutional involvement is suggested. The first projects may be smaller and less noteworthy than a faculty consulting project. But the intent, even the mere possibility of developing longer-term relationships with one or more external organizations raises the "ante" and introduces new factors affecting faculty participation. Similarly in a corporation or union, the individual project of a subordinate manager or official takes on different meaning if it represents the direction toward which higher level officials may want to move the entire organization.

Therefore the process by which chief executives – whatever their organization – or other policy-making officials reveal or hide their intentions and review and select partnership opportunities makes an enormous difference in the ways these activities are perceived and supported by others in the organization.

At times it is advisable to minimize the impact of particular projects on an organization. The special exceptions made to permit the project to accomplish its goals are specifically rejected as precedents. In other cases it makes sense to develop formal organizational policies and to support an activity as an example of the type of initiative desired.

Sometimes it makes sense to stress the ways in which the entire organization benefits from the side effects of a particular project and to establish special committees to oversee the activity, learn from it, and seek additional ways to involve others. At other times it makes sense to protect a project from too much attention, whether to protect a limited budget or to protect a politically sensitive project activity. The considerations are multiple. Yet from a strategic viewpoint, every collaborative project should be assessed on how its present location in the organization can best be used to touch and inform the lives of other members of the organization, and how its presence can be used to enhance and perhaps give new meaning to the central mission of the organization.

Level of Leadership

The question of who collaborates in education–work partnership projects and programs also must be answered in terms of the level or levels within an organization at which the partnership activity is initiated. Major differences in style and substance of partnerships are affected by the relative differences in power, prestige, resources, and visibility associated with different levels within organizations. These differences frequently determine who gets involved and in what ways.

Yet it is doubtful that a top level activity is inherently "better" than a lower level activity. Successful and influential partnership projects can be initiated as readily at the junior staff level as at the presidential level. Too frequently people assume that top level support is essential, an assumption that raises expectations yet may result in greater disappointment when success does not follow obediently the commands of those leaders.

Success and quality are functions of wise management (and good luck) at any level, built on a proper use of the levers of control available to those directing the collaborative effort. The impact of organizational level on program quality and success requires, therefore, some discussion of the available levers of control at each level. For purposes of this brief discussion, two generalized "levels" will be analyzed: "top level" initiatives and "lower level" initiatives. The intent of the comments that follow is to approach each organizational level objectively and without pejorative connotations. Different situations can make either level the target of opportunity.

Top level leaders, for example, tend to be very sensitive to failure. A leader knows that he or she has a limited stock of credibility. Many demands are made to tap that limited stock of decision-making opportunities. Consequently, the typical organizational leader wants ideas to be tested, to have all the risks identified and taken into account before decisions are made about the worthiness of a project or the amount of resources to be invested in it. Such thinking tends to err on the side of cautiousness.

Small, peripheral projects with which the leaders of organizations have little or no direct contact can play crucial roles in the development of partnership programs by testing and cleansing ideas of their more outrageous and ineffective features. Thus the interplay between top level and lower level initiatives is essential. Rapid progress and enthusiasm for partnership programs develop in situations where participants at the different levels of an organization understand and consciously employ the techniques of interaction between high level and lower level initiatives. Where chief executives and staff do not communicate, do not understand the opportunities and ploys available to them, or even disagree and work at cross purposes, partnership initiatives at any level are more likely to encounter frustration and failure.

Top level initiatives

The involvement of top level officials in a collaborative education–work project usually implies the making or anticipation of a decision related to one or more of six factors:

1 a major investment of financial resources;
2 a major shift in institutional mission (or the decision to reject a proposed shift in mission);
3 a major change in organizational practices;
4 a major personnel change;
5 a major public relations opportunity to represent the organization and take credit for some out-of-the-ordinary accomplishment; or
6 a major political move to assuage, or reward, some individual or group.

In other words, the involvement of top officials in a collaborative project probably has little to do with the substantive content of the project itself and far more to do with impact of the project on the organization. Dear though the topic may be to the leader's heart, the development of a new computer-assisted design program, the retraining of displaced workers, the institution of sound environmental practices, or the enrollment of assembly line workers in a technician-level degree program must take second place to the question of whether or not the proposed activity will enhance the survival, continuity, and growth of the organization in a constantly changing world.

Because individuals differ in their judgments regarding how innovative activities will serve to enhance or detract from an organization's mission or reputation, decisions about collaborative activities can be controversial. Support from the chief executive usually means that the organization's resources – its funds, personnel, reputation, and allies – either will be enlisted in support of a project (throwing the weight of the organization behind the project) or at least will be kept in a neutral position, allowing the project to prove itself without undue interference. But the very fact of top level support may arouse sources of hidden opposition. People who might have ignored a project operating modestly under the direction of a junior professor or manager will pay close attention to the same project if it appears to have the blessing and interest of the top executives. Is the project a harbinger of things to come? Is it a public relations exercise? If it were expanded, what would be the implications for the standard ways of doing things? If made permanent, who stands to gain, and who to lose? Would basic research be shifted into university laboratories? Would managers and union officials be accepted as adjunct faculty? Would affirmative action programs be taken more seriously?

In a word, projects can quickly become politicized once the top officials of an organization are involved. Sometimes politicization helps a project by setting policy or intimidating the informal opposition, those persons who delay actions and raise objections and generally undermine the ability of a project to perform. Sometimes politicization hinders project performance by making potential opponents more aware of the significance of the project's goals and practices, of the people the project proposes to serve, and of the points at which the project is most vulnerable to criticism.

Top level involvement in collaborative projects, therefore, is most justifiable when the skills and resources associated with an organization's top leadership are most in demand and can be most useful in practice. Of these skills and resources, credibility is the most important. The endorsement of top officials, their commitment to the goals of a project, their word that a project is of genuine importance to the mission and future of an organization, can carry enormous weight with funding agencies and prospective partner organizations and key personnel. The details of what is meant must be worked out according to the situation, of course. But the initial commitment to a project from top officers puts their credibility on the line and affects how seriously their commitments will be viewed in the future. Because it is preferable to avoid spending one's credibility, leaders generally prefer partnership projects that can manage on their own to find funding and produce desirable results without leadership involvement. The leader's skill and status are saved for other days and "bigger deals."

In addition to their credibility as leaders, that is, as people with the capacity to assure that things get done, top level officials are presumed to control resources. Smaller projects make relatively modest claims on an organization's resources. Larger projects, by stepping on more toes as it were, make larger claims: they need more attention from central administrative units, are more likely to require special dispensations from certain rules, and are more likely to make one group of people in the organization more noticeably enviable than the other groups. Leaders get called upon to balance these diverse interests and to assure an equitable distribution of rewards, or to rationalize the inequities in ways others accept as reasonable.

Involvement by top level officials is also necessary when changes in organizational mission are required. This frequently requires shifts in resources. The ability to shift mission and resources is entirely beyond the abilities of lower level staff.

All these strands of credibility, resources, and mission come together in the collaborative event made to order for the top level leader: the big deal. It may have been planned well in advance. Or it may be an opportunistic idea, casually mentioned over drinks or dinner with a fellow top level leader. The follow-up discussions, analysis, and planning may take years or only days. But the implications for the organization's future are large: money, prestige, the ability to attract staff and serve clients better all hang in the balance. At such moments the top level officer earns her or his pay by astutely conceptualizing, adapting, and negotiating to assure that the collaborative idea helps to shape the future course of the organization in desirable ways.

Two cxamples of the critical role of top level leaders in the success of new partnerships are the TECPLAY and Business Development and Training Center projects. The TECPLAY project of the National Institute for Work and Learning, in Washington, D.C., and the Charleston (South Carolina) Higher Education Consortium provided a computer-assisted program for upgrading basic skills and a comprehensive career development program to urban minority young adults. The short- and long-term success of the project is directly related to the roles played by the Mayor, the senior staff of Trident Technical College, the head of the local City Venture Corporation, and a number of community leaders. Their support and the resources they provided gave the project visibility and a solid footing which were central to its success.

The Business Development and Training Center (BDTC) at Great Valley Corporate Park in Pennsylvania is a cooperative joint venture of the Compact of Lifelong Education Opportunities and Rouse and Associates, an American real estate company. The BDTC brings aggregated learning, business development assistance, and learning services to employees and employers in the park. Credit and non-credit courses, workshops and seminars, career academic counseling, assessment of prior learning, and networking are offered through the BDTC. Without the support and resources of the head of Rouse and Associates, the Center would be little more than a good idea. James Rouse, the Chief Executive Officer of Rouse and Associates has provided space, financing, staffing, and, most important, visibility to the Center and its various activities.

Lower level initiatives

The ability to devote oneself single-mindedly to a project is one key resource that the top level leader can rarely provide. This, in contrast, is the most precious resource of people working at the lower levels of an organization. At any level and for any person, many competing demands on time and energy abound. But the top level executive has a job whose very nature requires multiple roles and responsibilities. Lower down the organizational ladder are located the responsibilities for actually implementing the details of specific projects, and, frequently, for creating the ideas that lead to other projects.

Small organizations such as small businesses, local unions, and smaller colleges have so many tasks to be done and so few people to do them that anyone with any enthusiasm is soon spread thin, with numerous responsibilities. In such cases it is hard to talk of organizational "levels." In part, this is the very reason the movement toward partnerships between education and work organizations has tended to focus on larger businesses and education institutions. Local unions and small businesses are so deeply and constantly involved in their primary "bread and butter" work that time and staff are not available to explore possibilities of partnerships, much less actually manage partnership projects. For these people to become involved in a collaborative education–work project means, by definition, that the purposes and activities of the project are directly related to the central purpose of their jobs and their organizations' missions.

Within larger organizations, smaller, less visible projects initiated by individual managers and faculty can and have proved exceptionally valuable. Like the inventor in the garage, testing and refining a product until it is ready for market, small collaborative projects enable people with foresight and motivation to put ideas into practice and to integrate the lessons of practice into new conceptualizations. Implementing the concept may take many months, during which new insights are seen, the strengths and limitations of partnership and personal abilities are revealed, and the world outside the project constantly changes.

But what if a project that seemed to set a crucial example turns out to be unimportant in the grand scheme of events? Or perhaps it is headed in the right direction but lacks some necessary ingredient. Or perhaps it is timely and does constitute an example worth replicating. The smaller project can take these risks at a relatively low cost to the collaborating organizations. Indeed, the mutual learning that occurs through the project and the trust established between professionals and organization administrators may be more valuable as a basis for future joint ventures than the substance of the specific project.

The smaller project initiated by an individual manager, researcher, faculty member, or union official will seem to lack the "clout" that is associated with more powerful positions in the organizational hierarchy. If the project director decides that an advisory panel would be useful to assist in securing access to information or critique the development of the project, less prestigious people will be attracted to the lower level project than if the invitation comes from a top level executive. All is proportion: technical expertise and lower level contact people may be more important to the success of the project than the visibility and temporary prestige of "names."

The top executive can more easily gain the attention of news media and more readily command the attention of the organization's own publicity staff. On the other hand, individual faculty and staff with strong reputations within their own technical fields will have easier access to those specialized audiences. Having the flexibility to call on technical and institutional authorities as the situation warrants, enhances collaborative projects by providng access to special skills and resources at all levels.

The lower level project is a valuable way to test the feasibility of ideas and of relationships between organizations. It is also a way of testing the ability of one's own organization to respond to the inevitable organizational problems of collaboration: scheduling, personnel, financial arrangements, decision-making and so forth. And the lower level project can be especially effective as a way of undermining the legitimacy of current practices and attitudes.

Whether one takes the viewpoint that the project is testing one's organization in a problem-solving way or undermining organizational practices in a confrontational, revolutionary way will depend in part on the personalities of the people involved and in part on the requirements of actual conditions.

In most education institutions, corporations, and unions, collaborative partnerships diverge from the standard operational procedures, the "S.O.P.s" of routine relationships and responsibilities. Few corporations rely on universities for the bulk of their research. Few colleges and universities rely on partnership programs with employers and unions for the bulk of their students, research opportunities, or curricular programs.

Inevitably, therefore, the individual who chooses to become involved in a partnership project is seeking to differentiate himself or herself from other faculty, administrators, or managers. Faculty in particular, because of the nature of college and university jobs and schedules, have time to pursue individual interests. These interests may take them into collaborative projects with populations (for example, migrant laborers, the unemployed, and welfare mothers) and organizations (for example, labor unions, civil rights organizations, community-based groups of whatever kind) that represent interests frequently in opposition to the dominant business and political powers. Or, as is typical of business school faculty, the individual interest of the educator might be entirely consistent with the interests of the dominant political powers and aimed at improving the functioning of those dominant organizations. It is natural in these choices that the character of the partnership should take on the core attitudes of the individuals and organizations involved.

Thus in some cases the individuals initiating lower level partnership activities use them to differentiate themselves from their peers in hopes of improving their visibility and approval in the eyes of higher authorities. In other instances, by seeking collaborative projects with organizations not viewed sympathetically by those authorities, the initiators are challenging the powers that be. In either case the rewards of partnership project are likely to attract entrepreneurial, individualistic persons. But the style of motivation and action will differ dramatically.

Collaborative activities, it seems, imply a certain level of confrontational spirit, either toward one's peers mired in routine or toward other organizations whose structures and behaviors have created the conditions which the collaborative project is meant to overcome. The Rural Education/Adult Development (READI) in the US state of Idaho project is one example of a new partnership that is characterized by a lower level initiative "on the margin" of its institution. Housed in the Cooperative Extension Service of the University of Idaho, the READI project helps develop computer literacy in rural adults. Working with local businesses and community groups, the project identifies ways technology can spur economic development in isolated rural communities. From its inception the project has been a lower level initiative of one committed energetic person who is "on the margin" of the Extension Service and the University. Another example is the "Beat the Streets" literacy program for street people in Toronto. Affiliated with Frontier College, street people who have gained literacy skills and personal control of their lives are "helping others to help themselves."

The level at which a partnership project is initiated and operated within an organization profoundly influences who conceives, who negotiates, who directs, who performs, who assesses, who represents, and who benefits from collaborative education–work projects and programs.

Depth of Collaboration

Eventually the question of who collaborates begs the question of how deeply felt within an organization are the values and practices of collaboration. Do partnership programs and, more to the point, the style and methods of reaching out to other organizations, affect an organization and its members superficially or profoundly? Are such programs praised as examples for emulation or are they restricted to the periphery of institutional attention? Are they used as catalysts for change within the larger parent organization? Or are they used for public relations purposes to demonstrate a degree of outward-looking concern while the rest of the organization is in fact shielded from the influences of their examples?

When used superficially, collaborative projects are not likely to be controversial. They do not challenge standard operating procedures and are likely to involve relatively few people. Scheduling, staffing, location, decision-making, assessment of results, and other matters requiring a sharing of viewpoints and authority among the collaborating organizations are carefully isolated to the collaborative projects. Implications for improvements in overall organizational performance are not discussed.

When used in more profound ways, the experiences of the organization in conducting collaborative projects are carefully examined for lessons learned. Standard operating procedures – whether dealing with personnel, paperwork, remuneration, or other relevant topics – are carefully reviewed and compared to those of other organizations. Inquiries about the project experience are encouraged. The board of trustees or directors is kept informed, and top officials are able to monitor the quantity and quality of the organization's efforts to establish and maintain collaborative relationships with other organizations. Members know that finding ways to work with other organizations is an acceptable means of solving problems.

An example of a new partnership that uses collaboration in a profound way is the Experienced Workers Re-Training Program of St. Louis Community College in the state of Missouri. The program involves a local partnership of business, education, labor, and government to provide outplacement services to workers and employers affected by structural changes in the local economy. In addition to helping workers and employers, the project has had a profound impact on the relations between the college and business sectors in the community, not only in delivering training programs that are responsive to business needs but in a wide range of other areas as well.

SUMMARY AND CONCLUSION

There are no simple answers to the questions surrounding collaboration. A college or university that bases its curriculum on cooperative education programs, requiring students and perhaps faculty to leave the campus and work at intervals in non-education organizations, is not necessarily a "better" or more effective organization than a college or university with a standard curriculum. It may operate on collaborative principles and may do a better job of serving those students who seek theoretical learning with work experience, but all this is done with trade-offs of time and energy that could have been spent on a traditional classroom curriculum.

A corporation that contracts with a university for a joint research program on computers or cosmetics is not necessarily better or more effective than its competitor that prefers its in-house research team. A company that joins a consortium of firms in supporting human development projects is not necessarily wiser than a firm that persists in going its own way. A union that develops a collaborative research and training project with a local college may in fact be spending resources better used on other union projects.

Partnership programs start from problems. Collaboration is a strategy for solving problems. The concepts of partnerships and collaboration viewed in the abstract are only solutions in search of problems. The benefits resulting from collaboration must be self-evident before a partnership program is initiated. By the same token, organizations faced with problems need to look beyond their own boundaries and the limitations of their own resources when searching for solutions. The partnership option should be considered on its own merits.

Who in an organization collaborates depends on much more

than the personality and motivation of individuals. Opportunities to initiate and participate in collaborative programs are directly influenced by an organization's mission, the locus of the collaborative activity within the organization, the level at which the individual works and at which the project is initiated, and the depth of an organization's experience with partnership projects.

REFERENCES

Doyle, Peter H. and Brisson, Candice (1985) *Partners in Growth: Business Higher-Education Development Strategies*. Washington, DC: Northeast-Midwest Institute.

Johnson, Lynn G. (1984) *The High-Technology Connection: Academic/Industrial Cooperation for Economic Growth*. ASHE-ERIC Higher Education Research Report No. 6. Washington, DC: Association for the Study of Higher Education.

Peters, Thomas J. (1982) *In Search of Excellence: Lessons from Best Run Companies*. New York: Harper & Row.

Commentary

Furthering Higher Education Partnerships

Beverly Witter Du Gas

> The winners in the new competitive environment will be the countries with the best educated work force and the most advanced technology.
>
> (David Vice (1987), President Northern Telecom Limited)

As we move into the era of the knowledge-based society, it becomes increasingly apparent that collaborative partnerships between government, universities, and industry are essential if we are to produce the cadre of scientists and scholars needed to advance our technology and a work force skilled in its utilization.

In a good many countries, collaboration between the three sectors is already taking place to further the advancement of knowledge and the preparation of skilled workers in a number of diverse fields. In Canada, one example is the government-initiated program entitled "Innovaction," which was developed by the Department of Secretary of State. This program was designed to bring together government, the private sector, and universities to undertake a broad range of collaborative research and development. Under the program, the Federal Government matches private-sector contributions to a granting council, such as the Medical Research Council, the National Science and Engineering Council, and the Social Sciences and Humanities Research Council which, in turn selects projects to be undertaken by university-based scientists. (Department of the Secretary of State 1987).

Another innovative approach fostering collaboration among institutions has been the establishment of Centres of Excellence at various universities across Canada. Their purpose is to foster research and the development of expertise in criticial areas of need. The government of the province of Ontario has established a number of such centers. One is the Centre of Excellence in Gerontology at McMaster University in Hamilton, Ontario. Its "raison d'être" is to promote multidisciplinary research to develop, and demonstration projects to implement, new and better ways of looking after the health and social needs of the growing number of older people in our society, with the concomitant aim of offering a better educational program for the workers needed to provide the health and social services.

Also in the health field in Canada, the Ministry of Health of Ontario has established two Teaching Health Units to bring together agencies providing community health services and the universities offering preparation for health professionals. The Teaching Health Units have a three-pronged purpose:

1 to enhance the quality of learning opportunities for students;
2 to foster collaborative research by university professors and health practitioners; and
3 to promote high standards of health service for people who live in the community.

In talking about collaborative partnerships, we should not forget the Cooperative Study Programs, which have emerged in the past two decades. These programs involve partnerships between universities and industry in which semesters of work in the field are alternated with semesters on campus. These cooperative study programs are not new – they have been around for a long time, under the nomenclature of "work/study" programs, or in the guise of required summer employment in the field in which the student was studying. What is new about the programs is their formalization and the granting of university credit for the work experience. The programs have enjoyed a growing popularity as graduates find they have considerable advantage in the job market over students in traditional programs because of their practical "hands-on" experience, and industries appreciate the advantages of recruiting an employee who is familiar with the workplace and does not require a lengthy – and expensive – orientation program.

Innumerable examples could be cited for collaborative partnerships occurring between educational institutions, as they try to provide more access to university courses and other forms of continuing education for their constituents. A province-wide system of five educational consortia has developed in Alberta, Canada. Each comprises the universities, colleges and vocational centers in its area and has as its mandate to provide instruction to geographically dispersed populations which have little or no access to programs available to urban populations. The expertise of faculty from the different institutions is shared and the latest in distance education technology used to deliver courses.

As we approach the twenty-first century, the future looks bright for collaborative partnerships. The barriers between "town and gown" appear to be disappearing and suspicions regarding government involvement in education are muted. "Incubators for small businesses" are being established on the campuses of some of our most traditional universities. "Joint appointments" are being made to a university department for people from the private sector, or from a public agency, who contribute to the education of students – and, university professors are being seconded as consultants to these agencies. Indeed, we are beginning to realize that, if we are to survive in a highly competitive world where knowledge is going to be the prevailing coin of barter, collaborative partnerships between government, academia, and the private sector must be carefully nurtured and encouraged to multiply.

REFERENCES

Vice, D. (1987) President, Northern Telecom Limited, as quoted in Burton, Lynn, *The People Prescription: Educating for the Knowledge-based Economy*, Canadian Labour Market and Productivity Centre, Ottawa.

Department of the Secretary of State (1987). News Release/Communiqué, August 19.

Conclusion: Developing Resourceful Humans

Adult Education Within the Economic Context

Lynn Elen Burton

Equating human capital to machine capital is a thing of the past. The purpose of this book has been to reach beyond the historic approach to human resource development to find a new vision of developing resourceful humans. The diverse and accomplished contributing authors have presented perspectives on various dimensions of this change. The linchpin of the emerging vision is the empowerment of people through lifelong learning.

THE WORLD OF TODAY

The future of work will consist of learning a living
(Marshall McLuhan)

In a world where nothing is certain except change itself, Marshall McLuhan's wisdom must move beyond "learning a living" to "learning for life." With this as given, adult educators are challenged to organize learning opportunities that are consistent with the work, learning, and life requirements of learners and potential learners.

Hierarchical corporate structures under the old economic order are being replaced by a spider web of activity whose strands begin in networks of communities and reach all over the world. A technology-induced redefinition and reorganization of work, coupled with the need to manage change, will inevitably break up the present boxes of school, work and retirement. The coming interweaving of work, learning, and life calls for new flexibility and the rethinking of our educational strategies. Teacher-centered, teacher-controlled approaches are increasingly dysfunctional as we move into the world of the twenty-first century.

Learning to learn becomes the cornerstone of learning for life. The traditional 3 R's of reading, 'riting, and 'rithmetic must merge with the 3 R's for modern living – reasoning, relating, and redefining.

THE IMPORTANCE OF LIFELONG LEARNING

The Learner Perspective

The learner is a consumer of educational services. It is incumbent upon the educational communities to ensure that this market is well served. Serving the learning community demands a sensitivity to the needs of this community. It also requires an understanding of the needs of potential learners and the provision of mechanisms to overcome any barriers to their fuller participation. Lifelong learning empowers people to act individually, and collectively, on their own behalf.

The Business Perspective

Local enterprises ensure community prosperity, but they need the help of adult educators. The Dofasco Steel Company slogan, "Our Product Is Steel, Our Strength Is People," translates into many different sectors. Working hand-in-hand with local enterprise, recurrent education ensures a ready and appropriately skilled labor force.

The National Perspective

Flexibility and balance are central to a changing world. To ensure prosperity, the work force must constantly retool. Maintaining a caring society requires a responsive educational system. Global competitiveness pressures and a changing environment present challenges to our entrepreneurial spirit and to our collective creativeness. Recurrent learning ensures continuing prosperity, and balance between consumer demands and the quality of life.

Lifelong learning equips us with the understanding of our national diversities and the qualities inherent in this mix. It is through understanding that conflict is resolved. It is through common values that our future as nations is assured.

The populations in developed countries are aging. Women and immigrant people are assuming new labor-force responsibilities.

The labor force requirements in traditional production and manufacturing industries are lessening, and at the same time, the service industry jobs are increasing. The introduction of new technologies and the constantly changing organization of work depends on the basic literacy and numeracy skills of the work force. Continuous learning is the essential prerequisite to a skilled and adaptable work force – the cornerstone of future national prosperity.

The Global Perspective

Complex global issues demand that citizens of the world pull in the same direction and learn to ensure that "the needs of the present are met, without compromising the ability of future generations to meet their own needs." Lifelong learning helps us understand our world and our place in it.

ADULT EDUCATION – REALIZING THE VISION

Excellent community-based adult eduction, cast within the context of strategic overall economic objectives, is indispensable to the success of individuals and society. In short, it is critical to "learning for life."

The learner must be at the heart of the educational approach. Learners' needs, motivations, desires, and experience must be central to the educational plan. Depending on the overall objectives, the organization of learning opportunities ranges from formal, to non-formal, informal, and on-the-job. The learner must be encouraged to assume responsibility for his or her educational success. The adult educator must work with the learners and the community to organize a quality learning experience.

The control implied in the traditional philosophy of human resource development must yield to the decentralized power inherent in the concept of developing resourceful humans.

REFERENCES

McLuhan, Marshall (1983), *Learning a Living in Canada*, Vol. 1. Report to the Minister of Employment and Immigration Canada by the Skill Development Leave Task Force. Canada: Minister of Supply and Services.

Glossary

Education is the way society organizes learning opportunities. The structure of the learning opportunities is often divided into formal, non-formal, and informal. The formal structure encompasses the traditional institutional providers such as public schools, colleges, and universities. The non-formal structure can be an organization such as the YM-YWCA which provides specific course offerings. The non-formal structure also includes employer led organizations. The informal structure is initiated by the learner or a group of learners who want to find out more about a particular topic area.

Learning is centered in the individual and/or group and occurs both in response to education and to self-directed learning needs.

Adult Education This term incorporates both the formal and informal learning experiences of adults. The formal sense of adult education refers to a specific set of curricula provided by formal institutions such as high-schools or universities. This formal sense of adult education implies a top down process of teacher to student. In a broader sense, adult education goes beyond this top down or transmission model. This model often is associated with the behavioristic and the Tylerian structural mode. A more democratic conception of adult education exists and is referred to as self-directed learning. This model of learning can exist within formal institutions or can be initiated by one individual or by a group of individuals (e.g. a book discussion club). Such individual or group initiated learning activities are initiated by adults and are legitimate parts of adult education.

Adult Learning Education and learning are not synonymous. Although both education and learning are processes, there are important differences in these processes. Education refers more to the transmission process. This process implies "sending" or "transmission" i.e., learning in the formal sense of "receiving". The center (locus) of education is generally with the teacher. However learning is an active process and includes the notions of self-directedness and discovery. This learning can occur within formal or non-formal educational institutions, or informally as in everyday life. The center (locus) of learning is with the learner/student.

Transaction implies two-way equal communication with shifting balance between the transmitter and receiver. Transformation, often precipitated by crisis, causes learner dysfunction, self-reflection, transformation and ultimately re-integration.

Adult Basic Education This includes the three Rs of reading, 'riting, and 'rithmetic as well as the three Rs of the future – reasoning, relating, and redefining. Adult Basic Education involves the very simple beginning of literacy and numeracy up to the high-school certificate level.

Human Resource Development (HRD) epitomizes the command-control model initiated by either an employer or teacher. *Developing Resourceful Humans* is the flipside or employee/student self-initiating empowerment model. HRD encompasses Human Resource Training (HRT) provided by employers in the employee development process. The HRT is delivered by the employer to the employees in order to achieve employer objectives. HRT programs can be delivered on-site or off-site within the formal setting of colleges or universities. It is possible and desirable for the providers of HRD/HRT to reach employer objectives while enhancing and facilitating the overall resourcefulness of the employees/learners. We can all gain by this expanded view of HRD/HRT both at the individual and the international level.

Developing Resourceful Humans refers to the encouragement of employee's or student's self-initiated learning which is directed to each individual's inherent resourcefulness in thinking, communicating, and action. It is often motivated by the student's awareness of his/her own deficiencies relative to particular circumstances and the need for improved competencies. Facilitation and/or support comes from the educator.

Education and Training There is an overlap in defining what constitutes education and what constitutes training. Education is often associated with the formal education system. Occupational, professional, or individual training is most often associated with work place applications within organizations employing individuals.

Index